THE IRON AGE
HILLFORTS
OF ENGLAND

A Visitor's Guide

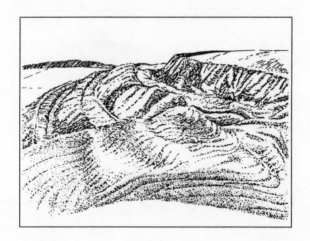

Other Books by the Author

McLaren; A Racing History, Crowood Press (1991)

The Elegance of Edwardian Railways: British Locomotives Portrayed though the Camera of James Grimoldby, Oxford Publishing Company (December 1993)

THE IRON AGE
HILLFORTS
OF ENGLAND

A Visitor's Guide

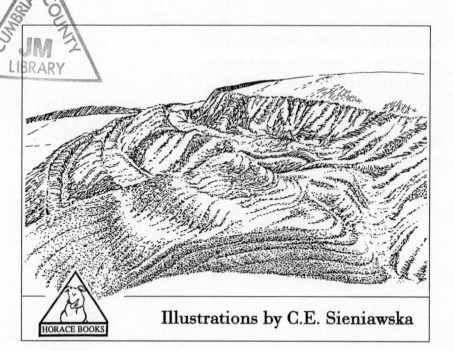

HORACE BOOKS

Illustrations by C.E. Sieniawska

Geoffrey Williams

Published in 1993 by
IMAGES

in conjunction with
HORACE BOOKS

British Library Cataloguing in Publication Data
A catalogue record for this book is available from the British Library

ISBN 1 897817 07 X

Designed and produced by Images (Publishing) Malvern Ltd.
Printed and bound in Great Britain.

Contents

Dedication

To Horace the horror,
30th August 1988 – 9th October 1991.
Thanks for three wonderful years,
all that fun and such enthusiasm.

The Author

Geoffrey Williams has been writing for publications for a number of years on a variety of subjects, which include various sports, history, politics and economics. He is the author of McLAREN: A MOTOR RACING HISTORY (Crowood Press), and has a book about railways, to be published by Oxford Publishing Company in 1993.

Geoffrey Williams was born in Lincolnshire in 1956, the son of a former champion boxer and musician, and educated at Hull University and Exeter University. He has spent his life engaged in a number of sports and physical pursuits which include motor racing, rock climbing and 13 cycle tours, on one of which he escaped from gaol in Hungary. He has now given up riding his luck, and enjoys the safety of the hockey field with Old Edwardian's Hockey Club, in his adopted city of Southampton.

Acknowledgements (and the rest)

Ever thought about writing a book? The first thing you will read and hear is not to pay towards the publication cost yourself; sound advice. 'If it is good enough, a publisher will accept and publish it, at his own expense.'

This is my third book, although the second to be published, and I approached a great many publishers (well over twenty) with the idea. A minority, but still more than ten, thought the idea good and were seriously interested, and these included some very big names in the publishing world, like . . . no I'd better keep mum.

Anyway, once they had done their sums on costs and projected sales and so on, each turned it down on the grounds that sales would not be sufficient (all right, one snooty publisher, a very well known one, thought my style to be 'too shallow'). In most cases, the editor/owner concerned was genuinely disappointed as they personally liked the book.

Despair had not quite set in when, by luck, I heard of IMAGES, and its founder Tony Harold. Quite simply, without Images, this book would still not have been published, and look what you would have missed. Cathy Whiting has done her level best to keep the book on an even keel ('Geoff, it's not a political manifesto'), but you know the saying about driving a horse to water and making it drink. In my case, Cathy was less of an editor, and more of a headhitter. Chris Redman has been responsible for (oh yes he has!), and has overseen all the illustrations for the book ('thank you, Lowry') Finally Anita Hill has been burning, and using up, the midnight oil while making this book into a sleek and ship-shape production. There have been many others behind the scenes who have contributed towards the publishing of the book, so don't just blame me.

Christine E. Sieniawska (I bet you can't pronounce that) has produced all the illustrations within the book, which were so good that I considered photographs unnecessary; in any case, I had trouble tracking down an Iron Age family group. Josh Sims contribution to the editing was worth every last penny (absolutely nothing), and I must say that he was a very convincing liar. Here are just some of his comments 'great', 'brilliant', 'lovely', 'what a load of bo . . . ' (how did that get in?).

Libraries were an invaluable source for both books and archaeological reports. Southampton University's Hartley Library either provided, or obtained from elsewhere, many important sources of information. In particular, I must thank all the unknown people who have partaken in the many archaeological excavations at hillforts down the years. It is they who have, quite literally, opened up a new world for us.

As with my previous books, thanks must go to the Librarian of my local Portswood branch of Hampshire County Libraries. Tim has always been willing to search out books requested, even from the depths of the county reserve collection, while giving his own suggestions ('clear off!') as to other possible sources. If all else failed, it was my local branch library that came up trumps.

Finally, and it was in the end, my thanks to Horace the horror, my dog, who came with me to almost all of the hillforts mentioned in the gazetteer. I say 'almost', because he was killed on a hillfort holiday, thanks to a driver too busy looking at my parked Riley car and not looking where he was going. When are we going to realise that to use a car is a privilege and not a right; that a driving test (repeated annually) of a standard at least that of the police advanced test, should be set; and that should be priced petrol to show it is a scarce resource not to be squandered? In 1993, there will be over 4,000 deaths on the roads, 50,000 serious injuries, hundreds of thousands of minor injuries, and millions of near misses, all caused by driver error. The cost in financial terms will be astronomic, in human terms it will be tragic. Just think, it could be you next.

Just one matter left to address. I could not understand how a book, on hillforts, could be enthusiastically received by certain publishers, and yet turned down as not being a commercial proposition. Of course, some publishers have swish offices, a good number of staff and other overheads. Then I discovered about the discount given to bookshops.

Generally speaking, your local bookshop gets 25% discount on a single copy, and 30-35% on two or more copies. Fair enough, considering the book might sell straight away, or it could be left on the shelves for some considerable time. Then, one of the larger national book retailers asked if I would like to open an account with them, and sent their standard terms. These were confirmed as usual by both my other publishers. This retail chain wanted a 45% discount, plus a 'sale or return' arrangement.

So, if you think books are expensive – and they are, that is one reason why. Just think, 45% of the price you paid for this book, or £6.28 per copy, could have gone into the retail chains' tills, who had no capital outlay, and bear no risk on un-sold copies. Aren't you glad you have not brought this book from such a store? Generally speaking, the author, who initiates the idea, touts it round the publishers, researches, writes and provides illustrations for the book, gets 10% of the cover price – £1.39½ (although this is not the case with Images). The publisher, who undertakes all editing, lay-out and printing, marketing and distribution costs, and takes the 'risk', gets the rest. Fortunately, most bookshops earn their cut, and these deserve mention here for bringing the book to your attention. Thank goodness genuine book sellers care more about books than money.

PREFACE

I was always brought up to look after and treasure books, and to ensure they are not damaged while reading them. As one gets older, books become less of an end in themselves, but more of a means to an end; a tool. This book is a tool, to be used, over and again.

True, you can read the opening chapters in the comfort of your own home, but essentially the aim of the book is to generate and enhance your interest in Iron Age hillforts, and to get you to visit them. That is why the dust-cover has been laminated onto the book, so that it will not be damaged by the wind and rain whipping round the hillfort ramparts, or when you accidentally drop it on the wet grass. As with most things, reading about them is one thing, but doing them is what it is really all about.

If you have never visited a hillfort before, or if you think you might have, but are not sure, then it is best to read through the opening chapters to find out a bit about the background of the Iron Age (can you state – without looking it up – between what years is considered the Iron Age?), and of course hillforts. All hillforts marked thus * denote inclusion in the gazetteer. It is then time to delve into the gazetteer itself, select your nearest hillfort, and to make your way there. One thing needs to be made clear at this point; that every hillfort in the gazetteer is 'free' (getting to be a rarity these days), but that someone, somewhere owns the land. Respect that, and if it says permission is needed to visit, which rarely is, seek that permission.

Once at the hillfort, the relevant gazetteer entry will not 'blind you with science', and reveal all the minutiae of its past. In nearly every case, no matter how heavily excavated, the relevant hillfort's history is not fully known, so a likely set of events is given. For some, that might mean a chronological run-down of the hillfort's past; for others, an 'educated' guess at what might have happened.

If you want to go beyond both the chapters and/or particular gazetteer entry, there are many archaeological reports available on those hillforts that have been excavated. There are also quite a number of books written by archaeologists either on the Iron Age, or hillforts. Be warned, these are mostly academic documents, and are of little value for general use. Still, should you feel a need to delve deeper into the subject, that is the path to follow. Ultimately, you need to go to an archaeological 'dig' yourself, or to join the Hillfort Study Group. For both of these, contact your nearest university archaeology department, and they will point you in the right direction.

Ultimately though, this book is all about getting out to see the hillforts, hence its sub-title 'A Visitors Guide'. I met an academic archaeologist while working on this book, who had undertaken several excavations, written numerous articles and books, and yet had visited far fewer hillforts in his life, than I had while writing this book. Obviously, he had given more to the archaeological world that ever I could, but not to go and see what you are really interested in seemed most odd; rather like writing about hockey, but never playing the game. Which reminds me, must dash or, I'll be late for the game. Come on Old Edwardian's let's dissect Winchester.

Part 1

IRON AGE HILLFORTS
OF ENGLAND

INTRODUCTION

Is 'History' of any use or relevance to us, or was it to anybody? Can we keep or derive any benefit from looking at the past, or are such activities just a 'past-time', at best, or an exercise in mere nostalgia? Of course, volumes have been written by historians about the value to society of their chosen subject, while countless hours have been spent waging the intellectual war on the question 'What is history?', all of which seems to have little meaning in the 'real world'.

The other night, for example, I was riding home after a hockey match and met some of my former pupils, now young men. They asked what I was writing about, and when I told them about this book) they said, in effect, '. . . oh, boring history, why don't you write something interesting, like . . .' They all enjoyed football, and watched Southampton F.C. regularly, yet did not know anything about the club's past, except that, ' . . . they won the cup ages ago . . .' (1976).

Taking football as an example, it can show, not only how history can teach us by looking into the past, but also enhance our enjoyment of the present. The F.A. Cup was won by southern amateur clubs in its first eleven years, from 1872. From then, until World War I stopped play in 1915, it was won by clubs from the industrial areas of the Midlands and the North every year, bar one. The Football League, begun in 1888, was won by teams from similar areas each year until that war. This tells us not only that the power-base of football was in the industrial heartlands of England, but that the professional game had completely over-shadowed the amateur one, and that football playing and spectating was also an important leisure activity.

That may well enhance our interest in football, but it is debatable if we can 'learn' anything from it, as many historians would have us believe. Whenever I consider that aspect of history, I am always reminded of the Marxist-Leninist parties who religiously followed the writings of those great revolutionaries, in the belief that Margaret Thatcher's 'dictatorial' government could be overthrown by following the same blueprint used by the Bolsheviks back in 1917. They did not take into account the fact that the 1917 Russian Revolutions were a freak of 'history', due to the immense losses of World War I. Not too much could be learned from those unique circumstances, that were relevant to the 1980s. So, by looking at the Iron Age, do not expect to learn too much of relevance for the modern world, but it might alter your opinion of where we came from, and also about the pre-Roman era as well.

One of the benefits of looking at history is to view and analyse change over a period of time. This can be applied to almost anything: cars, women's role in society, sport, and so on. However, looking at history can show how historians' interpretation of the past has changed over the years. Using the Iron Age as an example, until about thirty years ago it was generally considered that the Iron Age, in Britain, comprised three main periods, each of which could be sub-divided. These were labelled, not un-naturally, A, B and C by Professor C. Hawkes, an eminent archaeologist, and were linked into known events on mainland Europe.

In the mid-nineteenth century, a number of graves were discovered at some salt mines at Hallstatt in Austria. The bodies and grave-goods were from the late Bronze Age/early Iron Age, and Hawkes later equated this to his 'A' period. In the latter half of last century, another Iron Age site discovery was made at La Tene, in Switzerland, the numerous finds being of a later period than those at Hallstatt, and fitted into stage 'B' of Hawkes' labels. It was assumed by archaeologists of Hawkes' era, i.e. 1920s–1960s, that these peoples had arrived in Britain after 500 B.C. in a series of 'invasions'. These culminated in the Belgae invasions of the first century B.C., or Hawkes' 'C' period, for which documentary evidence can be found in Julius Caesar's accounts of his expeditions in Gaul.

This has all changed somewhat, and nowadays Hawkes' 'A, B and C' and the sub-divided Hallstatt/La Tene nomenclatures have both been dated further back in time, and are no longer considered to be accurate guides. The 'invasion' theory has been similarly discarded, except for possibly the arrival of the aforementioned Belgae, from the upper Danube region. Historical interpretation of these events has thus changed over time itself, but has not percolated down to schools and their portrayal of pre-Roman Britain, if at all.

Even as I write this, I have been asked to assist some Hampshire schools with a project on invasions, connected with visits to Maiden Castle*. When I mentioned that Iron Age Britain was not the victim of 'wave after wave of invasions', those teachers involved could have been knocked down by the proverbial feather.

So, let us have a look at the current state of play with regards to our own pre-history, at least in its most advanced stage, the Iron Age. The hillforts are the most visible, and widespread, of all Iron Age antiquities in our countryside, but remember, they were not all necessarily contemporary with one another. It is easy to over-state the importance of hillforts to the Iron Age, just like no image of mediaeval England would be complete without a castle, and probably high-rise buildings will come to be seen as typical of our age. Nevertheless, much of what is known about the Iron Age has come from excavations of hillforts and it is from these that you will come to appreciate that, while not on a par with the ancient civilisations of Greece and Rome, our pre-historic ancestors were not as far behind, as is often supposed.

CHAPTER ONE

The Iron Age:
Its Place in Time and Space

Can you, without looking down the page, put the following historical eras into chronological order? Mesolithic, Dark Ages, Bronze Age, Vikings, Paleolithic, Renaissance, Iron Age, Normans, Neolithic, Mediaeval and Romans. If so, can you give dates that would approximate to these? Then again, which of the above eras are pre-historic, and which are not? Well, without giving too much away, the Iron Age is part of Britain's pre-historic past, though that does not mean that the rest of the world was also in a pre-historic age.

'Pre-history' refers to the time before written accounts were made, and as far as Britain, let along England, is concerned, this means before the Romans arrived under Julius Caesar, in 55 B.C. Thus, man has only recorded his past in writing, in Britain, for about 2,000 years, a mere fraction of the time the land has been inhabited. Yet there is a tendency to group the long mass of pre-historic times together, and think of the pre-Roman man as being 'un-civilised' at best, or 'savages' at worst.

This is far from the truth, while it is best to put our forebears into context, by making comparisons with the rest of the world (*see table on p.21*). 'Pre-history' has been conveniently divided up into time-spans, and given labels, although any such dates are always open to contention.

PALEOLITHIC (OLD STONE) AGE: 500,000 — 10,000 B.C.
MESOLITHIC (MIDDLE STONE) AGE: 10,000 — 4,000 B.C.
NEOLITHIC (NEW STONE) AGE: 4,000 — 2,000 B.C.
BRONZE AGE: 2,000 — 800 B.C.
IRON AGE: 800 B.C. — 60 A.D.
(early Iron Age): 800 — 500 B.C.
(middle Iron Age): 500 — 100 B.C.
(late Iron Age): 100 B.C. — 60 A.D.
ROMAN PERIOD: 43 A.D. — 415 A.D.

Except for the occasional stone axe-head, or arrow-head, the only evidence in England of man's habitation for the former two periods is cave dwellings, such as Kent's Cavern in Devon, and these are extremely rare. The peoples of the New Stone Age though are quite different. Like their fore-runners, they too were mostly nomadic hunter-gatherers, using stone (flint) tools, but also leaving behind the first evidence of settlements, monuments and the ceremonial burial of the dead.

For a start there are the permanent settlements of the Neolithic Age known as causewayed camps. Not unlike mini-hillforts, these were often built on hill-tops, and usually comprised two or more concentric banks with causeways passing through. About a dozen have been discovered in England, the most famous being Windmill

Hill, near Avebury (Wiltshire), but others were built at, or near sites which were later used for Iron Age hillforts, very likely a pure coincidence. Some of these are featured in the gazetteer, at Maiden Castle*, no longer visible, and The Trundle*. The Windmill Hill site provided the first evidence of crops being grown, the first certain signs of settlement, but it is also possible that the causewayed camps themselves, which dated from c.4,000 B.C., were used for ceremonial purposes, rather than living in.

More impressive, and immediately visible, are the great henges from this period. Stonehenge, although not the stones, and Avebury are the most well known of these great monuments, but there are many others, such as Marden Henge and Woodhenge (all in Wiltshire). Many of these are connected to processional ways, such as the Avenue at Avebury, or the Dorset Cursus, among others. It is thought that these henges, cursus and avenues, as well as other monuments like Silbury Hill (Wiltshire), had some form of quasi-religious significance.

Silbury Hill

The formation and use of such sites still remains a mystery, as yet not understood, and the amount of labour required in their construction was considerable. They often displayed some form of planning; the Dorset Cursus, for example, was about six miles long. All sorts of weird and wonderful theories and explanations have been propounded, which include 'guides' for people from outer space. Do not be lulled into accepting any such mystical explanation though, as evidence for any form of all-encompassing use for these great monuments is, at present, merely an educated, or otherwise, guess.

Last, but the most widely distributed, of the remains from the Neolithic Age, are the long barrows, quoits of Cornwall or chambered tombs. Examples are to be found all over England, while some were later enclosed by a hillfort, like at Hambledon Hill*. Others, in particular Belas Knap and Hetty Pegler's Tump (Gloucestershire) and West Kennet Long Barrow (Wiltshire), are open for internal inspection.

The Bronze Age did not just arrive overnight ('I say, Ugg, did you hear that the Bronze Age began last week?'), and one might easily argue that any point from c.2,500 B.C. was the beginning of this period. In any case, there is evidence to suggest that a 'Copper Age' preceded the Bronze Age, bronze being an alloy of copper and tin. What is fairly certain is that at some stage between 2,500–2,000 B.C. an influx of people came to our island, identified by their distinctive shaped heads, and have become known as the Beaker people, after the shape of their pottery, rather than that of their noses. Whether these people over-ran, out-bred or were assimilated into the native population cannot be readily determined, but they seem to have been nomadic, possibly even relatively extensive traders in their pottery and bronze wares.

The most widely distributed of visible remains from this age are the round barrow burial mounds, either singular or in groups. These are of five distinct types: bowl, bell, disc, saucer and pond, all with, or without, a combination of surrounding ditches and banks. The distribution of these, and the lack of permanent settlements from the Bronze Age, suggests that the peoples of that period were highly mobile, and that a return to a specific site was only made for burial. It is also possible that many ancient trackways, identifiable as being pre-Roman, such as The Ridgeway, were established at that time.

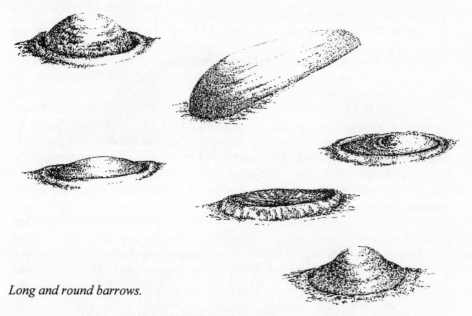

Long and round barrows.

Perhaps of more interest than mere burial mounds though, are the stone circles, stone lines and standing stones which emanate from this period. It was during the Bronze Age that Stonehenge received its various stages of standing stones, which culminated in its final form, the ruins of which we can see today. That is England's crowning glory of the age, but there are many lesser, though nonetheless noteworthy, examples, particularly in the South-West and North.

The first settlements of un-disputed antiquity began in the Bronze Age, some of which were either re-used, in the Iron Age, or indeed might have had a permanent and continuous settlement transcending the dates given above, such as Almondbury* and Mam Tor*. Some of these certainly pre-date 800 B.C., yet depending on the location, it does not follow that because the settlement was occupied during the Iron Age, the inhabitants were of an Iron Age culture.

Iron was probably introduced into England by traders from Europe, but somebody, somewhere in England could also have 'invented' it at about the same time. Iron is a much harder, and easier worked metal than bronze, and thus had considerable advantages, particularly for weapons. There is little doubt that its introduction would have had an impact on the lives of the native population, but of more importance was the arrival, probably as traders rather than invaders, of the Celtic peoples from mainland Europe. As with the Beaker peoples before, the Celts seem to have travelled inland, probably establishing a trading network, and visited the early settlements which we call hillforts. Iron-produced goods, offered the opportunity for improved weapons and a greater range of tools, and once people became 'settled' the race for possessions was on; the 'keeping up with the Uggs'.

It is likely that this scenario would have taken a considerable time, as the Iron Age did not come about over-night. In the far North of England, the inhabitants probably had far more in common with the Bronze Age peoples of c.1,000 B.C., than the Celts of the South-East, at the time of the Roman invasion of 43 A.D. The great North/South divide thus has quite a heritage.

The above has brought us to the threshold of the Iron Age, but before taking a serious look into that period of English/British history, we ought to consider the wider world beyond, against which comparisons can be made. Table 1 gives a general idea of how the rest of the world was faring, while we were safely, or otherwise, ensconced in our own pre-history.

The area to the north of the Persian Gulf, scene of so much strife in the last decade, can be noted as a probable cradle of civilisation. The Bronze Age in the Middle East was somewhat earlier than our own, c.3,200–1,200 B.C., and the first of what we might call city-states were established in Sumeria or Mesopotamia at the beginning of this period. The oldest known written records date from c.3,200 B.C., and although there are no continuous or comprehensive records extant, pre-history ended over three thousand years before ours did.

Stone henge

DATES	ENGLAND	EUROPE	WORLD
500,000-10,000 B.C.	Paleolithic (Old Stone) Age	Axes c.25,000 B.C.	
10,000-4,000 B.C.	Mesolithic (Middle Stone) Age	Hunter-gatherers	
4,000-2,000 B.C.	Neolithic (New Stone) Age: henges, long-barrows, caves, concentric camps nomads, flint tools.		c.3,200-1,200 Middle East Bronze Age. c.3,000-2,000 B.C. Egyptian pyramids; Sumeria/ Mesopotamia
2,000-800 B.C.	Bronze Age: round barrows log boats, stone circles etc. religion, first hill enclosures.	1200 B.C. Fall of Mycenae. c.1,000 B.C. Aryans arrive from Asia.	c.2,000-1,500 B.C. Phoenicia, Troy, Minoa, founded, 1262-1252 B.C. Tutankhamun rules Egypt. c.1,000 B.C. David fights Goliath.
800 B.C. – 60 A.D.	Iron Age: 800-600 B.C. large hill-top enclosures, light defences. 600-400 B.C. Plateau/contour hillforts, possibly not permanently inhabited, better defences. c.400 B.C. territorial 'capitals' of permanently inhabited hillforts. c.300 B.C 'cliff-castles' of South-West. First century B.C, oppida building begun. 55/54 B.C. Julius Caesar's Roman army invades the South-East. 43 A.D. Claudian Roman invasion of England.	776 B.C. first Olympiad. 753 B.C. Rome founded. c.750-650 B.C. Homer writes Illiad and Oddessey. 490 B.C. Battle and Marathon. 390 B.C. Celts sack Rome. 279 B.C. Celts attack sanctuary at Delphi.	800 B.C. Carthage founded. 6th century B.C. Confucius writes analects in China. 264 B.C. First Punic War, Carthage/Rome. 214 B.C. Great Wall of China begun.

Simultaneously, and quite probably unknown to each other, at the other end of the 'fertile crescent', the Egyptians were building their first pyramids in c.3,000 B.C. Once again, although at a later date, these people had begun to leave written records, and to leave their pre-historic period behind. It is quite a salutary thought that, while our ancestors were busy building the great henge at Stonehenge, the Egyptians were not only creating the pyramids, but the various sculptures in stone and precious metals so widely known today.

About 2,000 B.C., while parts of Britain were entering the Bronze Age, the Babylonian Empire, as a sort of successor to Sumeria, was coming into its own, while the civilisations based at Troy, Mycenae and the Minoan Empire, on Crete, were being founded. As for the Egyptians, although most of their monuments had been built, they were to rise to their greatest heights over the next thousand years, with Tutankhamun being Pharaoh in 1250 B.C. The seafaring civilisation of Phoenicia came into being during the second millennium B.C., as did the first flowering of the Greek city-states, but not before sliding back into illiteracy (or pre-history?) with the fall of Mycenae in c.1,200 B.C.

Thus, by 1,000 B.C., while we were probably still mostly nomads, or building our first permanent settlements, much of the Middle East and the Eastern Mediterranean world was into its Iron Age, with the independent city-state, or indeed empire, well and truly established. The Judean tribes were becoming more settled, with David killing Goliath c.1,000 B.C., while 200 years later the city of Carthage was founded, and began to form an empire.

The written word was now beginning to come into vogue in the ancient world, and while Europe saw the rise of the Celts, out of the Aryans from the central Asian steppes, Homer was composing the *Iliad* and *Odyssey,* c.700 B.C., and Confucius writing his analects shortly afterwards. It is indeed to these ancient civilisations that we look for the first written accounts of the Celts. In 390 B.C. the Celtic 'barbarians' crossed the Alps and sacked Rome, an action that would not be lightly forgotten, nor forgiven, and may well have been the catalyst for the establishment of the empire. The Greeks were also having to come to grips with the war-like people from the north, and managed to beat them back when the Celts attacked Delphi in 279 B.C.

It is to a Greek, an Athenian in fact, named Pytheas, that the first written account of England is accredited. He sailed with the Phoenicians to Britain, and wrote about the voyage and the tin trade with Cornwall. This took place c.325 B.C., and while the Cornish people were engaged in foreign trade, it was not they who were undertaking the 'adventurous' deeds.

England next appears in literature with Julius Caesar's account of his 'invasions' of 55 and 54 B.C., while he also mentions the earlier invasions of the Belgae, after his army had driven them from mainland Europe. That is rather jumping the gun though and, having seen that the island off the North European coast was something equivalent to a Third Word country today, let us return to our shores and investigate Iron Age England.

It is not known how the Iron Age came about, nor why the Celtic peoples should have become so dominant north of the Alps, and in England. Iron, and its manufacturing techniques, probably reached central and northern Europe from the Mediterranean region, through trade. It has already been noted that the Phoenicians were trading with Cornwall for tin, and may have been for many centuries. Could iron not have been introduced by the south-west 'back entrance', as well as the 'front door' of the Straits of Dover? By whichever route though, iron was introduced on these shores by c.800 B.C.

The introduction of iron, remembering that it took many centuries before it found its way to the North of England, does not necessarily herald the dawning of a new age though, just as computers have not transformed daily life to the extent portrayed in some science-fiction novels in the last twenty-odd years. Thus it was in the Iron Age, as communities both grew in size and became permanently established, whether based in hillforts or not. Again, this change did not happen overnight and, as has been mentioned, permanent hill-top enclosures had been established from c.1,000 B.C. Why this should be so, is not certain, but from c.1,200 B.C. the climate became both colder and wetter, and did not begin to improve until c.800 B.C. That, as you will have noted, is the convenient 'start' of our Iron Age.

Those hill-top enclosures, which dated from c.800 B.C., tended to be of two types: the large, lightly fortified enclosure, with a sparse population, like Leckhampton*, or the small, strongly fortified enclosure, such as Almondbury (Phase 4)*. Later, the contour hillfort was developed, c.500 B.C., with better defences than the large enclosure, mentioned above, and these were not necessarily permanently occupied either; Figsbury Ring* was one such example.

From c.400 B.C. onwards, more stoutly defended, and larger hillforts were built, with regional variations, making the best use of the local terrain, like the cliff-castles of Cornwall. The growth in the scale of the hillforts, and thus the need for greater manpower to build, extend and maintain them, suggests that the rise of an aristocracy, or warrior-class, went hand-in-glove with this ancient 'construction boom', although that cannot be determined with any certainty. Quite naturally, given the labour required to build a hillfort of this kind, they became permanently occupied, but from c.100 B.C., some were being abandoned, especially in the South.

What is unusual about such actions is that it coincided with what has not been ruled out as a form of invasion by the Belgae, a more war-like type of Celt from South Germany, from c.100 B.C. Little of our Iron Age past has been determined with absolute certainty, and words like 'probably', 'possibly', 'may have been' and so forth, have been quite liberally used (to a greater or lesser extent!). That is not surprising really, as written accounts are few and far between, while an archaeologist can only use what he does, or does not, find to piece together some form of picture. So, perhaps if there were enough Belgic peoples coming over to constitute an invasion, one might expect to find hillforts being either built or strengthened, and not abandoned.

Contrary to this, some evidence of hillforts being up-graded, possibly in the face of the Belgic threat, can be found, like Battlesbury* and Scratchbury*, to name just two. The Belgae, for their part, seemed more inclined to go in for a different kind of settlement to the hillfort, the 'enclosed oppida', or fortified town, built to a much larger scale. Indeed, at The Trundle* there is evidence of a move being made to the lower ground near Chichester, possibly after the Belgae had overcome the original Celtic inhabitants. The enclosed oppida were often built to a scale that dwarfed even the massive Maiden Castle*, and were characterised by a series of linear dykes and banks. Only Dyke Hills and Bigbury which could possibly be considered as enclosed oppida, have been included in this book, but others are to be found at, or near, Chichester (Sussex), Colchester (Essex), Silchester (Hampshire), with possibilities at Oldbury (Kent) and Salmonsbury (Gloucestershire), all except the last, being in the South-East.

When Caesar invaded the picture was beginning to change, and ninety-odd years later when the Romans made their full-scale invasion in 43 A.D., it had changed still further. The Belgic tribes of the Atrebates, Regni and Catuvellauni were well established in the South-East, warring amongst themselves as much as the earlier tribes, and may have been pushing into the Midlands (see Bredon Hill*). The tribal plan of Britain c.0 A.D., will give some idea of the extent of each tribe's control, although it is not known, except for the Belgae areas, what sort, or extent of any centralised rule was apparent. Remember, of course, the further north one goes, the less 'Iron Age', in all facets, each tribe was.

The arrival of the Belgae was not all bad for the locals though, as they brought a couple of items along that began to have a far-reaching effect. The most important was the wheel (and not the square one, as in the film 'Carry on Cleo'). It is almost impossible to determine how widespread was the use of the wheel for transport by the non-Belgic tribes, although the Iceni, Boudicca's tribe, certainly used chariots against the Romans; but it was unlikely that it was used in the manufacture of pottery, before the Belgae arrived. This, of course, enabled pottery to be manufactured on a large, more standardised scale than hitherto (Belgaeware!), with consequent benefits for trade, leading to the establishment of an exchange economy.

Pottery of the middle Iron Age.

The Belgae also introduced their sturdier plough, which was more suited to the heavier, clay soils of the valleys and lowlands of the South-East. This may help to explain the earlier ploughing of hills, with lighter soil, and thus the location of the hillforts. Evidence of the growth of an exchange, as opposed to a barter, economy has also come through finds of, initially Belgic, coins, and other tokens of exchange, particularly in the South and East of England.

Such evidence, along with other incidentals like jewellery, decorated weapons and domestic utensils, suggests that the southern half of England, at least, had reached a standard not dis-similar to that recognisable in the mediaeval period, over 1,000 years later. Permanent 'towns' existed, where trade and manufacture took place, while warrior-leaders occupied hillforts as the centre-piece of an area, with its surrounding farms and field systems; a not un-recognisable scenario from the mediaeval baron with a castle at the centre of his lands. The late Iron Age peoples even had the Druids as their religious leaders, a position similar to that of the Roman Catholic church during the mediaeval period, although not on such a lavish scale. One wonders whether the 'common man' of the late Iron Age was a serf, tied to the land, as was his mediaeval counterpart. There is evidence of slave-chains and trade, from the earlier Iron Age, but this could simply be for law-breakers, or prisoners from conflicts.

The further north one looks, the less organised the tribal system seems to have been. The Brigantes, for example, was more a loose confederation of peoples, than a cohesive tribe on the scale of the Atrebates. In the far North of England, the tribes were more akin to the Bronze Age than Iron Age, in their use of metals, pottery, a lack of a medium of exchange and from what can be determined of their organisation. These differences in the deportment of the various tribes showed themselves in the reaction to the first certain invasion of this island, the arrival of the Romans. Some were in favour, like the Atrebates, others against, such as the Catuvellauni; others almost ambivalent, the Iceni; and others totally divided, like the Brigantes. At least we know that the Iron Age human response to change was no different to ours!

So what caused the fall of the Iron Age, and when did it happen? Obviously, the Roman invasion saw the usurping of the fairly absolute power of the tribal aristocracy, with a Roman Governor appointed to represent the Emperor. The leaders of the Atrebates/Regni tribes, for example, seem to have done rather well out of Roman rule, and quickly assimilated themselves into the norms and benefits of Roman life. The leaders of tribes who fought against the Romans did not fare so well, naturally, and if they were granted a bit of foreign travel after their ultimate defeat, and an organised parade through the streets of Rome, they met their end very soon afterwards. Likewise, the religious leaders, the Druids, did not last long, and did not get the 'foreign travel' either.

Did life for the archetype 'common man' alter much, though? True, there were towns on a more lavish scale than hitherto, but these were not for him, and as for the road network, these were mostly used for military purposes, and the common man continued to use his trackways. He probably still lived in his round, or later rectangular, hut, perhaps even in the, then un-fortified, hillfort as before, worked the fields, either by himself, or in common with others from his village, and paid his dues, in whatever form, to the Romans, rather than to the former leaders. Swap some of the titles around, and our common man would probably recognise the lot of the mediaeval serf without too much difficulty. Indeed, as feudalism was only officially abolished in Russia in 1861, and even then it took decades to finally disintegrate, he might not have felt out of place there.

The Iron Age, as such, is usually thought to have ended in England in the decades following the 43 A.D. Roman invasion. Known to both the Greeks and Romans as 'barbarians', the Celts were subjugated to Roman rule on mainland Europe south and west of the Danube, and in England south of Hadrian's Wall, as a rough guide. However, as with the rugby team, the 'barbarians' could not be kept down, and an even more war-like lot finally forced the Romans to abandon Britain in the first half of the fifth century A.D.; 'accurate' dates for this are sometimes bandied about but, as with the demise of the Iron Age, the Roman life-style did not just collapse, but disintegrated gradually. Eventually, these 'barbarians' sacked Rome itself, and the Angles, Saxons and Jutes came to pillage and settle here, forcing the Celts and Romano-British into Wales, Cornwall and Ireland. Europe now entered the Dark Ages; a kind of post-history pre-history, if you see what I mean.

From being a central part of European pre-history, i.e. illiterate barbarians, the Celts, banished to the extremities of Europe, were little pockets of literate 'light', amidst the darkness of 'Barbaria', i.e. Dark Age Europe. Quite a cultural transformation. It was not too long before the Celtic Christians of Ireland made their way back to mainland Britain, and established religious houses, only for the next wave of barbarians, the Vikings, to arrive. The Saxons managed, in the end, to stave off the Viking take-over, but not the arrival of the Normans in 1066, and before we know it we are into the mediaeval period.

Through all the above, the plight of the common man, should he have survived all the invasions, would not have altered much. Indeed, when it comes to the question of, 'when did the Iron Age end?', we have two points to look at. One is the use of iron as the technological catalyst of the age, the second being the society and its norms.

Taking the former, it is known that iron began to usurp Bronze from c.800 B.C., hence, although not universal throughout England, the beginning of the Iron Age. Iron was not really replaced until last century, with the advent of steel (a derivation of iron), and even then iron was still widely used this century. Using the technological aspect as a rule of thumb, one could then argue that it was only the advent of plastics and the nuclear age, which finally saw iron and steel replaced from its pre-eminent position.

Of course, you might say, that is all very well, but our society hasn't much in common with that of the Iron Age. Oh no? Okay, where do you live? Your house is probably of rectangular shape, like those of the Roman period and, unless you are lucky, it will not have a much greater floor area than a decent sized Iron Age hut, and if you live in a modern 'box', probably much less. Should you work for yourself, well, so did many Iron Age farmers and craftsmen. Perhaps you work for firm, one of those large ones that have been equated to the feudal barons, both for their scale, and the remoteness of 'management', or the chief of a large hillfort, like Midsummer Hill*. Or perhaps you work for a small firm, something similar to the chief of a smaller hillfort, such as Burrough Hill*.

Religion might not be as popular as it once was, but how do our 'rulers', in political life and work, survive? We pay taxes for the privilege of allowing them to pursue their own ego-trips, or our work provides the profits for the company to pay such people. In the latter case, this has probably not changed at all, while in the former example, our Iron Age 'common man' probably had a proportion of his produce taken 'in kind', as in mediaeval days. Comparisons could also be drawn in activities like the family and sport (c.400 B.C. the Greeks were playing a form of hockey, while our ancestors were going out for a 'raid'), but these only serve to confuse the issue.

Despite all the above, for the purposes of looking at hillforts we will stick to the orthodox, and say that the Iron Age ended in the mid-first century A.D. A gradual, uneven change took place over the 850 or so years of the English Iron Age and, despite the shock' of the Romans', and subsequent, invasions the lifestyle probably continued in this format, at least until the Industrial Revolution, beginning in the late eighteenth century. The change in Iron Age society, and the differences throughout Britain, let alone England, can be seen in the diversity of hillforts, and their subsequent development. Indeed, it is these great ruins of our (mostly) hill-tops that are not only the lasting monuments of that age, but have come to epitomise what is understood by the Iron Age.

CHAPTER TWO

Peoples and Society in the Iron Age:
Who, When and How

'I'm here at a hillfort in southern Britannia, and we've been under siege all day long. The barrage from the neighbouring Belgae tribe has intensified in the last half hour, the sling-stones inflicting many casualties: men, women and children alike, and even one of our own R.B.C. crew. Several of the thatched, wooden huts have been set ablaze by lighted spears thrown over the ramparts, but teams have been despatched to contain the fires.

'Amidst all the confusion, the Belgae have captured many head of cattle and sheep, not rounded up as they approached. This is a major loss for the local people, who have only just re-stocked their herds after the destruction caused by a similar assault last year. Considerable damage to crops has been caused by the fighting, and the total cost to the people of the hillfort, even if the attack is repulsed, is likely to be high. Relief supplies will almost certainly be needed over the coming winter.

'The south of Britannia has become an increasingly violent place, with the Belgae tribes trying to gain land to the west and north, despite fierce resistance. It is a seemingly pointless fracas, in a forgotten part of the world, overshadowed by the glorious successes of Julius Caesar, in Gaul. It is quite possible that Caesar will soon turn his attention to this corner of "Barbaria".

'This is Katia A.D., for the Roman Broadcasting Corporation Six o'clock News, in southern Britannia, 56 B.C.'

Perhaps the above is over-dramatising events a bit, but without a doubt there was a good deal of unrest in the South of England during the first century B.C. The arrival of the Belgic Regni/Atrebates and Catuvellauni tribal peoples from Europe was only one cause of this, and for up to three centuries before there had been an increase in inter, and intra, -tribal disputes.

At the heart of this friction lay a symptom not unknown to us today, a rise in the population. As the previous chapter showed, evidence of small, permanent settlements had begun in the middle Bronze Age, and by the time of our arbitrary change to the Iron Age, c.800 B.C., lightly defended, large hill-top settlements had become well established. Once people begin to settle, and establish territorial claims to the land, it is usually the case that attempts are made to improve one's home, and belongings. The permanence of the home also encourages a more domestic outlook on life, while a settled background is more of an incentive to breeding. than having to carry ones off-spring everywhere.

Not surprisingly, any population figures for the Iron Age can only be vague guesses, as indeed are population trends. For a start, drawing comparisons by the number of burials is not easy as, unlike people of the Bronze Age, those of the Iron Age did not usually mark graves with a large barrow. Cremation seems to have been the most popular method of body disposal in the Iron Age, like today.

The population of England and Wales in 1991 was about 50 million, that of England being about 47m. The figures for England and Wales had previously been 1951 = 44m, 1901 = 32m, 1851 = 18m and 1801 (the first year of the Census) = 9m. It has been estimated to have been about 5.5m in 1750, and had remained at a similar level for several centuries before.

The 1991 figure for England and Wales, represents about 620 people per square mile, placing these countries behind The Netherlands and Belgium as the most densely populated in Europe. Population growth has thus been massive, but pales in comparison with modern India. The population on Independence in 1947/8 was about 350m, whereas the combined population for the three countries, which comprised the India of the British Raj, i.e. India, Pakistan and Bangla Desh, is currently about 1.1 billion, and rising at about 2.5% per annum. These figures need to be borne in mind when considering population growth in the Iron Age.

People at work.

The Domesday Book of 1086 A.D., the Norman census of land and people, gave the earliest indication of the population of England. Analysis of this gives the persons per square mile in different parts of the country as South = 21-7, South-East = 25, Cornwall = 13, South-West = 23-9, Marches = 23, Upper Thames = 32, East-Anglia = 41-6, Fens = 23, Midlands = 28, North = 5. These figures may well reflect the population spread of late Iron Age England, which was about half that of the Norman period, probably about 1-2m.

29

Excavations of hillforts have revealed that the above population density figures do not tell the whole story. Excavated hillforts of the South that have hut circles, show an average of about 5 huts per acre. Given a 'guesstimated' average of 3-5 persons per hut, this gives a population density of 9-16,000 per square mile, if the whole of the interior was similarly occupied. However, certain hillforts of the Welsh Marches had a more regimented, grid layout of huts, which would give a population density of about 45,000-60,000 persons per square mile, in other words, little different to our cities today. So, although the overall population was small, even in relation to the amount of usable land, a form of 'population pressure' could probably be felt within settled homesteads, hillforts or otherwise.

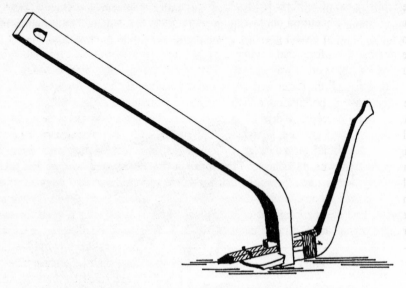

A bow ard – wooden plough of the late Iron Age phase consisting of a beam, to which oxen were harnessed, and an iron coulter.

It is likely that, with the increase of permanent settlements, the population grew modestly throughout the Iron Age. This can be deduced from the gradual drift away from the higher, light-soiled ground, to the heavier, more productive, clay soils of the valleys and lowlands. This would have been a slow, and not universal, transition inhibited by the agricultural equipment then in use. The 'Celtic fields' of the later Bronze Age and early Iron Age, (these are roughly square fields of between ½ – 1½ acres) were well suited to the plough then in use. This would have been a hand plough in the earlier times, developing to a foot plough with beam and coulter, and pulled by two oxen. That still only broke the surface of the soil, so the Celtic fields were ploughed first length-ways, and then width-ways. A move to the heavier soils of the lower ground was thus not to be taken lightly.

The intensive farming of the celtic fields, or the 'run-rig' system of a small field for crops surrounded by a larger one, mainly for cattle, led to soil erosion, and falling yields. More land for cultivation would thus be required to feed a stable population, but if that was growing too, as with many Third World countries today, problems arose. A possible solution to such a problem is shown in the South, South-West and Chilterns, from early in the Iron Age. Linear dykes had been dug in many places, cutting across the former celtic field systems, signalling that a re-distribution of the land took place. This can be seen today at sites such as Quarley Hill*, and the un-finished hillfort of Ladle Hill*, and had a similar effect to the 'enclosures' of the eighteenth century Agricultural Revolution.

Hand in glove with the re-apportioning of the land, was the change in emphasis from arable to cattle and sheep farming, especially in the South, while from c.550 B.C. onwards the former hill-top enclosures were being replaced by the more defensive hillforts. Furthermore, there is good evidence in the South to suggest that the establishment of hillforts led to the dividing of the land into zones, of about 40 square miles, each centred on its main hillfort. Even this was not enough to satisfy the need for land to feed a growing population, and it was after the building of the more defensive hillforts that raiding a neighbour's land and stock came more into vogue (or was it the other way round?). This is still depressingly evident today.

Thus far, until the latter half of the second century B.C., the Iron Age had seen a steadily growing population establish itself in permanent, defensive sites, mostly hillforts, with a perceptible drift away from the higher ground to the valleys. As one would expect, these gradual, general trends, enacted over several centuries, caused a change in the social structure of Iron Age society, just as the drift from the countryside to towns, throughout the world in the last two centuries, has had a similar effect. It is quite probable that the more mobile, nomadic peoples of the Bronze Age had a considerable degree of equality among each group. Permanent settlement, and the marking out of individual plots of land, with a need for more centralised organisation, almost inevitably leads to the rise of the director, or leader.

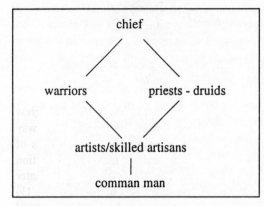

In the modern world we hear how, for example, certain tribes of Africa are ruled by 'elders', while others are governed by 'warriors'. Among the Celts, an apparently war-like race, it would seem that a 'warrior class', that is the strongest, came to the fore to assume power. This would have been perfectly natural, given the times, as even today it is common to take a similar course by appointing the best player as the team captain, for example. Once a structure has become accepted, so a form of 'pecking order' becomes established, with off-shoots for those with a natural intelligence above the norm (learned/religious class), and those with an aptitude for making things (craft/art class). It is not a particularly great step to enforce this social hierarchy through the offspring, and before you know it there is a lineage system which maintains the status quo.

If the above sounds a bit too theoretical and convenient, especially as archaeologists are not yet able to dig up evidence of social structures as readily as they can other artefacts, neither is it pie in the sky. Examples that fit the above hypothesis can be found in many tribes and societies down the years, but something more specific can be found in the social hierarchy of Celtic society, in the Dark Ages, from Irish literature. Here, a king ruled over a rigid, hierarchical structure of nobles, free-commoners and un-free. Each of the three classes was sub-divided, the nobles: warriors, men of learning, priests, specialists and master craftsmen; the 'free-commoners': peasant farmers and basic craftsmen; and the 'un-free': the vast majority.

The Irish-Celtic social structure is broadly similar to that of the Celtic tribes of Gaul, as described by Julius Caesar in the account of his conquest of Europe and, one might surmise, equated to the position among the tribes of England. It may well have been the case that, during the Iron Age, the power of the warriors grew and the 'un-free' found themselves increasingly in a position not unlike that of the mediaeval serf, that is tied to the land and dependent on the lord, or warrior, for protection. Certainly the growth of the permanent hillfort settlement, and the primitive form of land management that was exercised, points towards a greater direction of Iron Age society, and therefore the existence of a ruling class. This probably resulted in the establishment of the tribal areas, shown in the last chapter, although these would have been quite fluid.

Central to Iron Age society was the family; more the 'extended family' of several generations (grand-parents/parents/children), than the 'nuclear family' associated with modern industrialised society. That, in itself, would enforce the rigidly hierarchical caste system and, especially in the later Iron Age, would have virtually precluded social movement. Indeed, the economy of Iron Age Britain would have centred on the family, a fairly self-sufficient production unit. Above this, the population of a hillfort would also have been an almost self-sufficient unit, at least during the middle Iron Age, c.500-100 B.C. As mentioned in Chapter 1, the extent of slavery, if any, cannot be determined. Caesar made reference to the slave-trade, and slave manacles have been found at Bigbury* hillfort, but these are almost in isolation, and could easily have been used for prisoners.

With the arrival of the Belgic peoples in the late second century B.C., from what is now Belgium and Holland (whether by invasion, or in dribs and drabs), the tribal system seems to have become more formally established. By the time Julius Caesar popped over for his second visit, in 54 B.C., it is known that the (Roman-friendly) Regni/Atrebates held sway in central South England, while the more war-like Catuvellauni occupied much of the Home Counties. In Kent too, Caesar was confronted by woad (blue) painted Belgic warriors, but these only appear to have been near the coast.

It may be that the arrival of the Belgae, caused from a loose confederation of hillforts in a given area, the founding of the tribes, as shown by the map in the previous chapter. In the first century B.C. there was a move away from hillforts to the lower ground, and the establishment of the aforementioned enclosed oppida, at least in the Belgic territories. In opposition to this, the Durotriges and Dobunni tribes appear to have improved the defences of certain hillforts, while evidence abounds as to other neighbouring tribes casting a weather-eye over Belgic expansion (see Wandlebury*).

As the first century B.C. wore on, even after Caesar had routed the Catuvellauni, tribal tensions grew with the latter tribe, united under their leader Cassivellaunus, stretching their tentacles further afield. Even the Atrebates complained to Rome about their neighbours' expansionist aims in their direction, and this real, or perceived threat would have been something of a forcing-ground for tribal unity. This trend is enhanced on the one hand by the Iceni of Norfolk, where a relatively large population existed, with hardly any hillforts, and tempered by the fact that '11 kings' allegedly threw their hand in with the Romans, in 43 A.D. That does not sound as though the tribes were too unified.

Be that as it may, 'one swallow does not make a summer' and the general trend of society becoming more centralised, under an established ruling class, does seem to be a feature of Iron Age England. This at least was the case in the South, but the farther north one looked not only was there less emphasis on a central ruling body but, along with the comparatively sparse population, the economy would appear to be less developed, at least by the first century B.C.

As with most Third World countries today, the economy of Iron Age Britain was based on agriculture, at a subsistence level. That a surplus was extracted can be shown, not only in the proportion of effort given over to defence, mainly in hillforts, but also the existence of both the ruling class and the religious leaders (the Druids), with their attendant luxury goods, such as jewellery. There is little evidence of a means of exchange, prior to the Belgic introduction of coins, c.100 B.C., so it must be assumed that barter was the normal means of trade. Presumably the warrior class extracted a proportion of the crop as payment for offering protection, while it is likely that, as in India today, cattle and sheep might have been considered as status symbols.

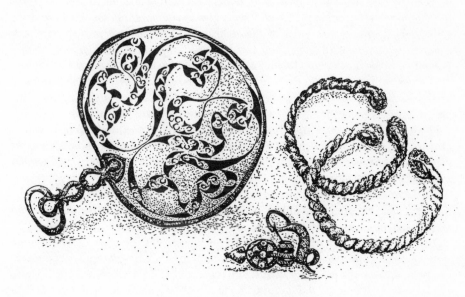

Mirror, brooch and gold torcs.

33

The re-dividing of the land with dykes, from c.500 B.C. onwards in the South, mentioned earlier, could be interpreted as an attempt by the newly established warrior class to, not only assert their control, but also improve productivity. Put simply, if agriculture in Third World countries today could extract the crop yields common in England, let alone the prairies of the U.S.A., there would be little problem in feeding their ever-growing populations. That was the problem faced in Iron Age England, especially in the southern half of the country. A growing population, stable or falling yields on the higher ground, and a finite amount of land suitable for tilling with the light ploughs of the time, all combined to enhance the change to an hierarchical society.

We have seen how man replaced hill-top enclosures with the more defensive hillforts, while there was a similar, although by no means universal, movement away from the smaller celtic field systems to the larger, dyke-enclosed fields, probably for stock. This new field system was still not able to provide the necessary food for a steadily growing population.

For a population to grow, either the Birth Rate must rise, and/or the Death Rate fall. As recently as the eighteenth century, the average lifespan in England was no more than forty years, compared to nearly eighty years today, so one might assume that the figure for the Iron Age would have been lower. With the aforementioned agricultural problems, the Death Rate would not be expected to fall. We must therefore look at the possibility of a rising Birth Rate.

The great rise in the population of England and Wales between 1750-1870 came about with the Birth Rate fluctuating between 32-36 live births per 1,000 of the population. On the other hand, the Death Rate fell, although not continuously, from 32-21 deaths per 1,000 of the population; in other words, people lived longer, on average. The subsequent increase in population has come about despite the Birth Rate falling to fourteen, as the Death Rate is now about eleven. In the three countries which now make up the India of the British Raj, the massive growth has been achieved with both Birth Rates and Death Rates falling from the high forties to a Birth Rate in the thirties, and Death Rates comparable to that of England and Wales.

It was quite different in the Iron Age, and to cause a rise in the population a rise in the Birth Rate must almost certainly have occurred. As we have seen, this probably came about through the establishment of the more permanent settlements, dating back to the Bronze Age. Food produce would thus need to keep pace with a growing population, and we must also assume the occurrence of periodic famine, or plague, as these were a feature of life in Europe until two centuries ago, and remain so elsewhere, even today.

I have suggested that crop yields fell, as the land was over-worked, and the need for crop rotation and fallow periods was not fully understood; a two field system did not really cater for this, and more marginal land was brought into cultivation. Needless to say, there are no figures available for crop yields from the Iron Age, but some idea can be gained from those of more recent times. Crop yields can be measured as a ratio of 1, that figure representing the seed corn. Today, yields can be very high indeed, with ratios of up to 50:1 being obtained. It was not always thus, and in the mid-eighteenth century wheat yields were about 7:1. Two hundred years before, yields were only about 3.5:1 for wheat, and were lower still for barley, oats and rye. One might assume that yields were much the same, if not lower, in the Iron Age and, as yields probably fell, it might have been the case that in some years little more than the seed-corn was produced.

Having seen how the celtic fields were farmed early on in the Iron Age, with the light plough, we ought to look more closely at the major industry of those times. Today, fewer than 2% of the British population is engaged in agriculture. In the Iron Age, that figure was probably nearer 98%. Corn crops would have been developed over the centuries from grasses, and by the Iron Age would be recognisable to us today. Wheat, oats, barley and rye were the main crops, and as such formed the basis of the staple diet. Spelt wheat was introduced during the Iron Age, which not only produced a better flour, but also allowed for an autumn and spring sowing and enabled more land to be tilled. Spelt wheat was well suited to the heavier, more productive clay soils of the lowlands, which were increasingly being brought into use. It may have been the gradual move to the lowlands, along with the use of a sturdier plough which gave the option of opening up further land, that caused the abandonment of certain hillforts.

Root crops, such as turnips, swedes, and so on were not grown, but beans, lentils and peas were. These would have provided not only vegetables, but winter fodder for the cattle. The keeping of livestock was the other major farming activity. Until the introduction of cotton and man-made fibres, animals provided clothing, while bones were used for tools. Meat would have been a luxury, especially in the South and South-East, and whole herds would not have been slaughtered each winter, but the dairy produce would have been valuable. As has been suggested, the cow might have been a status symbol, and also served as a draught animal.

It is likely that cattle and sheep would have been allowed to roam the hills each spring, with the linear dykes and banks acting as ranch boundaries, and they would have provided good manure for the land. Many hillforts, or hill-slope forts, of the South-West were a combination of defended land for both animals and people (*see* Clovelly Dykes*, or Tregeare Rounds*). That part of England seems to have witnessed the increasing importance of cattle and sheep during the Iron Age.

Sheep are a hardier, more independent animal than cattle, and appear to have become more common in the South and South-East, especially on the hills. Wool was, of course, vital for clothing, with its annual 'crop'. Pigs were also kept, particularly near the forests where the great scavengers came into their own in foraging for food, especially in the winter. The rubbish they were happy to eat soon turned itself into high protein meat and fat.

Mixed farming was the norm in both the Midlands and the Marches, presumably with regional variations. In the former region, there was a marked drift to the lower ground, with linear ditches, rather than celtic fields, proving dominant. In the more 'backward' North, it was thought that the keeping of livestock was the norm, but limited, recent evidence has revealed both the clearing of the forests and the increasing importance of crops, especially in the late Iron Age.

Each region thus had its own agricultural variations, and this was repeated again with its distribution. By c.100 B.C., the livestock based agricultural economy of the South-West seems to have been geared more to the trading of its produce. It is quite possible that Clovelly Dykes* was even a sort of 'export depot' for this purpose. Elsewhere, the agricultural economy was probably not quite so enlightened, and produce may have been for re-distribution and own consumption in the South and the Marches. In the Midlands and East Anglia, production seems to have been for a community's own needs, while that of the North was probably basic subsistence agriculture.

The arrival of the Belgae c.100 B.C., seems to have coincided with the introduction of the heavier plough; this was better suited to the clay soil of the lowlands, but was still without a mould-board to turn the soil after cutting the surface. It was, nevertheless, a major development, with a probable widespread use, at least in the South. The heavier, clay soil of the lowlands was more productive than the light soil of the higher ground and, apart from opening up more land to be tilled, the yield-ratio would almost certainly have risen. It was possible that the population further increased in the first century B.C., although peace did not reign as the Belgic peoples were arriving.

In comparison with agriculture, other economic activity would have been pretty minuscule. Two industries probably dominated non-agricultural activities: metal-work and pottery. The latter was almost certainly undertaken on an individual 'family' level, each region developing its own style. Another important introduction by the Belgae was the potter's wheel, and, prior to the Belgae's arrival, almost all pottery would have been hand-made. Wheel-thrown pottery was something of a revolution though, and facilitated manufacture on a larger, more standardised scale than had hitherto been possible.

Pottery of the middle and late Iron Age phase.

Metal-making, however, must always have involved a degree of specialism, whether in bronze or iron. For a start, ores needed to be extracted, and mention of tin-mining in Cornwall was made in the previous chapter. The manufacture of metal-wares would have been a skilled trade, geared mainly towards war. The main manufactures have been found to be swords, daggers, helmets, shields, plus certain tools, such as axe-heads, and other utensils, like cauldrons, horse/chariot fittings, sickles and so forth. Much of this manufacture was carried out in the Sussex Weald and Forest of Dean, both areas being rich in ores, and certainly involved an element of trade.

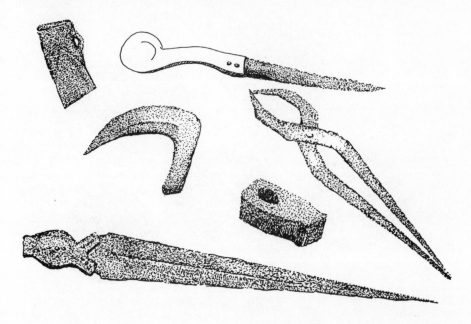

Iron tools: – axe, saw, sickle, hammer, tongs, sword.

Other economic activity would have been undertaken which involved a degree of specialisation, like salt extraction, boat or jewellery manufacture. These would have been on a local, small-scale level. The final introduction of the Belgae was to have a far reaching effect though, even if only in the South and East of England, at first, and probably on a restricted basis: money. Coins began to appear from the end of the second century B.C., along with the first Belgae peoples. The introduction of a means of exchange gave a significant spurt to economic expansion, as say brought about by the potter's wheel, probably an equivalent of the great consumer credit boom of the 1970s/80s.

That does not mean that the economy 'took off' to any great degree, nor 'slump' as in recent years, but money would have been another nail in the coffin of an egalitarian society, and another enhancement to accumulate. Trade would have benefited considerably, thus creating more homogeneous tribes; coins do not appear to have been used to any great degree in inter-tribal trade and, for example, coins of the Atrebates have rarely been found outside their 'area'.

Coins also need minting, yet another specialist task, and a mint has been discovered at Hengistbury Head*, for the Durotriges, while that of the Dobunni tribe appears to have been at Bagendon (Gloucestershire). As an example of the use of coins in trade, Durotriges coins are rarely found in Dobunni areas, but the reverse is certainly not the case. Foreign trade did not rely on coins though, and routes through France and Spain to either the South-West, or the South, had been developed at the dawn of the Iron Age. The nearer route, across the Channel from Kent, would probably have been used even earlier.

Early British coins.

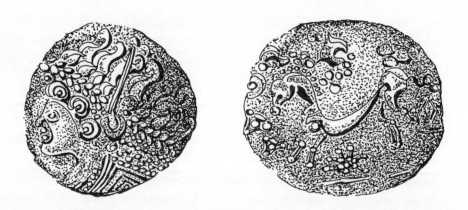

Gallo – Belgic coins.

Amphorae jars.

No doubt, foreign trade would have dealt more in luxuries, such as weapons, jewellery and suchlike. Hengistbury Head* and nearby Poole (Dorset) were developed into trading ports, with raw materials being exported, and other semi-raw materials being worked up into finished goods for either home consumption, or re-export. Wine, imported in distinctive pot jars called amphorae, seems to have been a particularly favoured luxury, in both the South and South-West. This is evidence not only of foreign trade, but also of a class wealthy enough to acquire such luxuries.

After Caesar's invasions of 55 and 54 B.C., Hengistbury seems to have declined as a port, and the centre for an increased, foreign trade was shifted to Essex, and strangely not the direct route via the Straits of Dover. Strabo, a Greek geographer who wrote in the first century B.C., says that the British exported grain, cattle, iron, hides, hunting dogs, precious metals and slaves. Imports included wine, pottery, jewellery, glass, ivory and olive oil; a relationship not unknown today, with many Third World countries exporting raw materials to and, importing finished goods from, the industrialised countries.

Leaving the economy behind, there were other aspects to Iron Age life with which we would have been familiar: religion and war, the two often in-divisible. As we have seen, the rise of the permanent, defensive settlement gives us enough evidence to suggest that all was not 'hunky-dory' throughout the Iron Age. There are many examples of hillforts having seen action, (*see* Bredon Hill* and Almondbury*) but not perhaps as many as might first be supposed, given the vast number of hillforts.

No doubt, as the population grew and the warrior class sought to flex their muscles, or at least get the people they were supposed to be 'defending' to undertake the fighting for them, there was also a 'raiding season'. Many of the bronze and iron wares that have been found are connected with a less than peaceful existence, while it seems that chariots were quite a feature right into Roman times. Indeed, it is said that the Catuvellauni had 4,000 chariots ranged against the army of Julius Caesar.

The Celts seem to have worshipped 'Mother Earth', and many swords have been dredged from rivers, presumably having been thrown there, either as an offering by the owner or, more likely, on his death. Their religious leaders were the Druids, with their holy island of Mona, modern Anglesey. Again, the existence of a religious leadership implies some form of social hierarchy, but these were something else. The Romans were convinced the Druids indulged themselves in human sacrifice, perhaps even cannibalism, were wary of the political nature of the religion and were quick to abolish it soon after the invasion of 43 A.D., despite their tolerance of conquered people's religions, like the Jews.

Without there being a shred of evidence, it is possible that something recognisable as a universal Celtic language was spoken throughout England, and possibly even the British Isles, at least by the time Caesar arrived. Of course, it could also be that many different languages were spoken, but Welsh and Gaelic can be dated back to pre-Roman times, and may well have been understood in the Iron Age. Being pre-history, or course, there is no Celtic writing, although some Belgic coins carried inscriptions, usually of a kings name, and then in what was probably Latin.

The above over-view of Iron Age Britain probably conceals as much as it reveals, but one thing is crystal clear, and that is it was constantly changing, if not on the scale we are used to today. Iron Age Britain on the eve of the Roman invasion of 43 A.D. would have seemed almost as different to Iron Age man of c.800 B.C., as that of today for someone transported in time from 1750.

Far from being 'un-civilised', Iron Age society in the first century A.D., especially in the southern half of England, had many of the traits so obvious in our own world. True, it might not have been as advanced as Rome, and was essentially still pre-historic, but it was increasingly poised to make that leap from the 'dark' into the 'light'. I wonder how advanced English society would have been in 1066 if neither the Romans had invaded, nor had Britain subsequently sunk back into the Dark Ages, in many respects a regression of several centuries.

Invade the Romans did, although it seems that a considerable number of kings were quite happy with the situation. The Atrebates, for a start, were allies of the Romans and the Roman presence was minimal in their area. The Durotriges did not fare so well though, and many of their hillforts were put to the test, and failed miserably. Resistance to the Romans seems to have been at its greatest and farther away from the South and South-East they went. Ultimately, of course, the Romans conquered all of England and Wales, but not Scotland, and history records the massive impact they made. One has to wonder though, was the impact that great for the common man,? As was suggested in the previous chapter, his lot probably changed very little, but as history records, the Iron Age was at an end, along with pre-history.

CHAPTER THREE

The Hillforts of the Iron Age:
What, Where and Why

Man has a great habit of attaching labels to all sorts of things. Unfortunately, many of these headings tend to be too general, for example when we refer to 'man' it can mean, literally a 'man', or any combination of race and gender from new-born to the oldest aged human being imaginable. In other cases our labels can be ambiguous; for example, when does a town become a city, or a village a town? If you told a foreigner that you come from the city of St Asaph, in Wales, that person would, no doubt, assume you lived in a bustling population centre, and not the tiny group of houses that surround the small cathedral, with a population lower than quite a number of villages.

'Hillforts' is a simple, straight-forward title, bereft of any such confusion, you might think. 'It's a fort on the top of a hill, surely', you might reply, if asked, and with a bit more awareness you might add, 'dating from the Iron Age'. Well, you would not be wrong but, as you will see, that would only be part of the answer. There is no set definition, and even historians and archaeologists would argue among themselves as to what constitutes a hillfort.

One thing is clear though, and that is a hillfort must have been a fortified settlement, whether permanently lived in or not. As to size, that poses a problem. Is a farm 'homestead', surrounded by a small earth bank, a hillfort? That is certainly a matter for debate, but the issue has been side-stepped as far as this book is concerned, as the smallest hillfort included in the gazetteer is Honnington*, at just over one acre. At the other end of the scale, Stanwick* is the largest hillfort, although it was built after the Romans invaded, and neither is it on a hill. Confused?

In 1962 the Ordnance Survey published a map entitled 'Map of Southern Britain in the Iron Age'. Excluded from this was all of Scotland (as ever) and the English counties of Durham, Northumberland, Cumberland and Westmorland, the latter two now forming part of the new administrative area of Cumbria. This map gave a total of 1,366 hillforts for its area, of which 796 were in England. Since that time, certain hillforts have been found to have possibly been built after the Iron Age, such as Clare Camp (Suffolk), while others have been re-designated as heralding from the Iron Age, like Carlwark*. If those hillforts from the omitted five counties are included, mostly in Northumberland, the total for England would have been about 950.

The O/S map further sub-divides the 1,366 hillforts into 'Large', i.e. over 15 acres, 'Medium', 3-15 acres and 'Small', under 3 acres (there are 640 acres in a square mile). They also sub-divide the hillforts as to the scale of the defences into 'Univallate', i.e. with one defensive wall, and 'Multivallate', with two, or more, defensive walls. The hillforts of Southern Britain, including Wales, divide up thus:

HILLFORTS (1,366)	MULTIVALLATE (34%)	UNIVALLATE (66%)
LARGE (10.5%)	44%	56%
MEDIUM (33.5%)	41%	59%
SMALL (56%)	28%	72%

As can be seen, the vast majority of hillforts are less than 15 acres in area, although there are considerable variations depending on the region, which will be dealt with later. Of those which are 'multivallate', a considerable proportion are thought to have originally been 'univallate' hillforts, that had been given extended defences at a later date.

A hillfort could be anything from a defensive enclosure surrounding a few huts, the equivalent of the hamlet, to a massive structure, probably comparable to a modern city. Some were undoubtedly the equivalent to the 'city-state' of the ancient world, perhaps like those of Sumeria, Yarnbury Castle* fits the bill. Others were the stronghold of a local chief, something similar to a minor Norman/mediaeval Knight, like Chun Castle*.

In all cases though, whether large or small, the building and maintenance of the defences must have taken a considerable proportion of the productive time of those for whom it was intended. This will be dealt with in more detail in a later chapter, but the building of a hillfort, its size bearing some relation to the number of people it was intended to protect, probably took no more than 20% of total available labour time, say over two years. This equates to the proportion of defence expenditure in the government's budget. Once built, a hillfort's maintenance would probably be of a similar value to the 7% of our Gross National Product spent on defence. So although hillforts can look mighty constructions, they were as cost effective as modern defensive measures; this says more about the money that is frittered away on defence nowadays than in the Iron Age, remembering how much greater the economic 'cake' is today.

It would be fair to say that the majority of hillforts were built after 500 B.C., yet on mainland Europe more hillforts had been built in the first half of the millenium. In the latter half, while the Celts and earlier peoples of Britain were settling down and building these defensive structures of ever increasing size and scale, the European Celts were 'up and awaying' in what appears to have been a great social movement, and abandoning their homes and hillforts. Ultimately, as we have seen, some of these, especially the Belgae, arrived on our shores in not inconsiderable numbers.

The inhabitants of our islands had been building hillforts for several centuries before 500 B.C. though and, with those built in the later Iron Age, have left a considerable variety of defensive camps which come under the heading hillfort. Before we look at some of these types, it is important to remember that what we can see today are 2,000+ year-old *ruins*, many of which have been abandoned for that length of time. Our climate is not kind on such remains, with or without human defacement, so what we see today, impressive though they may often be, are not in 'mint' condition. Consider what your house would look like if you abandoned it now, and came back in 4,000 A.D. It is also worth remembering that not all the hillforts were contemporary with one another. Some were abandoned centuries before others were built.

As a generalisation, it is possible, as with most building structures, to guess the age from the visible physical remains, and also to put it into some chronological sequence for its class, whatever the structure might be: castles, country houses or hillforts. The large, lightly defended *palisade enclosures* that transcended the Bronze Age/Iron Age, like Rams Hill (Berkshire), or the small strongly defended enclosure, such as Almondbury* (phase 4), both usually on hill-tops, were the first true hillforts, although not exclusively so. It is quite likely that their defences were built for protection against wild animals rather than man, except perhaps against a brief raid. The large ones were lightly populated, and it may be that few were ever permanently occupied.

Next came the *'contour'* hillforts, which usually consisted of a bank and ditch following a contour to surround the summit of a hill. Many of these were circular, like Figsbury Ring*. A variation of this type was the *'plateau fort'*, which would also often have a single rampart and ditch, with two opposing entrances, like the first Yarnbury Castle*. Dating from about the sixth century B.C., contour forts often had a permanent population, of greater density than the earlier palisade enclosures, and few, if any, were developed from these. They tended to be smaller, and their defences were periodically refurbished.

The middle Iron Age, c.500-100 B.C., saw the abandonment, re-building or increasing in size of the contour hillforts, while some of the earlier ones were brought back into use, having been abandoned; Hod Hill* is possibly an example. During this period, distinctive regional styles began to develop, and in the latter half many 'univallate' hillforts were given improved defences and became 'multivallate'. During that period the tribal areas of the pre-Roman period, as seen in Chapter 1, began to germinate as certain hillforts became a focal point for their area, at the expense of others, especially in the South, like Beacon Hill*.

Finally, the last 150 years of the Iron Age saw some hillforts abandoned, and the growth of the enclosed oppida, mostly on the lowlands in the Belgae areas. In the Durotriges area, and also in the South-West, hillforts were not only occupied during this period, but many received up-graded defences, like Hod Hill* or Maiden Castle*, and this trend could be seen all over the country, as at Wandlebury*, Mam Tor*, Stanwick* and Old Oswestry*, among others. These later defences, or up-gradings, tended to be simple earth banks and ditches, although of considerable size and depth, some of which appear to be unfinished, possibly as the enemy arrived too soon, as at Spettisbury Ring*.

The above might enable us to distinguish a hillfort by its era, in the same way as we can tell the difference between houses from Tudor, Edwardian and modern Britain. As with houses, though, there are many different types of hillfort, often distinguished by their period of building, but also by intended use, fashion and the local terrain. After all, defences suitable for a hill-top would be unlikely to suffice at sea level.

The earliest 'hill-top enclosure' had much in common with hillforts of a later date, that had far superior defences. Its primary attribute was its strong position, usually on the top of a hill, hence the name! Despite their relatively early date, many had an impressive 'box' type, spoil-filled rampart, revetted at the front and rear by either timber, or stone, depending on availability. Gateways tended to be of the simple 'straight through' type, protected by a double gate, some having small guard-chambers. Most of these were abandoned, and remains are slight, hence none have been included in the gazetteer, but there are many examples, such as Rams Hill (Berkshire) and Ivinghoe Beacon (Buckinghamshire).

There are a number of sub-divisions for what might be described as the typical 'hill-top' hillfort. The 'contour' hillfort is one which encloses the summit of a hill with man-made defences that follow the contours, as at Cow Castle* and Yeavering Bell*. Another variation is one that encloses the summit by the man-made defences linking up natural advantages, such as rocky out-crops, as at Carlwark*, or utilising natural steep slopes, as at Caer Caradoc (Clun)*.

A further variation on the hill-top theme is the hillfort whose ramparts follow a contour for most of the way, and then descends to drop 'off the shoulder' at one side, as at Old Oswestry*. Another, more common variety is the hillfort that does not enclose the whole summit, as at Quarley Hill*, which would result in a hillfort of massive proportions. Then there is Midsummer Hill*, whose defences enclose two hills. The last of the hill-top' divisions is that of the 'ridge-top' hillfort which, rather than enclose the whole ridge, has stout defences facing the level approaches and lesser ones that face the sides which afford a degree of natural protection; Oldbury Castle* is representative of this type.

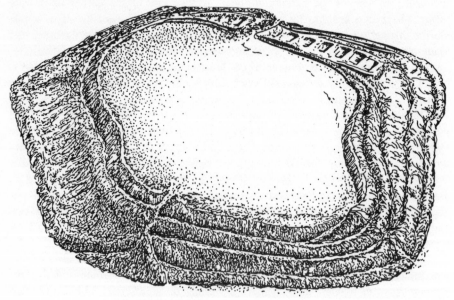

Old Oswestry hillfort.

Hill-top hillforts, whether of contour or any other type, are usually quite large, especially in the South, and can be seen throughout the country. Many were the focal point of a particular area, such as Cissbury Ring* or Danebury (Hampshire), and a good number of these had their own field-systems, or were at the centre of a cross-dyke field system, as at Quarley Hill*. It is by no means certain that all were permanently occupied, although those still in use in the first century B.C. usually were. Not surprisingly, this general type of hillfort was the most common, and some of the following types were variations on this theme. Natural advantages were often utilised, or defences adapted to suit the terrain; as in World War I, trench warfare was the norm in Flanders, mountain warfare in the Alps and a more mobile war on the plains and marshes of the east.

Undoubtedly some of the most spectacular hillforts, if not always with the most outstanding defences, are the 'promontory' hillforts, and the 'cliff-castles' of Cornwall, and also South Wales. These can be divided into two types; those on the coast, and those inland. Often, man-made defences for these are relatively slight, amounting to little more than a series of cross-dykes at the 'neck', the natural advantages of a steep slope, or cliff affording protection elsewhere.

Inland, Leckhampton Hill* is a good example, with man-made defences on two sides, and near vertical rock faces on the other two; nearby Crickley Hill (Gloucestershire) is similar. A more unusual type of promontory hillfort, which could also be described as a contour fort, is that at Uleybury*. There, all four sides are well protected with man-made defences, while the narrow strip of land adjoining the main range of hills has additional protection. Another variation is Dyke Hills*, which might be an oppidum. The River Thames 'protects' two sides, the River Thame another, while the land approach is defended by massive cross-dykes.

Not all promontory forts have a natural visual advantage over their locality. Dyke Hills*, for example, is overlooked by the Sinodun Hills, on which sits Sinodun hillfort. That is a bit of an 'odd-bod' though, but Hamble Common Camp (Hampshire) is only a few feet above sea level, its cross-dykes running from the River Hamble to Southampton Water. Perhaps the most important promontory fort was also in Hampshire, but is now supposedly in Dorset, at Hengistbury Head*. The English Channel protects two sides, Christchurch Harbour one, and cross-dykes cut off the land approach. Once again though, much of Hengistbury is less than 50 feet above the sea.

The numerous cliff-castles of Cornwall are rather different, usually affording prodigious views, even if overlooked from the land, many being virtual, if not actual, islands. Trevelgue Head* is in fact an island when the tide is in, protected by numerous banks and ditches, albeit of nigh impregnable proportions, and although any would-be attackers could see everything that was going on inside the hillfort, there would be nothing they could do about it.

Another hillfort peculiar to Cornwall, and the South-West, if not exclusively so, is the 'hill-slope' fort, with or without multiple enclosures, and the *multiple enclosure* hillfort, not always on a hill-slope. To confuse matters further, the multiple enclosure hillfort, usually on a hill-slope, is called a *rounds*. The *rounds* tend to be quite small hillforts, comprise two or more concentric banks and ditches and are almost certainly fortified, combined cattle enclosures and homesteads. Quite why they should be on the slope of hills is not known, but many are, such as Tregeare Rounds* and Warbstow Bury*. Other similar hill-slope forts can be seen at Buzbury Rings (Dorset) and Goosehill (Sussex), despite their rarity outside the South-West. As a Cornish alternative though, Castle an Dinas* encloses the summit of a hill, although this might have been more of a local stronghold than was the case with most rounds.

Multiple enclosure hillforts are again mostly seen in the South-West. Not all are of the rounds type, but they are usually associated with the keeping of livestock. As a result, such a fort comprises several enclosures, one of which was for the humans, and the other(s) for the animals. The best example is Clovelly Dykes*, which is a rounds with a number of enclosures attached, and another is to be found at the opposite end of the county at Milber Down (Devon). These tend to date from the third century B.C., with their 'extensions' being added later.

Combined hillforts/cattle enclosures are not totally unique to the South-West though, and there are examples of hillforts with a cattle enclosure attached, as at Conderton Camp* and Winklebury (Wiltshire); while others, such as Casterley Camp (Wiltshire) had their main enclosure sub-divided to accommodate livestock. At the opposite end of the country, in Northumberland, multiple enclosure hillforts of a more unusual kind can be found. These have circular enclosures side by side, with additional protection around the outside and, in plan, look like a pair of spectacles. Old Berwick* is an outstanding example, while another is featured at Wooler*; both of these being sited on the top of a hill.

The remaining types of hillfort are less common, and do not necessarily command their surroundings to the extent that the aforementioned types do. As its name suggests, the 'plateau' hillfort is built on level ground and may be overlooked, although it might just as easily overlook nearby ground. Arbury Banks* is an example of this type, overseeing ground to the north, but with the hills to the south peering down on it. Sodbury Camp (Gloucestershire) faces level ground on three sides, with no natural advantages at all, but overlooks the Severn valley to the west, as it rests on the escarpment. Cherbury Camp* is even more unusual, in that it is a 'valley' hillfort. That does not mean it is overlooked on all sides, for the valley in question is between the Marlborough Downs and the Cotswolds, formed by the River Thames and its tributaries, and is several miles wide. Nevertheless, its three ditches were often transformed into moats in the winter, and it could only be approached from the north-east.

Hillforts, therefore, come in all shapes and sizes, just as the ruins themselves range from nothing visible at ground level, to the massive remains of Maiden Castle*. Having looked at the different types of hillfort, it is apparent that people from each region of England tended to adopt a certain type of hillfort, dependent on their needs and the terrain. Height was a critical factor, but it was the relative, as opposed to absolute, height that was important. Warham Camp*, in Norfolk, for example is less than fifty feet above sea level, but is equal to, or even higher than most of the surrounding land. On the other hand, Ingleborough*, at over two thousand feet, dominates its immediate surroundings for a radius of several miles, but mountains to the north rise higher.

Starting with East Anglia, the distinguishing factor about this region is its lack of hillforts and, as with the Midlands, no particular trend can be distinguished. There is a concentration of about fifteen hillforts in the Peak District, mostly with a single, stone-built or -faced rampart, and these are usually on hill-tops. There is not a great deal to see northwards from there, until Northumberland is reached, and one must assume that the majority of people lived in defended farms and villages.

The hillforts of the Border country tend to be small, occasionally of more than one enclosure, of considerable number and with a fairly even spread of medium and large hillforts, like Yeavering Bell*. It is likely that these larger hillforts represented local trade and/or administration centres, while the bulk of the population was scattered in small homesteads.

Moving south, there is a concentration of hillforts along the north-west escarpment of the Cotswolds, none on the south-east, and a number in the south, around Bristol. Many of these are large/medium in size, and over 40% are multivallate, although those in the south of the area tend to be smaller. Those on the north-west escarpment form a chain, each visible to its neighbour, although as they were not all contemporary with each other, it was doubtful that they were built with any form of semaphore signal system in mind. Quite a cross-section of hillforts are represented in the Cotswolds, and there are a number sited in the Upper Thames area, which include the possible oppidum at Salmondsbury (Gloucestershire), and Bagendon (Gloucestershire).

Over to the west, and probably a reason so many of the Cotswolds were sited to face the direction, lies the Welsh Marches. As far as this book is concerned, the hillforts of Wales are 'out of bounds', but that was certainly not the case in the Iron Age, and those hillforts just over the border today would have been very much a part of the scene. One reason the Marches was probably such a volatile area was that the area to the south and west of the River Severn saw a meeting of the areas of three tribes: the Dobunni, Cornovii and the Silures. North of that river the Cornovii met with the Ordovices and Deceangli tribes, and although it would be overstating the case to suggest that these tribes were all homogeneous units, their very fragmentation probably only served to make matters worse; a situation probably not unlike that in the former Yugoslavia today.

Many of the Marches hillforts in the north are in Wales, but those in the south are more evenly distributed. As with the Cotswolds, there is a good proportion of large hillforts, the majority having mulltivallate defences in the south, with the reverse being the case in the north. The majority of the rest are medium-sized hillforts, with a consequent high population density.

Wessex, the central South part of England is, in many ways similar to the Marches, with regard to its hillforts. The downlands that stretch from Sussex in the east, to Berkshire in the north and Dorset and east Somerset in the west are covered with hillforts. Almost one in three are large hillforts, while barely 10% are small, and many of the large hillforts had their own delineated territory. As a generalisation, those hillforts to the east of the Hampshire Avon were univallate, while those to the west were multivallate. This was especially true of the large hillforts, and while many to the east fell under the Belgic Atrebate control in the first century B.C., those to the west fell into the Durotriges area, and remained fortified until the Romans swept through.

The South-East can be similarly divided up. The Weald and North Downs, to the south of modern London, had a few large hillforts, mostly multivallate with a few univallate ones nearer the River Thames. East of Beachy Head, there was hardly a hillfort to be seen, and to this day little is known about the Cantiaci tribe which occupied that corner of England. The South Downs, on the other hand, is cut through by four rivers, and these seem to have divided the range of hills up into convenient areas, each with its own large, univallate hillfort overseeing a number of smaller univallate hillforts. There are only three multivallate hillforts on these hills. Finally, the Chiltern Hills are also home to a number of hillforts, with twice the national average of large ones, but many are clothed in Beech trees, for which the hills are renowned.

Cornwall is home to more hillforts than any other county in Britain, while Devon is second, although way behind, as far as England is concerned. With over 300 sites in the South-West, only seven are large, and of these four are promontory hillforts, with over 60% being small. Despite the rounds type being synonymous with Cornwall, this type of hillfort is in fact heavily out-numbered by the univallate type. Not surprisingly, many hillforts, of all types, are spectacularly sited.

We have not yet addressed the crucial question of 'why build hillforts?', as there must have been a number of reasons why people from the Iron Age expended so much physical hard graft. After all, few people today would willingly spend a proportion of their lives labouring away at something which had no perceptible need, or benefit. The defence budget is one of the largest items of government expenditure, and as this comes out of the exchequer and our general taxes, so we all contribute whether we like it or not. Prior to the growth of government activities which 'care' for the population, especially since World War II, such as the N.H.S., education and social welfare, the defence budget had always been the single highest element in government expenditure. That could be mirrored in most societies throughout history, and Iron Age Britain was no different.

At some stage early in the first millenium B.C., the Celts began to arrive on our shores, probably for trading, rather than more sinister, purposes. Nevertheless, co-incidentally or not, people began to settle in semi-permanent groups, and once you start doing that there is a need to offer some form of protection, both against wild animals, and outsiders who might take more than a passing interest in your possessions. After all, we lock our doors, chain our bikes up and such like. A wooden fence surrounding a hill-top often sufficed at first, a *palisade enclosure*, while an earth bank and ditch would serve a similar purpose. Once built, the semi-permanent camp takes on a more established position.

As ever, with the 'haves' and 'have nots', those who 'have not' would not be above a bit of cattle rustling or land stealing, while the "haves" natural inclination is not only to have more, but to protect their possessions. Remember though, few of these early hill-top enclosures were developed into more heavily fortified hillforts, and most were abandoned. Could the arrival of the Celts – not as an invasion force one must add – have combined with the poor climate to lead to a more violent society, and a rise in theft of land and cattle? A natural response to this would have been the building of the early hillforts, though why so few in East Anglia and the extreme South-East, even in the early Iron Age, remains a mystery.

Many hillforts were not permanently occupied though, and some of the more exposed ones would have been distinctly in-hospitable in the winter. These would have acted as a refuge for the surrounding area although, unless the locality was exceptionally trouble-free, the hillfort could not have just been left empty. Others might have served as an equivalent to a mediaeval baron's castle, the hillfort being a local chief's stronghold to which the locals retreated at the first sign of trouble.

Hillforts could also have been developed out of a local meeting place, the focal point of a locality, or perhaps a sacred site, possibly like Danebury (Hampshire). No doubt some settlements developed into a full hillfort, like South Cadbury* or Mam Tor*, while Quarley Hill*, and probably the un-finished Ladle Hill*, grew at a meeting of ranch boundaries. If, as was mentioned in the earlier chapters, a warrior class developed, some form of restrictive pressure would have been imposed on the ordinary people, probably not unlike Feudalism in mediaeval times, with the chief offering protection in return for a proportion of the community's labour time. A set of physical defences would be a pre-requisite of such a system.

Once a warrior class is in existence, it usually likes to flex its muscles occasionally, and no doubt raids were carried out on other groups of people, who would have responded by creating their own defensive hillfort. Perhaps a pre-historic 'arms race' was an accepted feature of life, and if you did not possess any defences you were done for.

As the Iron Age progressed, there is evidence of more specialist use for hillforts. It is possible that some in Wessex were 'paired', with one being on lower ground and more suited to grain produce and storage, while the neighbouring one was on higher ground near the cattle enclosures; Beacon Hill* and Ladle Hill* might be a possible example of this. There is also evidence to suggest that some hillforts were built as fortified storage centres, such as Croft Ambrey (Herefordshire), where rows of compact buildings might have been used for grain storage. Such specialisation could only be contemplated where a unified tribe existed, and this seems unlikely, on the whole, in Iron Age England.

Some 'mystical' people who tend to look beyond the more conventional archaeological and historical interpretations of hillforts, burial mounds and such-like, often have other, more fanciful ideas. One theory suggests that the Iron Age peoples simply adopted, and adapted existing earthworks. These had supposedly been built to enhance the hills, a sort of landscape sculpture, to magnify the currents of natural energy that flowed through the earth, and which periodically came to the surface; a kind of pre-historic power station. These ancient peoples were supposedly, and probably, more at one with the earth and its natural forces than we are today. It is thought that pre-historic, mostly Neolithic, man derived some gain from the earth's magnetic forces, and this forms part of the Ley Theory, which will be referred to in the appendix.

The mystics may, or may not have a point, but certain hillforts have had 'finds' carbon-14 dated[1] to the Iron Age, and there is no doubt that nearly all were built in the first millenium B.C. In any case, although some hillfort ramparts might appear as beautiful landscape sculpture today, they are ruins, and would have appeared distinctly more menacing, and less artistic, 2,000+ years ago. As for citing imponderables, such as many hillforts have no evidence of habitation – few that have been comprehensively excavated have not come up trumps in this respect (Castercliff* is a possible exception); or that the defences would require tens of

---

[1] A scientific method of measuring the age of organic matter, and especially useful to work out the date of, say, charcoal found in a hillfort rampart.

thousands of defenders to man them effectively, which shows a lack of insight into how British Iron Age people fought, as cited by Julius Caesar and other 'classical' sources – merely shows that the mystics fraternity have come up with good theories only because they have not fully researched the subject.

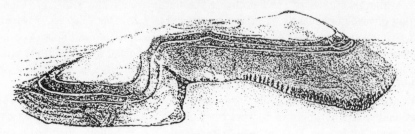

Hambledon Hill.

In any case, hillforts were not static entities, despite the physical constraints imposed by their defensive boundaries. Many multivallate hillforts were, as we have seen, developed from univallate ones, with the addition of extra lines of defences to the outside, while Wandlebury* was developed by having additional defences built on the inside. Some hillforts were considered to be too small, and so their defences were either partially or totally dismantled, and a stronger set built to increase the size of the hillfort, as at Yarnbury* or Scratchbury*. An alternative to this was the over-ambitious hillfort, which was rebuilt on a smaller scale, such as Winklebury (Wiltshire).

As with most things in life, some things grow at the expense of others. This is easily seen if we look at towns. Take Birmingham as an example. Two hundred and fifty years ago Birmingham was little more than a village, and certainly could not compete with nearby towns such as Warwick, Stratford, Tamworth and Lichfield. Thanks mainly to the Industrial Revolution, and the complex of canals that gave it the euphemistic title of the 'Venice of England', Birmingham grew massively to become not only England's second city, but the heart of the West Midlands administrative area, until recently. A similar phenomena can be detected among hillforts and their surroundings, particularly in Wessex and the South Downs. Some seem to have grown in importance, at the expense of their neighbours, some of which, unlike the towns surrounding Birmingham, were abandoned.

Trade, and/or the location of the most powerful of the warrior class in any given area, were probably the major causes of the above trend, but that does not necessarily account for the growth in the scale of defences. The 'chicken or the egg' argument comes up here, as to the cause of the pre-historic arms race. Did slings, and the deadly accuracy with which they could be used, cause the building of multivallate defences of a greater depth, or did such defences call for the invention of the sling as a weapon to overcome them, or was neither the case? We cannot hope to find the answer to that question, but slingers platforms existed at some gateways, like at Danebury (Hampshire). Certainly Iron Age man does not seem to have had the weapons to overcome the best defences, other than surprise, or by burning the gates down, as at Bredon Hill*.

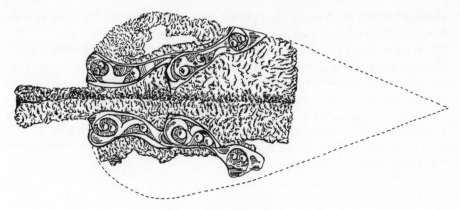

Ornamental spear head

Modern towns tend to attract trade and, particularly in the pre-motor car age, form a focal point for their surrounding area, where farmers send their produce, and craftsmen their wares. Hillforts, especially in the mid-to-late Iron Age, would have served a similar purpose. The land around the hillfort would have been used for either crops or animals, probably being worked either communally or by a pre-historic version of feudalism. Craftsmen, if they existed in a particular locality, such as metal workers, jewellers and so forth would probably have lived in the hillfort, these being specialist tasks.

Although many hillforts do not, on the surface, appear to have been heavily populated, where they can be seen there are few signs of huts outside the hillfort, lower down the hill, for winter habitation. That is not surprising, as the land has probably been farmed during the intervening period, but the same is true of many hillfort interiors. On the other hand, hillforts where there are numerous hut circles, like Yeavering Bell*, Hod Hill*, Midsummer Hill*, do not have a similar amount nearby. This suggests that certain hillforts were centres of trade, agriculture and order, where the people lived and went out each day to work on the surrounding agricultural land, sort of pre-historic commuters.

That situation could change though, for the higher the hillfort's population, probably related to its size, the greater the area of cultivation would be. Thus, it could be that for a large hillfort, say Maiden Castle*, the farthest fields would be several miles away from the hillfort, beyond what would be an economic daily 'commuting' distance, on foot. Once a hillfort came to dominate a particular area, could it be that the people who worked the land for the hillfort lived in a few huts, or a small enclosed farm, only while the land needed tending? After all, if there was an annual raiding season would you want to be living on an isolated farm unattached to either of your hillfort neighbours? At least if the alternative were true you could retreat the several miles to safety, or even act as an 'early warning system'.

Ultimately, once the tribal system seems to have become more established, c.100 B.C., there was a movement away from hillforts, especially in the South and South Downs, though by no means universal in the former area. St Catherine's Hill (Hampshire) currently being threatened by the proposed M3 extension through Twyford Down – was abandoned in favour of the valley settlement of modern

Winchester. That happened in other places, such as The Trundle*, but many hillforts remained occupied right until the Romans arrived in the immediate vicinity.

Hillforts in the Durotriges and the Dobunni tribal areas, the South-West and the Marches remained in use until the, occasionally bitter, end. The long, gradual development of the Iron Age hillfort reached its climax in the South, and possibly the Marches in the first century B.C. Thereafter, developments seem to have been hasty, especially re-fortification, or simply 'treading water', seemingly waiting for the Romans to arrive. It is significant though, that few attempts to overcome hillforts were made by the Romans east of the River Avon. Perhaps, like the sinking ship, they had all been abandoned by then.

CHAPTER FOUR

Hillforts in Detail:
Defences, Entrances and Internal Residences

No matter how important an historical site might be, it is the size and scale of the remains that reflect the level of interest in it. An historically significant monument, with impressive remains, will obviously appeal more than an equally spectacular site without any 'history', but if there is little to see, no matter how important the site, genuine interest remains limited.

Take the Battle of Bosworth field for example. It was here, in 1485, that King Richard III and his supporters lost out to the followers of Henry Tudor, who was crowned Henry VII on the field of battle, while Richard was reputedly left to cry out 'A horse, a horse, my kingdom for a horse'. The site is thus one of the most important in English history, but there is limited visual interest except for a few fields. On the other hand, nearby Kirkby Muxloe Castle, quite apart from being unfinished, is a virtual non-entity in historical comparison, yet has much more to see when you visit it.

Mention has already been made in a previous chapter that, when you go to visit a hillfort, what you see are 2,000 year-old *ruins*. As the main materials for construction in the Iron Age were wood, stone (where available) and soil and rubble, one can see that the life-span of such materials, except stone which has often been removed, is limited. The ruins of hillforts thus range from nothing more than crop markings, only visible from the air, to ruins of considerable size. Unfortunately, the passage of time and nature have taken their toll on many hillforts, and some that are of considerable historical or archaeological importance are hardly worth a visit. As far as the gazetteer section of this book is concerned, I have concentrated on hillforts with often impressive remains, and as a result some with an importance nearer that of the Battle of Bosworth field than Kirkby Muxloe Castle, have been omitted.

It must be remembered that, as with most fortifications down the ages, the main objective of any hillfort was to provide an effective defence as economically as possible, which just goes to show that the modern emphasis on keeping costs down is nothing new. While it might have been the case that some form of over-aggrandisement of the defences, either as an additional deterrent or simply a display of status, occurred, the extra work as a total of the whole would, no doubt, have been fairly marginal. It is only recently that many of our major buildings, as well as smaller ones like houses, have the architectural merit of a matchbox, and are shoddily put together with low quality materials. Thank goodness our forebears took more pride when they built our great civic buildings, universities and such-like.

The different types of hillfort are usually defined by the form the defences have taken. Univallate hillforts, i.e. those with one rampart, comprise about 2/3 of all English hillforts, although that fraction is reduced for large and medium sized hillforts. In most cases though, multivallate hillforts usually began life as univallate hillforts, and had their defences extended, either during one period of use, or after they had been abandoned and were re-used. Some hillforts seem to have been abandoned on more than one occasion, like Blewburton (Buckinghamshire).

For those readers who lived through World War II, and the two decades before, you will realise more than most the value of building up defences in peaceful times, as opposed to when the Luftwaffe was raining bombs down on munitions factories. Since that time, the 'Cold War' was deemed a sufficient excuse for keeping defence expenditure at high levels, but now that is over and successive governments claimed threat to our shores from the former U.S.S.R. has past, so all three services are currently in the throes of making 'cuts'.

The building of hillforts was little different, and the people of the Iron Age would have been faced with a similarly contradictory position of the best time to build a hillfort being when there was no hurry; that would mean during peaceful times (as during the 1920s and 1930s, after 'the war to end all wars'). Thus a great deal of collective effort would have to be expended in providing a defensive structure that might never be used in one's lifetime, and who wants to do that? If, however, you wait to build a hillfort until it is needed, you may end up not finishing the job before the enemy arrived, as may have happened at Ladle Hill*, or not completing the strengthening of the defences, as at Hod Hill* and Spettisbury Ring.*

One might well assume that hillforts were either built, or strengthened, at a time of modest unrest, rather than outright war. On the other hand, if a group of people decided to settle at a permanent site, and it was the norm for the area to have a fortified hillfort, there would be a good chance of those people also building a fortified settlement, a hillfort. This was a similar situation to that of the U.S.S.R., after World War II, having to get its own Atom Bomb. The Russian army might have been the biggest and most powerful after the war, but without the 'A' bomb it was at a distinct advantage to the West.

It is thus the defences which form the most impressive remains of hillforts, in general. We have seen that the palisade enclosures are the earliest form of hillfort, but that few remain to be seen. On the whole, many of these were simply a wooden fence surrounding a section of hill-top, often without any supporting ditch. Occasionally, a double fence system might have been used, possibly to prevent a rampant wild animal getting a clear run at the fence defending the interior; but as these would have been mostly built of wood, there is seldom anything to see, on the surface at least.

When one visits a hillfort today, with very few exceptions in England, the defences are mostly grass covered mounds and ditches, both of which are weathered to a greater or lesser extent. If one cleared out the ditches and re-furbished the rampart to its former height, you would soon have a pretty formidable set of defences. You might also think that the simple pile of earth and spoil, the 'glacis' rampart, was the earliest form, but this has been shown not to have been the case. Many hillforts began life with a box rampart as its primary defence. This would mostly be a wooden frame built around and over the heaped spoil dug from the ditch. The main advantage would have been of height, up to about twelve feet above ground level, while the width of the 'box' could be similar to the height.

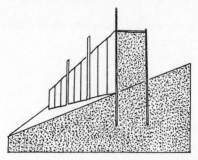
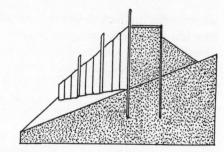

Box Rampart

A ditch, usually of 'V', or more rarely 'U', shape would have been dug outside the line of the rampart, but on steep ground the spoil from the ditch would have been thrown outwards, down the hill, to build the rampart. A further outer ditch would thus have been needed. The revetting of the rampart would have been wood, although sometimes a dry-stone facing was used, and a vertical face presented to the outside world; a stepped-stone inner rampart was built at Rainsborough (Northamptonshire.). Needless to say, after a winter or two, at the most, the internal spoil would soon begin to bow the wood, or to push the dry-stone wall out, precipitating the collapse of the rampart. To alleviate this disaster, wooden horizontal 'ties' were placed through the spoil to connect the inner and outer revetting, although one must assume that this was learned by bitter experience, in the early Iron Age at least. To prevent the collapse of the rampart into the ditch, a 'berm' was necessary between the two. Hillforts which used this form of defence include Leckhampton* (stone-faced) and Hod Hill*.

A variation of the box rampart is the 'wall' rampart, which presents a vertical wall to the outside, but often has a sloping rear. The front revetting would still need to be 'tied' into the rear revetting, hidden beneath the spoil, or horizontal beams would be needed at the front. A ditch and berm would have been similarly used, as with the box rampart, while the rampart would often have had a parapet and walkway on the top, as before. Wandlebury* had this type of rampart, but this was unusually built very late on. Both the box and wall type of ramparts were incorporated into univallate and multivallate defences.

You would not expect to see the remains of a box or wall type rampart today, the wood having long since perished, although the holes in the ground can often be seen when excavated, and the stone has either been overgrown, like at Castle an Dinas*, collapsed, as at Rainsborough (Northamptonshire), or stolen. Chun Castle* still has its stone walls intact to a fair height, while the collapsed stone walls can be seen at Yeavering Bell*. Mostly, we are left with the grass covered mounds.

Such grass clothed ramparts make it difficult to distinguish between box and wall ramparts, and glacis ramparts, at least on the surface. These latter ramparts were, quite literally, simply the stone, spoil and earth dug from the ditch and piled up. To be effective, these needed to be 'high', with a steep slope from the bottom of the ditch to its summit; 'wide', to prevent the base being eroded away and the whole thing collapsing; and 'handsome' – not strictly essential, but some did have a parapet on top, as in the flint one at Hod Hill*. Mention of this last hillfort also emphasises the point that hillforts sometimes had two different types of rampart, while others were rebuilt with different types of defences than before.

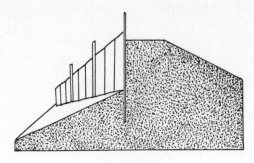

Wall rampart

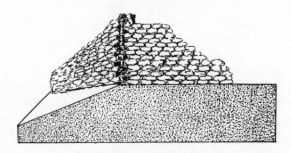

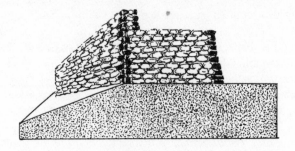

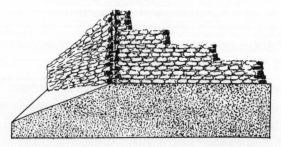

Different versions of stone faced wall ramparts.

Glacis ramparts are surprisingly common, and in many multivallate hillforts the outer, if not the inner, ramparts are usually of the glacis style. This suggests that the glacis style was more common in the middle and later Iron Age, and many hillforts that were hastily refurbished in the face of the Roman II Legion in the South-West, such as Hod Hill* and Spettisbury Ring*, simply had the ditches dug out and the spoil piled high onto the rampart. This was a far from successful expedient at that time.

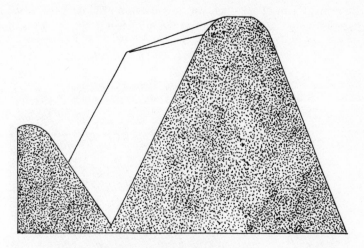

Glacis rampart with 'V' ditch

On the other hand, if you want to see just how effective glacis ramparts and ditches could be, even in their present ruinous state, just try and 'storm' the defences at Maiden Castle*, starting from outside the farthest ditch. Oh, and remember that sling-stones and spears would be raining down on you, as well. Some glacis ramparts were revetted at the back, presumably to prevent their collapse onto an internal building, as at Maiden Castle*. Also, glacis ramparts were often built on top of a collapsed earlier rampart, even if this had been a box type, for example, as at Hod Hill*. Whatever the rampart though, it had to be sturdy enough to withstand a frontal assault.

A major weakness of the timber-faced box or wall rampart was its susceptibility to fire. Such ramparts, even stone ones with timber lacing, have been either deliberately, accidentally, or possibly spontaneously, destroyed, often leading to the abandonment of the hillfort in question, as at Almondbury* and Leckhampton*. Untreated, exposed timber does not last forever either, and the timber revetting must have required periodic replacement, possibly every twenty-five years for the stoutest timber, but rather less for the rest; in other words, a major re-build would probably have been required once in an average Iron Age lifetime, rather like replacing Polaris with Trident.

Very few hillforts were defended simply by a rampart, the earliest bank at Castercliff* being an exception. As a general rule, for every rampart, of whatever type, there was a corresponding ditch, the spoil from any additional ditch usually having to be put somewhere. There are many exceptions though, such as

Abbotsbury* with two banks and one ditch for much of the circumference, and Figsbury Ring*, with its, possible, quarry-ditch set back well into the interior. A number of hillforts have a quarry-ditch immediately inside the rampart but, as at Figsbury Ring, this was not, of course, part of the defences.

Apart from the aforementioned 'V' and 'U' shaped ditches, flat-bottomed ones were used, particularly from the middle Iron Age onwards. This was probably as much to do with local tradition and the terrain, as with one type being superior to the other. The primary aim of the ditch was to prevent a head-on 'rush' at the rampart, and considering they could be anything from 6-20 feet deep, and 15-40 feet wide, they could prove to be a tough obstacle.

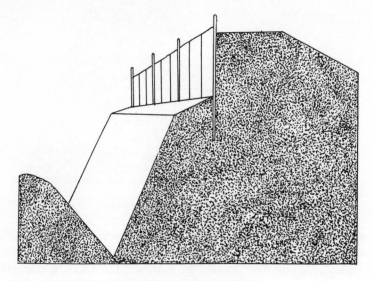

Wall rampart with 'V' ditch.

Many ditches are quite silted up today, and all would have needed constant dredging and clearing during the Iron Age. Nevertheless, many are still of considerable proportions, and if you want to see just how formidable a deep, flat-bottomed ditch could be, just go to the re-constructed defences at Stanwick*. With a glacis rampart it was the norm for the slope from the ditch bottom to the top of the bank to be continuous, but there are exceptions where the angle of the slope changes, as at The Trundle* and Caer Caradoc (Clun)*. As with the box type of rampart, it was not unknown for a glacis rampart to have a berm between itself and the ditch.

The clearing of the ditch(es) often resulted in the formation of a secondary bank on the outside of the ditch, hence its name, the 'counterscarp bank'. These vary considerably in size, from little more than a low mound, to a bank of substantial proportions, which led early archaeologists to describe some univallate hillforts as multivallate, as at Beacon Hill*, or confuse the number of ramparts a hillfort has, as at Yarnbury*. Not surprisingly, most hillforts feature a counterscarp bank to their outer ditch, while some with defences more widely spaced also had them for an inner ditch, as at Castle Ring*; this feature was another hindrance to a potential attacker, which came about through routine ditch clearance. Not to be sneezed at.

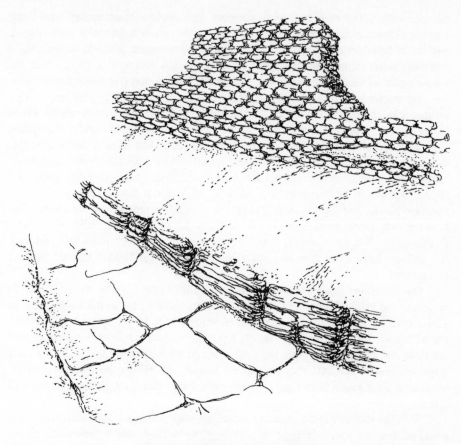

Stanwick defences re-construction.

The above concerns the main defences only, but some hillforts had need of additional space and annexes were built, at a later date, perhaps even in the post-Iron Age. The best example of this is at Clovelly Dykes*, where the original rounds type hillfort received three almost rectangular enclosures to the west, and a semi-circular one to the east, probably built in several stages. The defences for the outer enclosures were built to a similar scale to those of the original rounds, but more often the annexes, being post-Iron Age, are banks to mark out the annexe, as at Yarnbury* or Stanwick*.

Other variations on the need to enclose further space can be found in the use of cross-dykes/banks, as at Chanctonbury Ring*. Here the ridge-top plateau on which the hillfort stands is cut off by banks at both the east and west, although in this particular case, the cross-banks might be older than the hillfort. There is also the possibility of the existence of a satellite, or subsidiary hillfort, either for use as an out-ranch or defensive camp for people working on out-lying land, as an early warning system (unlikely), or for other specialist use. These may exist at Martinsell/Giant's Grave* and Yarnbury*, with a small camp 450 yards to the north.

The defences are the outstanding feature of a hillfort, and the most likely part to be seen today. The combination of rampart type ditches, counterscarp banks, the number of lines of defence and their dispersal, either close together or wide spaced, has left a bewildering range of hillfort ruins. With certain hillforts undergoing a metamorphosis through several types of defence, it is almost possible to trace the whole gamut of these defences at one site, like at Blewburton Hill (Berkshire).

No matter how powerful the defences though, a means of gaining access to a hillfort was necessary. It was the entrance which, if not planned carefully, could easily prove to be the vital chink in the armour that would render all efforts expended on building the ramparts and ditches useless. Just witness the lengths that the greatest of mediaeval castle builders went to, with elaborate barbicans, draw-bridges and portcullises to protect their entrance. Even today, at Army posts and Police Stations in Northern Ireland, an array of look-out towers, cameras, fences, concrete blocks and zig-zag approaches are all used to protect the entrances. This was the one likely weak-spot in the defences of a hillfort, as with most static fortifications. Not surprisingly, therefore, these were kept to a minimum and very few hillforts have more than two entrances; even the great Maiden Castle* has just that number.

On the other hand, when you visit a hillfort, care needs to be taken to recognise the original entrances, as many hillforts feature gaps in the banks made at a later date. Hod Hill*, for example, has what appears to be six entrances. Only two are of certain Iron Age vintage; one is Roman; two mediaeval at the earliest; and the final one may be Iron Age, but could also be of Roman antiquity. As the later 'gaps' are usually just that, they are easy to identify, but where the original entrance was either little more than a gap, or has been badly damaged, difficulty may still arise.

With the palisade enclosures, a simple gap, with perhaps a section of fence that could be dragged across at night, or if danger approached, would have sufficed. As with this type of fortification, nothing of note remains to be seen on the surface, but a similar entrance would have been adopted for the earliest box rampart defended hillforts, of a simple gap in the defences. Wood would have been the main material used, but entrances permitted, even encouraged, a degree of innovation and individuality. This has often resulted in the entrance being the most fascinating part of the hillfort ruins to be seen today.

For a start, the ends of a rampart, whether of box, wall or glacis type, would need a considerable amount of strengthening, to prevent a lateral collapse into the entrance gap. This often meant, even with the earliest hillforts, that the ends of the rampart were expanded, and a heavy timber, or more rarely stone, frame was built to define the passage, usually of a considerable height. The single or double gates, not necessarily hinged, would have been positioned between the two rampart ends, and the defenders would have enjoyed a height advantage over any attackers on the immediate approach to the gates. That simple 'straight-through' entrance would have allowed for a head on, direct approach to the gateway, at which an attacking force could charge with impunity. In addition, wooden gates are prone to burning, and one would assume that an attacking force would have aimed to set fire to the gates.

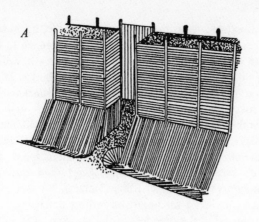

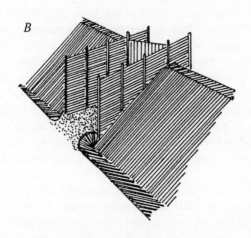

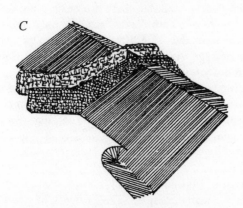

Reconstructions of possible entrances:-

A   *Palisade gap*
B   *Palisade gap with extensions*
C   *Stone wall entrance passage*

To counter this threat, extensions to the passage were made, again usually timber-faced, either/or fore and aft, to deepen and narrow the approach to the gates. The gates themselves were often divided by a central post, a row of which might also have been used to divide the entrance passage, as at Blewburton Hill (Berkshire). This form of entrance had the advantage of forcing any attackers into a narrow confined area, overlooked by the defenders who could throw objects down onto them. Although preferable to a simple gateway, this type of entrance still did not prevent any direct charge on the gates. Despite this, entrances of either the simple straight-through, or the straight-through with side extensions types, can be seen at hundreds of univallate sites, like Chanctonbury Ring*, and certain multivallate hillforts, such as Prestonbury*, or Badbury Rings (Dorset).

Hand in glove with the need for improved hillfort defences, as the Iron Age progressed, went the need for a more defensible entrance. The next step in the development of entrances, and one that is widely visible today, was probably the introduction of 'in-turned' rampart ends, as at hundreds of hillforts, including The Trundle*, and more rarely 'out-turned' rampart ends, at Battlesbury*, or even a combination of both, as at Bredon Hill*. This simple expedient of extending the ends of the rampart round, usually inside the hillfort, allowed for not only a particularly long entrance passage, some being in excess of 100 feet, but also facilitated the introduction of certain 'accessories', some of which had been used on the earlier entrances, such as two sets of gates, guard huts and chambers and bridges. The depth of the approach was the principal defensive measure, and one might imagine that the long, narrow, congested approach would become a drain on the morale of an attacking force as missiles rained down from above, cutting the attackers to pieces. On the other hand, the gates were still exposed to the direct approach.

Right from the early Iron Age, hillforts had been built with additional defences to the entrance. Leckhampton Hill* had guard chambers built into its entrance passage, from possibly as early as the seventh century B.C., and these were a feature of many Marches hillforts. Free-standing guard huts, usually, but not always, outside the gates, may have been widely used, but these are much more difficult to trace, even by excavation. Post holes of a considerable size, the only sure evidence of the use of gates, also exist at a number of hillforts which were probably used for a bridge over the entrance passage. As with all timber constructed features, these are not visible today, but Rainsborough (Northants.) had one from at least the fifth century B.C., while Midsummer Hill's* south entrance also received a bridge at one of its many re-builds. Some hillforts might also have possessed an archway as well, possibly on which to display heads; a gruesome Celtic act, that was still performed until just over 200 years ago. It is likely that such 'accessories' existed at many other hillforts.

The use of such adornments, along with the regular re-building of the entrances, like the probable seventeen of Midsummer Hill*, gives a very strong hint that these hillforts, at least, were permanently occupied. The existence of guard chambers also suggests that the inhabitants were either organised enough to have a rota for guard duty, or that a warrior class existed to undertake such tasks. Furthermore, guard huts also point to the gates being permanently manned with, as in mediaeval walled towns, a check being made on all visitors.

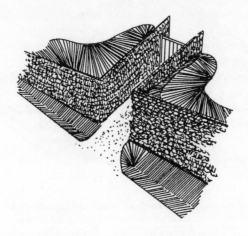

Entrance – in-turned ramparts.

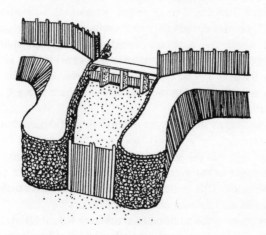

Long entrance – passage with bridge, eg Bredon Hill.

Once again though, even with a long inturned passage, double gates, guard chambers and huts and a bridge, a head-on approach to the gates was not prevented, and the entrance was still susceptible to a determined charge. Any further defensive improvements to alleviate that problem would require considerable labour on the part of the inhabitants, and the end result would also inhibit the ease of their own approach. At Blewburton Hill (Berkshire), a gully was built inside the entrance to force any attackers to change direction after breaking through the gates. This was quite rare though, being an early example, and it was more usual to take measures to prevent a direct approach to the gates themselves, often taking the opportunity to increase the number of ramparts at the same time, though not always.

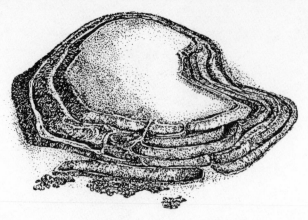

Western entrance of Maiden Castle – maze like approach.

The simplest method, which required two ramparts, was to stagger the entrances through the ramparts, thus forcing an attacker to turn and present his un-defended side to the defenders. This could be undertaken with both wide-spaced ramparts, as at Clovelly Dykes*, or with normal defences, perhaps best seen in the stone ramparts of Chun Castle*, where the attackers would also be confined to a tight space. Multivallate defences also allowed for in-turns of a considerable length, and several sets of gates to be used, as at Old Oswestry*, where the length and steepness of the western approach, quite apart from the possibility of there being three sets of gates, would be highly effective.

Quite often though, to improve the defensibility of the entrance, out-workings were needed, to channel the approach and prevent a charge. Obviously a steep approach precluded this, but the south-west entrance at Hambledon Hill* has a long passage at a right angle to the gates, formed by the extension of the outer rampart well beyond the entrance. This is almost a mirror image of the north-east entrance at nearby Hod Hill*, and also the east entrance at Oldbury*.

More commonplace is the addition of cross-banks, as at Uleybury*, to prevent a direct approach; an offset passageway through additional banks, as at Abbotsbury*; a large independent out-working, as at Yarnbury*; horn-works, like Beacon Hill*, which also had its rampart ends looped round. At hillforts with more than one entrance, a combination of any of the above-mentioned entrances were often used, which will add to your interest, as the entrances are often the best signs of ingenuity in any defensive structure, hillfort or otherwise.

Even these did not always suffice though, and some entrances developed into highly complex, maze-like approaches. Yarnbury* is impressive enough, but the pick of the bunch are the complex, twin-portal entrances at Maiden Castle*. At both of these a winding, twisting approach is made, overlooked by guard and slingers platforms, to hinder an assault. A similarly complex entrance, though on an altogether smaller scale, overlooked by a central slingers platform is the final development at Danebury (Hampshire). These were all designed to withstand an attack in large numbers, and the 'war grave' at Maiden's east entrance is possible evidence both of an attack by the Roman II Legion, and the ultimate failure of even these advanced defences to hold out.

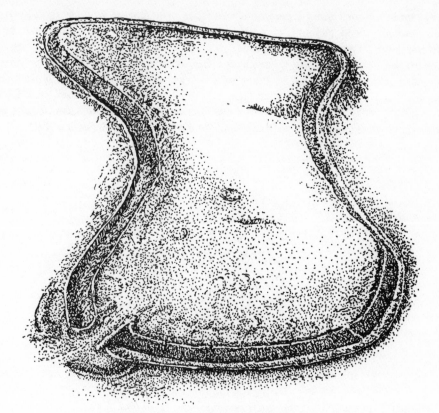

Entrances – horn-works Beacon Hill.

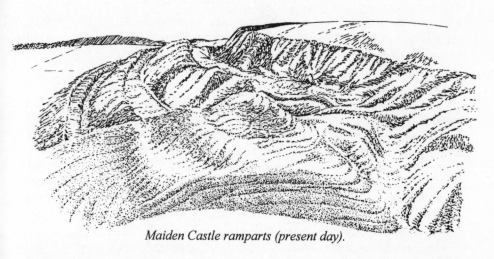

Maiden Castle ramparts (present day).

It must be remembered that entrances were in constant use, especially if the hillfort was permanently occupied. A further hindrance to both an attacking force, and also day-to-day traffic, was *chevaux de frise,* usually made up of large, pointed stones to prevent horses or chariots charging the entrance or defences. Wooden stakes were also probably used, although there has been no evidence of such use in England, but it was more commonplace in Europe, with some examples to be found in Irish, Welsh and Scottish hillforts. Of much more benefit, was the metaling of the entrance passage with stones. Some of these were carried on into 'streets', as at Maiden Castle*, or Hod Hill*, but no such metalled tracks from the Iron Age are visible on the surface today. The importance of a metalled entrance to a hillfort can be seen in the numerous entrances that were re-metalled over the years, as at Bredon Hill*.

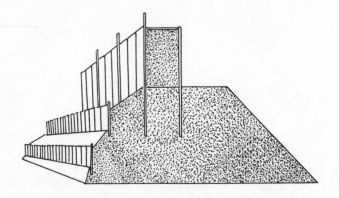

Box rampart with stakes out of ditch chevaux de frise.

The interior of the hillfort was the most important, for it was this area where people lived, and which the defences protected. Regrettably, most interiors have little to show today; Iron Age buildings, pits and tracks often being ploughed over down the years, or their remains being so slight as to have all but vanished. On the whole, it would be fair to say that the internal layout of those hillforts that have had a part of the interior excavated, a distinct minority, resembles more the uneven scatter of an African tribal village today, than the regimented grid pattern of Roman towns. There are exceptions though.

Most hillforts for which some knowledge of the interior layout exists, have a seemingly random, dis-organised scattering of buildings, such as can be seen in the hut platforms at Hambledon Hill*. Other hillforts have a regular, ordered street pattern, like Danebury (Hampshire), while Croft Ambrey (Herefordshire) and possibly Midsummer Hill* had a rigid grid layout. Hod Hill*, on the other hand, has what appears to be a random spread of huts, but these were originally arranged around two quite distinct tracks which led from the north-east entrance. A final type of internal layout is that of huts all together, and large areas of the interior either unused, or for non-residential purposes, possibly like Cissbury Ring*.

One would expect the internal arrangements to develop over time, and to reflect the use to which the hillfort was put. In a rounds hillfort, only one enclosure would contain huts, whereas if the hillfort was possibly either a barracks or a huge granary – two suggestions put forward for Croft Ambrey (Herefordshire) – then one would expect a high concentration of buildings. If a hillfort were to be used purely as a refuge for people from the surrounding countryside, then one would not expect to find much evidence of permanent huts, and this has often been the case, although there are mitigating factors. On the other hand, if a hillfort was a warriors stronghold, or at least the 'seat' of a chief, one might expect to find the remains of the occasional large 'civic' building; on this count there might well be further evidence to be uncovered.

The traditional, British Iron Age dwelling is the circular hut, about 20-40 feet in diameter, although some are considerably bigger. This might not seem particularly big, but in fact a 40 feet diameter hut would compare favourably in area, with a modern 'family' house, minus the bathroom and hallway. As with most other hillfort structures, the building material reflected that which was available in the locality: stone on the hills, and wood and wattle and daub in the South and Midlands. No evidence is available, but roofs must have been of thatch, although turf might have been used in certain places.

With the exception of Chun Castle*, no hillfort mentioned in the gazetteer has the remains of the built-up hut walls still standing. A reconstructed example can be seen at Singleton (Sussex), and the Hampshire Iron Age Farm near Petersfield, while in Cornwall two English Heritage administered Iron Age village sites can be seen, at Carn Euny (O/S map 203, ref. 402289) and Chysauster (O/S map 203, ref. 473350). The walls, which were usually between 3-5 feet high, were built of either timber, or stone, while wooden rafters would have been used to support a, presumably, conical shaped roof. Additional internal upright post-holes have occasionally been found, to offer further support for the roof.

The huts were usually entered by a single entrance, while many had a small 'hall' to allow for two doors, thus keeping potentially dangerous draughts out. Dangerous? Just think of the consequences of a gust of wind catching the flames from the fire, and the effect on the thatch! Hearths have been found in many, but not all, huts that have been excavated, but what is very difficult to determine is the internal layout of the hut. The most likely theory is a large communal area in the centre, with the edges partitioned off into individual 'bedrooms'. The partitions would probably have been of cloth or skins, and have left no trace. All in all, one would expect them to be little different, except in shape, from a village hut of the early Middle Ages.

Although huts cannot normally be seen nowadays, traces of hut circles, that is the wall footings, and hut platforms, the base cut into a steep slope on which a hut was built, can still occasionally be found. In nearly all cases they are, like the defences, clothed in grass, but the size can be made out. There seems to be no particular region better than another for such sightings, the main factor being the subsequent disturbances of the interior. Thus traces of huts can be seen either in large quantities, or covering a significant proportion of the interior at Hod Hill* (South), Chun Castle* (South-West), Midsummer Hill* (West) and Yeavering Bell* (North), and at other sites in the gazetteer.

Square, or rectangular buildings appear to be quite rare in Britain, although more common in Europe. Another feature of the English hut, over its European counterpart, is the relatively large size. There is no obvious reason why rectangular huts were not built, except perhaps tradition, but they have only been found as a tiny proportion of round buildings. However, take the typical log cabin. This does not need nearly so many posts dug into the ground as a round hut, if any, so traces of a potentially common abode would be non-existent to excavators.

Chieftains hut.

Another possibility, at least for some hillforts, is that, as in certain Central African tribal villages today, only the leaders had their huts in the centre, while everybody else had theirs around the outside. At least some European hillforts have been found to have had timber buildings erected in a 'lean-to' fashion against the rampart, possibly as at Almondbury*. This type of building leaves little or no evidence of its existence, and if this was common-place, then hillforts for which no trace of huts have been found, the majority, might have had a similar housing layout for the 'masses'. If this were not the case, one major difference between the Iron Age and today was the egalitarian nature of the huts as, on the whole, it is difficult to detect an area where warriors, or leaders, might have lived apart from the masses.

Quite apart from living accommodation, the storage of food was an important consideration in a permanent settlement, such as a hillfort. Mention has already been made about the possibility of the closely packed buildings of Croft Ambrey (Herefordshire) and Danebury (Hampshire), being used as grain stores. Certainly, grain has been stored in buildings raised from the ground on stilts, right up to the modern day. In most hillforts the most obvious place used for storage, of both grain and possibly salted meat, was in pits. As can be seen from the drawing, these could be of unusual shape, and were sometimes over six feet deep. Some were lined with stone, while wicker-work might have lined others, as at Conderton Camp*, but above all else, they needed to be sealed, probably with clay, to prevent the food decaying.

Care will have to be taken at certain hillforts not to confuse the site of pits with those of huts, for they are sometimes indiscriminately placed. Many pits have also been found that were filled with rubbish. These would have formerly been storage pits that had 'gone off', after a period of time. Again, these are placed hap-hazardly between the huts and, one might surmise, would have been something of a nuisance to the occupants, especially at night. Pity the poor devil who fell into one of these when it was full of stinking rubbish, or worse!

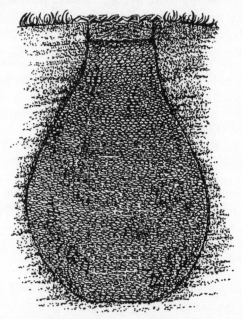

Cross-section of a storage pit filled with grain.

One would assume that communal, perhaps civic, buildings would have existed in a permanently occupied hillfort. Detection is the obvious problem, and few hillforts have been found to contain such buildings, with certainty. A large building within a hillfort is not unusual, but clues to a probable use are hard to come by. There are exceptions though, and the site of Iron Age temples have been detected at a number of hillforts, including Maiden Castle* and South Cadbury*. Unfortunately, these cannot be readily distinguished on the surface.

Much easier to see, in most cases, are features that are most definitely not of the Iron Age. Of particular interest are those which already existed on the site before the hillfort was built. These can be divided into two categories: those visible when the hillfort was built, and those probably not. In the latter category fall the aforementioned Neolithic concentric camps, especially those at Maiden Castle*, Hembury Castle* and The Trundle*, although this latter must have been visible as uneven ground, as it still is today.

From the former category, some hillforts contain a number of pre-Iron Age features. A Neolithic long barrow sits distinctively on the summit of Hambledon Hill*, and can be seen for miles around. Lesser ones appear at Warbstow Bury* and Hengistbury Head*. Some hillforts also contain examples of a pillow mound, as at Midsummer Hill* and Maiden Castle*, but they are difficult to detect at both of these sites. Also from the Neolithic Age are the many flint mines visible on the surface at Cissbury Ring*.

Far more common are Bronze Age round barrows. These can be seen at several hillforts, sometimes in prominent positions, as at Trevelgue Head*, and at others in considerable numbers; there are seven inside Scratchbury*. Quite why these features were enclosed within the respective hillforts defences is unclear, but it could quite possibly be that, as there was no harm done, nobody was particularly worried.

Quite naturally, one would expect to see all manner of post-Iron Age features within a hillfort, but some are of historical, and visual importance. Abandoned, presumably Iron Age, defences are to be found in the interiors of a number of hillforts, after they had been expanded. These include both partial defences, as at Oldbury* and Scratchbury*, and complete defences, as at Castercliff* and Yarnbury*. There are also abandoned defences to be found outside the later, smaller, hillfort, as at Bredon Hill*.

Undoubtedly the most spectacular Roman feature in a hillfort, is the fort built into the north-west corner of Hod Hill*, which utilised some of the Iron Age defences. Roman temple footings can be seen at Maiden Castle* while they are overgrown at Chanctonbury Ring*. The Normans knew a thing or two about using other sites for their own ends but, perhaps surprisingly, hillforts were not usually adapted to their needs; probably because the Saxon population no longer lived anywhere near them. However, motte and bailey castles were built at Herefordshire Beacon* and Almondbury*, but only the earth motte, and bailey banks, exist nowadays.

Features of interest which can be seen of a later period, some of which were placed there simply to take advantage of the hillfort's location, while others used the ruined defences, include a church and mausoleum at West Wycombe*, two villages at Stanwick*, a farm at Clovelly Dykes*, an obelisk at Oldbury*, a folly at Bredon Hill*, radio masts at The Trundle*, a coastguard lookout at Hengistbury Head* and, most important, pubs at Ham Hill (Somerset) and Almondbury*.

So far, we have dealt with the main features, visible or otherwise, of hillforts but, as with all pre-historic, and later buildings, the methods of construction are quite fascinating. For a start, despite the use of iron, tools were limited and usually consisted of animal bones and antlers to serve as picks and shovels, while baskets, and possible boards, for carrying spoil and stone would have been needed. Another important task concerned the cutting down of trees, so stone, and very occasionally iron, axes would have been used. At the heart of all construction though, was sheer hard, physical graft.

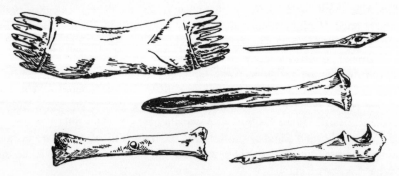

Bone tools:- Needle, gouge, awl weaving comb and bobbin.

70

Fortunately for us, not all hillforts were completed, which has enabled archaeologists to piece together the tasks and method of construction. Most of these had additional defences that remained incomplete, whether because the enemy arrived a bit smartish, or because the threat had gone away, is not usually known, as at Cranbrook Castle*, or Warbstow Bury*. However, the best example of an unfinished hillfort is that at Ladle Hill*, and its gazetteer entry includes details of the method of construction.

At Ladle Hill, the work was carried out by gangs of workers who cut a marker-ditch to define the area, but pegs or stones could also have been used. Then a ditch was dug outside the line of the rampart, with the spoil and soil being piled inside the space left for this. Chalk blocks were then cut out of the ditch to be placed on the intended line of the rampart and, had the builders got that far, the spoil would have been placed on top of this, and probably the front, if not the rear, would have been timber revetted. This was quite possibly a normal method of construction, in chalk country.

Ladle Hill encloses 7 acres, and with a 'guesstimated' population of about 150, which equates to about 120 man/days labour per day, given that women and children could also have done their bit, the hillfort would have taken about 120 days to build. With a hillfort of double the size, 14 acres, and given a population/area ratio of the same level, i.e. 240 man/days labour per day, such a hillfort would only take about 90 days to build, as the defences to enclose 14 acres are only 50% bigger than for 7 acres.

Conversely, with a hillfort of half the size of Ladle Hill, at 3.5 acres, and thus a population/area ratio able to provide 60 man/days labour per day, the defences would take 180 days to build, as the defences are still 75% of those of Ladle Hill. All this is a very general calculation, but it does show the benefit of building a bigger hillfort, and an approximation of the time needed to build the basic defences, without gateways, additional ramparts and huts to live in. That time might not seem to be too long, but when other more important, agricultural tasks had to be undertaken, it can be seen that the building of a hillfort was not to be taken lightly. All the more reason, you might think, for it to be permanently occupied, and not left to decay and to be used only in 'emergencies'.

There was thus, probably, more variety in hillfort building than in mediaeval castles and towns. In some respects they are typical of the pre-historic world, yet the scale of the defences often overshadow those of more than a thousand years later, while the basic living accommodation of the common man would probably not be out of place in the early mediaeval period. We tend to think that it was the Romans who first planned our towns and paved our roads, but such tasks had already been undertaken, albeit on a smaller scale. When one considers matters such as these, quite apart from the size of our modern 'box' houses being no greater than an Iron Age hut, it makes one wonder just how little we have advanced in over 2,000 years, in some respects.

CHAPTER FIVE

Hillforts in Action:
A blast from the Past

Can you define what constitutes a town? Sunderland has recently been granted a charter and has become a city, presumably on the grounds of its population. On the other hand, there are several cities with a much smaller population, most notably Ely with a population only 10% of that of Sunderland, and which have a cathedral. At the other end of the scale, I have heard of several villages that each lay claim to being the largest village in England; these include Yate (Gloucestershire), Shepshed (Leicestershire) and Cottingham (Yorkshire).

Are they really villages? Yate covers about the same area as Stroud, while Shepshed, although smaller, is similar in size to Ashby de la Zouch. Cottingham, on the other hand, is not only of a similar size to Barton upon Humber, but is joined to, and is in effect, a suburb of Hull. There is a similar conundrum regarding the use of hillforts; can a large hillfort be considered a town, and is a small hillfort an equivalent to a village?

I tend to think of a village as being a small conglomeration of houses, with a few local services (if it is lucky nowadays) and a church. The earlier hillfort, perhaps like Figsbury Ring* or the early Yarnbury Castle*, served as a focal point for its immediate locality, and was something of a self contained unit, probably more like an eighteenth century village than one today.

A town can be a gathering of houses with anything from just a few thousand, to hundreds of thousands of people. Often a town, or city, can be a focal point for quite a large area; a market for agricultural produce, and a manufacturing centre for both its surrounding area, and much further afield, especially if the town specialises in a form of manufacture, like shoes from Northampton, and cars from Coventry. Certain larger hillforts, especially in the middle-late Iron Age to c.100 B.C., had much in common with a more modern town, sometimes as a focal point for a large area, others as a specialist in a type of production, or as a combination of both.

A typical large hillfort of c.100 B.C., like Battlesbury* or Hod Hill*, would probably act as something akin to a 'capital' for an area of 35-40 square miles, at least in the South of England. It would often have grown at the expense of other hillforts in its area, some of which about 300 years before might have been at least the equal in size and stature. In certain respects the large hillfort would have served many of the duties expected of the earlier village type hillfort, such as the seat of a warrior, meeting place or trading centre and refuge. In others, the change in size and status of a hillfort would have meant that other duties, such as tribal organisation, religious centre and manufacturing, could have been carried out within, or from, the large hillfort.

We saw in earlier chapters that the Iron Age was anything but static, even discounting regional differentiation. It seems that, except in areas where conflict was still a regular occurrence, like those bordering on the advancing Belgic peoples, there had been a perceptible move away from the single large hillfort, and that defences were no longer given the importance formerly attached to them. This may have been due to the cohesiveness of an area, enhanced by the rise of one hillfort over the others, or perhaps the establishment of the tribal system mentioned in Chapter 2. In such a scenario, the influence of the large, formerly predominant, hillfort might have waned, and the last 150 years prior to the Claudian Roman invasion did see the abandonment of many hillforts.

On the other hand, hillforts were occupied in many tribal areas where they had been well established, right up to, and beyond, the arrival of the Romans. The large hillforts continued to play a major role within their sphere of influence, while others which served a single function, such as an 'invasion' beach-head, possibly like Bindon Hill (Dorset), a meeting place/refuge, or perhaps a religious centre, were abandoned. No single hillfort has, as yet, produced enough evidence to confirm, with certainty, what daily life would have been like for its inhabitants, but the body of evidence from many hillforts is growing, and a fairly general picture can be constructed. To have a look at such everyday life, let us again enlist the assistance of our intrepid, roving Roman Broadcasting Corporation reporter, Katia A.D., as she visits a fictitious, large hillfort, on the downlands of Southern England, in about 125 B.C., before the Belgae arrived in Britain, in force.

'After many days following a river upstream from the coast, we've made our way onto the higher ground which overlooks the valley. Our arrival was expected and, after being met at the river bank, we were pointed in the direction of the main hillfort, which is roughly at the centre of an area bounded by river valleys, and given the assistance of a guide.

'We made our way through the lower ground which was split into two-field systems used for growing corn, mostly wheat and barley. Men, women and children all undertook a variety of tasks in those fields, the former mostly working bare-chested, it being one of the warmest days we've experienced on this island. There didn't appear to be any great urgency about their activities, and most people stopped work as we passed, there being a distinct feeling of 'nervousness' in the air.

'Also on the lower ground, there was evidence of the large numbers of cattle we had come to expect, carefully herded into large areas bounded by ditches. These were tended by a few men all of whom seemed to take great pride in their work, perhaps in the manner the chief slave of a distinguished senator might regard his tasks. When asked about the number of cattle normally attended to, one man replied that there were usually more than we could see today, but that many had been moved to the high ground by the hillfort, as there was a probability of danger.

'As the day progressed, and we slowly gained height over the river on which we'd arrived, we passed many a cluster of huts, situated near to the land which the occupants worked. These were a considerable distance from the hillfort, and the residents only made their way there on infrequent occasions. It was at such a place that we were to spend our first night.

'The hut allocated to our party of six was slightly larger than most, circular, and built of wooden posts set into the ground, with the gaps filled with woven branches and reeds covered in clay, a mixture known to the locals as "wattle and daub". The conical shaped straw, thatched, roof was supported on long stout timbers. It was only possible for the tall, blond Celts, with their sharp blue eyes, to stand around the central area of the hut, but sitting upright on the rush covered, earthen floor was easy enough, even by the walls.

Round Hut

'Dinner that evening was taken with the four families who lived in the group of huts we, and our guide, were to stay at. The meal comprised bread and meat, the latter in copious quantities – above the norm so I gathered. It was quite apparent that a "show" had been made for us, as guests. Milk and water were provided as liquid refreshment, while later a drink peculiar to these islanders, made from grain, and called "beer", was brought forth. The climate of the island is too severe for grapes, and wine, although occasionally brought from mainland Europe, is definitely not available in this tribal area.

'Our hosts for the evening were neither slaves, nor the equivalent of our citizens, falling somewhere between the two. They worked the land and looked after their chief's cattle, in exchange for which he, and others of similar exalted stature, granted them protection. Despite the presence of the official guide, this latter point was treated with a good deal of sarcasm as, in most cases, it was the men-folk who did the bulk of the "protecting" themselves. Only three weeks before they had been summoned to the hillfort to prepare to fight off the tribe from across the valley to the north. This had proved to be a false alarm, but rumour was presently rife that they might be summoned again, at short notice.

'These people, having returned from their daily work, transformed their appearance for the evening by the donning of gaily woven tunics, fastened by clasps and brooches of quite exquisite beauty; this despite their lowly stature. The men were clean shaven, while most sported a long moustache, and as the evening wore on so their tales of heroism grew as long as the hours. Animals were kept as objects of pleasure and pride, rather than a source of food, and our hosts had a variety of dogs, fowl and even hares, for the children. Having seen the children to bed, the women gave an initial impression of being subservient to their men-folk, somewhat dispelled by the time the men were ordered to their beds, in view of the tasks they had to undertake the following day.

'A meal prepared from grain, called porridge, was provided to help us on our way to the hillfort, the next day. Most had already set off to undertake their necessary tasks by the time we were ready to leave and, being Spring, there was a variety of work to be done. This included digging out the field-dykes, repairing huts, as well as the more normal agricultural duties.

'Our guide took us along the many tracks between the field-systems where, again, people were busy tending the crops. We gradually made our way to the higher ground where arable gave way to grazing land. Sheep were very much in evidence, while near the hillfort cattle were being carefully tended; the rumours of an attack from another tribe were being taken very seriously.'

Katia A.D. and her crew have now arrived in the immediate vicinity of our fictitious hillfort, and we will join her for 'live' coverage as they make their approach and enter the hillfort.

Celtic Warrior

'Welcome to this historic moment as R.B.C. brings you to the heart of a typical hillfort "town", in the South of Britannia, an island off the north coast of Europe. We have been accompanied by our local guide, and although our presence is expected, we all have to undertake the normal entrance procedure for visitors. We have now reached the point where our track has been joined by several others, from different directions, for the final approach to the entrance. The entrance track is paved with stones right through to the interior, and as we make our way along, it is difficult to make myself heard over the noise of the numerous cattle that have been herded in, what appear to be temporary, corrals in view of the heightened hostility from a neighbouring tribe.

'We are now approaching the outer set of gates, which are open, and from a bridge over the entrance a number of men, each armed with a spear, a long sword and carrying a rectangular shaped shield with rounded corners, are taking more than a passing interest in our party. There is a wooden guard hut on either side of the gateway, outside the gates, from which a guard is advancing towards us, watched by his companion. He is asking our guide who we are, what we are doing here and on whose authority our presence has been granted. Obviously, the replies have been satisfactory as he has beckoned us to pass through.

'This is the moment we have travelled to this island for, as we enter a long, quite narrow, stone faced, high sided entrance passage, from which we will gain entry to the hillfort. The defences at this point are even more impressive than the two ramparts and ditches, the innermost topped with a stone wall, which form the main defences. Indeed, with the heightened walls of the entrance passage, the scale of the building work would not look out of place in a town near Rome.

'Several guards are lined along the parapet at both sides of the entrance passage looking down at us. We are now approaching the second set of gates, which also has a bridge over the top. There are a number of guards looking down at us from this great wooden structure, but no heads are displayed, as we were told to expect. Further guards have emerged from guard chambers built into both sides of the passage, and they are coming forward to meet us.

'Our guide has spoken to them and we are being gestured to pass through the great wooden gates. Two of the "guards" have now joined us, and are to be our new guides while we stay at the hillfort. As he bids us farewell, our earlier guide confirms that the extra number of guards on duty is due to the heightened state of readiness in case of a raid.

'Once inside the gates, the passage opens out to reveal the great interior enclosed by the defences. I can see three paved tracks that lead away from the entrance in different directions, although other, non-paved, paths also lead among the circular huts, from where a number of people, undertaking domestic tasks, have stopped to watch our entry. The interior is almost flat, and we are being led along the track towards the centre of the hillfort. Most of the huts appear to be clustered around the perimeter of the defences, and are quite close together; I would imagine that the population density, though not on a level with our great cities, is high.

'I have just asked a guide about the closely spaced, rectangular buildings on wooden stilts away to our right. He told me they are granaries, and we are going over to inspect them. A cart hauled by two oxen is being loaded with baskets of grain from the granaries. This is to be distributed around the huts for use today and tomorrow morning; there does not appear to be any money changing hands in this transaction. I am now inside one of the rectangular buildings, which are built of wooden posts and the local wattle and daub, but are smaller than the circular huts; the grain is piled loosely, right up to the rafters. The guide has just explained that grain stored in these is for ordinary daily consumption. He has gestured us away from the granaries to some open ground nearby.

'I am now standing on the clay-sealed cover of what is, according to a guide, a grain storage pit. The harvested grain has been threshed, and is then stored in these pits, of which there are quite a number in this area alone. A guide has just pointed out many other open areas, not all near the granary buildings, reserved for storage pits, both for grain and salted meat. These pits are not opened until there is a need for the grain, and then all the contents are removed and taken for storage in a granary. The residue "crust" of grain around the edges of the pits, which are deeper than a man is tall, is used as fodder. The pit can be used again, but after several years is only suitable for the disposal of rubbish.

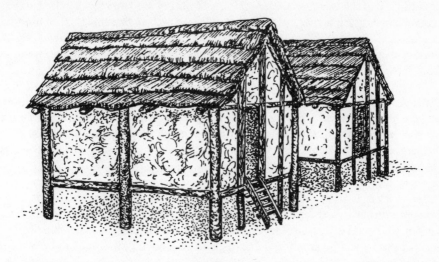

Granaries.

'We have re-joined the main track of the interior, and are approaching a group of huts, no larger than the norm which, so I have been informed, are for the Chief and his fellow warriors. Our quarters are among this large group. Just before we reach these, a further track leads off from the right to form a processional way to three rectangular wooden buildings. These house the shrines of the tribes-people, while a small group of normal circular huts nearby belong to the priests, known as Druids.

A Celtic chariot.

'Parked by the huts of the Chief and his retinue, are two lightly built chariots. A guide explained that there are many others, but the warriors are all out patrolling the area in view of the expected raid. Amidst these huts is one large rectangular building around which much activity is centred. A guide explained that this is to be used for the feast tonight, both in honour of our visit, and to gird the warriors for the deeds of bravery they will be expected to perform, in the event of a raid. With that, we have been shown to our quarters and provided with two servants to look after our needs.'

Katia A.D. has been thorough in the description of the goings-on around a hillfort, but she has not yet had a chance to meet the ordinary residents. Let us now join her as she, accompanied by her guides, goes among the people and their huts. Remember though, Katia A.D. does not speak Celtic, and her guides will act as interpreters.

'I am in a large group of huts where activity is almost at fever pitch. Iron ores, brought in from far off to the east, are being smelted and the blacksmiths are busy making the peculiar long swords, iron tips for spears and other innumerable objects, such as chariot and horse fittings. Each item takes a good deal of time to be worked into the required shape, and the iron workers do not have time to talk with me; the more items made, the greater the number of men who will be able to resist any raid. Normally used to making highly decorative brooches and weapons, the present manufactures are strictly of utilitarian quality.

Daily work in a hillfort.

'Further along, women, children and some men are undertaking more routine and mundane tasks, such as grinding corn, patching up huts and baking bread. Many tasks require a good deal of manual labour but, unlike with the metal-workers, there is no real sense of urgency, people being willing to chat. Others are busy cutting wood into the required lengths, to be used to shore up the defences, on which many of the men are currently employed. The standard of carpentry is very high, and seems to be quite a universal skill, among the men. There is a surprising, neat orderliness about the way the inhabitants undertake their work. Children, in between their tasks, are running about challenging each other in mock single-combat duels. My guide has explained that the purposeful "busyness" of the inhabitants, is solely due to the expected raid.

Grinding querns.

'I can only say that these people seem a world apart from the "barbarians" who sacked Rome and occupied our lands just over 250 years ago. They seem quite happy and settled and, for most people, seem to have an egalitarian society, each being prepared, and expected, to assist in a variety of communal tasks. I am now going to return to my quarters to await the great feast to be held tonight.'

Such a feast would not have been a rarity in Celtic society, for public display, of both material possessions and personal abilities, was very much a part of the Celtic way of life. This particular feast had an additional importance, for not only were guests present, in the form of Katia A.D. and her R.B.C. crew, but also reputations needed to be enhanced and fighting spirits lifted, through stories of great deeds of derring-do. Let us see what Katia A.D. has to report of the evening's events.

'It's now well past midnight and the feast, attended by most of the warrior-class among the tribe, is coming to a raucous close. The personal attire of those present was even finer than that of our hosts for the previous night. Everyone wore jewellery and functional items of considerable splendour and craft, while the Chief drank from his ceremonial gold goblet. Food, in particular meat, was served in lavish quantities, washed down by that native drink called beer.

'Almost from the outset, glories of past generations were recalled and regaled, while each warrior tried to out-do the others both in the story they could tell, and their boasts of personal triumph. As the beer flowed, so the stories of heroics flowered, but I received no answers to my questions regarding the tribe from which a raid is now regarded as being almost certain.

'It was pointed out however, that, in this tribe at least, the Chief is elected annually from, and by, other members of the warrior-class, with spiritual guidance offered by the Druid religious leaders. This guidance is, I gather, usually followed. The Chief himself brought the feast to its climax with a tale about how he slew the leader of an opposing tribe last year, while on a raid. This so demoralised the opposition that they turned and fled, leaving behind a great many cattle which were captured. It is feared that revenge will not be long in coming.'

There was to be no 'encore', but it had proved to be a memorable evening for Katia A.D. and her companions. It was to be though, but a precursor for the events of the following day, and we will now join Katia A.D. 'live' on the inner rampart in the early afternoon.

'I was awoken this morning by frantic, almost frenzied, activity within the hillfort. A large group – one would hardly call them an army by our own glorious standards – approached from the north, led by chariot-mounted warriors, with support from infantry and cavalry. A massive effort was made to get all cattle and people within the confines of the hillfort, while the warriors and others prepared to go out and meet the enemy. The sheer number of cattle, and all the excitement, has caused organisational problems within the hillfort, but eventually "our" warriors, supported by all the able-bodied men, emerged onto the plain outside the entrance, and drew up in ranks opposite the enemy.

'The invaders created an almighty din with long trumpet-like instruments, and war cries, while individual warriors came forth from their ranks to boast about their great deeds, and to taunt and belittle 'our' warriors. From my vantage point on the defences, it all looked like a bit of good natured fun, but eventually one of our warriors was engaged in single combat, and was slain by several savage sword blows. Tension rose still further when our warrior's head was severed, and the victor paraded up and down the ranks waving his trophy.

'Two more of our warriors went forth in single combat, one losing his life, and his head, and the other getting back to the ranks severely wounded. The boasts of the previous night were beginning to seem fool-hardy. As the third of our warriors finally retreated, so spirits seemed to flag, while those of the enemy were lifted sky-high. The Druids of both sides now intervened, seemingly in a bid to halt an immediate battle, and as a form of compromise our Chief went forth to join in single combat with his opposite number; to do or die.

'Our Chief was deposited in the field by the chariot, and finally joined by the opposing chief. They began to shout and taunt each other at first, and eventually, almost tentatively, joined in combat, cheered on by roars from the men of both sides. This proved to be an even, increasingly violent, contest with both men fighting bravely, their personal and tribal honour at stake. Eventually, our Chief went the way of his other warriors, but before his head could also be severed, the field was engulfed by the rushing mass of the opposing hordes.

'As they charged towards the hillfort, many of our men, disheartened by the demise of their leader, turned and fled towards the open gates. Most got in, but the outer gates were bustled closed before the mass of the enemy arrived, leaving some to fight to a very bitter, decapitated end, and a few to flee as best they could. The ramparts near the gateway were already manned by those too old, or infirm to fight, and also some women, and these were reinforced by those who escaped from the field.

'Slings became the main offensive weapon on both sides, the defenders firing down on the attackers with lethal accuracy, while the attackers tried to clear the defences around the entrance. It soon became clear why, as chariots were driven up to the outer gates, and stooks of burning straw were piled up against them. Eventually, the gates began to burn, and groups of the enemy ran forward, with shields over their heads, to try and force the gates. They took many casualties, but the gates were forced open about an hour ago.

'Since then, a similar attack has been pressed forward in an attempt to set fire to the inner gates. This time though, the scale of the defences in the entrance passage have proved too much and, although I have been unable to get to the defences at that point, I am reliably told that there has been a wholesale slaughter of the attackers within the entrance passage. Certainly, the spirit of the attackers has diminished somewhat, and they have resorted to throwing the odd lighted spear over the ramparts in the hope of setting fire to some huts; not without success, but the fires have been easily contained.

'As I speak now, the opposing forces are beginning to make their way from the scene of the battle, leaving many a headless corpse behind. Once the attack on the inner gate had been easily repulsed, they seemed incapable of revising tactics to attack at another point, or even throw a "dummy" attack, much to my R.B.C. crew's surprise, and the relief of all, especially as there is no direct water supply within the hillfort. A few opposing warriors have remained behind, having faked an attack on the entrance, and taunt our defenders in between the odd shower of sling-stone volleys. The rest have rounded up what few cattle were left outside the defences and are driving them away.

'It has been a bad day for the inhabitants of this hillfort, having lost their Chief, several warriors and others and had the entrance damaged, the outer bridge also having collapsed after the gates fell. On the other hand, the defences were not breached, but the raid was very much that, more of a sport than a truly organised assault. Whether such defences, and defending tactics, could withstand a sustained siege as applied by the Republican Army is doubtful. We had intended to leave here tomorrow, and in one respect, the sooner we get out of the war-zone the better. On the other hand, we do not want to be the first Roman heads to be displayed over the entrance of an hillfort in this inclement land. This is Katia A.D. for the Roman Broadcasting Corporation, Britannia.'

Of course, all the above is quite fictitious, and certainly raids were not an everyday, or even annual occurrence. However, the above reports do convey an impression of what a hillfort and its surroundings might well have been like, while the form the battle took might not be too far from the truth, at that time. As we know all too well, time waits for no man, and while the above is based on numerous, mostly archaeological, sources, details of life and warfare of the Belgic tribes can be gained from written accounts, not least from those of Julius Caesar and his English campaigns of 55 and 54 B.C.

Caesar, in the accounts of his northern Europe campaigns, differentiated between the war tactics of the Belgae in Gaul, and Britain. In mainland Europe, Caesar described the tactics of Belgae laying siege to a hillfort, and these differed considerably from those described by Katia A.D. For a start, the defences were encircled, and a missile barrage of sling-stones and incendiary darts was used at several points of the defences, to clear them of defenders. Then at one point, a group of attackers, under heavy covering fire, approached the defences with shields held aloft, to either set fire to the wooden defences, or to undermine those of earth and stone. Entry to the hillfort, on the occasion described by Caesar, was gained. These were tactics the Romans themselves also used.

In complete contrast to the battle reported by Katia A.D., and tactics adopted by Celtic tribes on the European mainland, the Belgic Catuvillauni tribe, after having failed to halt Caesar's forces in open warfare, resorted to what amount to guerrilla tactics. The oppidum capital of the Catuvellauni, north of the River Thames, was defended by a combination of felled trees, rivers and streams, marshes, ditches, earth banks and palisades; quite different to the great, inflexible defences of a hillfort.

Having harried the Romans by using quick raids, particularly on foraging and advance parties, the Catuvellauni utilised these same highly mobilised strikes to defend their woodland fortress. That this was ultimately unsuccessful does not tell the whole story, for the Romans had been demoralised by the regularity and speed of these guerrilla-type attacks.

It is reasonable to assume, given no other evidence, that the Belgae used similar tactics in any skirmish with the resident Celtic tribes of England. Whether such tactics could have been successful against a hillfort is not entirely relevant, for the Belgic peoples might have been raiding the resident Celts on the surrounding land. If a confrontation similar to that witnessed by Katia A.D., was entered into, then by a series of rapid strikes, and feinting retreats to draw pockets of Celts away from the main forces, and then to be cut down (a tactic used by the Normans at the Battle of Hastings in 1066), the Celtic forces could easily have become demoralised, and retreated to the hillfort. This would have been fine, providing the defences held out and no siege was laid, for defenders would have been trapped inside, and few hillforts had a permanent, internal water supply.

Our emphasis on aspects of war and confrontation in this chapter, both during the middle and late Iron Age, no doubt over-states the importance of such matters in society. Hillforts, by their very nature, had defence as a major priority, and with Celtic society, both in the Iron Age and later, often being considered as heroic, so such emphasis has not been misplaced. 'Epic' encounters, both of the single combat and raid nature, abound in Celtic legends and mythology. These mostly referred to the warrior-leaders and not to the common man, in the same way that the champion sportsman, top actor or famous musical performer is regaled in modern society, while the likes of you and I go about our daily lives in relative anonymity (sorry Prince Charles, I did not expect you to buy this book!)

A study of known aspects of Celtic society, through the accounts of Caesar and his adventures, Irish society until the Middle Ages or even the Arthurian legends, stripped of all their romantic nonsense, suggests that Celtic people were extrovert, romantic and had a sense of both hierarchy and fairness, in an egalitarian way. One could assume that, in the face of any evidence to the contrary, English Iron Age society was fairly similar. Perhaps a social structure not dissimilar to feudalism existed, at least in the South, and this seemed to assist the age of chivalry and valour in the Middle Ages; could this have not been the case in the Iron Age?

The common man led a mundane existence in the Middle Ages, but life cannot have been all work and no play. Life for the great majority in the Iron Age was probably fairly similar: routine tasks carried out on behalf of a senior ranking class who supposedly ruled and protected in return, with some time set aside for individual or group leisure and perhaps tending one's own 'luxuries'; not a great deal of difference from today, if you strip away the fripperies. Remember, it is only in this century that social mobility through effort and ability on anything approaching a large scale has been possible, and even now many 'haves' do everything in their power to hang on to what they have got, and to get more, at the expense of the 'have nots'.

Anthropological studies of man have shown many similarities, and differences, between social hierarchies and relationships in non-industrial societies and our own. The same is true for daily tasks, except that in some hunter-gatherer tribes only about two hours per day is spent on tasks necessary for survival, as opposed to the large proportion of earnings from our eight hour working day that go towards similar needs. Given the existence of such similarities, between societies separated by thousands of miles of land and sea, and thousands of years in civilised 'development', it is not beyond the bounds of possibility that Iron Age society had much in common with ours, on a day to day basis.

That cannot be stated with absolute certainty; still less can many of the exact similarities and differences with our daily life be made. The dominance of industrial, commercial or administrative work in our lives would have been matched by the predominance of agricultural tasks for the Iron Age man. True, we have many more alternatives in life today, but quite a number of these are more passive than active, such as watching a play or television, or even going to a pub. It is perhaps the latter activity that would fit easiest into the daily life of the Iron Age common man, although participating in sport, music and other performing arts would also have figured high in this category.

Whatever the daily routine of Iron Age life in England, it is the defensive nature of the hillforts, in particular, but also fortified farmsteads and hamlets, that remind us of the, possibly exaggerated, violence of that time. Perhaps such defences distort our mental image of those days, for real evidence of attacks on hillforts are few and far between. Unlike with Mediaeval and Norman castles, few hillforts readily show the scars of a siege or a battle, except for the occasional burnt stone from a gateway, or the slighting of ramparts.

As when visiting a castle though, an insight into daily life at an Iron Age hillfort will enhance your visit, enable you to go back in time and to find an empathy with the people who lived then In any case, to get a good impression of the noise, and especially the smells, that would have gone with daily life in an hillfort, you ought to visit the Jorvik Museum, in York. A Viking 'Dark Age' village re-construction it might be, but you will have your eyes, not to say nostrils, well and truly opened.

CHAPTER SIX

Hillforts Beyond the Iron Age:
Back to the Future

We saw in the last chapter how hillforts fared in a simulated attack in both the later Celtic and Belgic periods of the Iron Age. Although evidence exists of the burning of gateways at hillforts, and a subsequent sacking (Bredon Hill* among others), the number of examples found of such actions, against the number of entrances excavated, is still relatively small. Hillforts, we might thus assume, were generally up to the job they were designed for.

On the other hand, that is comparable to saying that the mediaeval castle was right up to the mark until the advent of gunpowder. The tall, massive keeps of the mediaeval castle, a symbol of strength in pre-gunpowder days, was an easy target for even the earliest cannon, as many of the ruined examples up and down the country show; not all were slighted in the Civil War. To counter this technological and tactical change, new castles were built as low, squat affairs, hardly imposing structures but able to withstand a certain amount of artillery bombardment.

The advent of the sling, as we have seen, may have led to, or stemmed from, the increasing use of multivallate hillfort defences in the middle Iron Age, but a far sterner test awaited these great fortifications in the late Iron Age. The arrival of the Romans, first of all in 55 and 54 B.C. under Julius Caesar and then the Claudian invasion of 43 A.D., saw the Celtic/Belgic peoples faced by a highly disciplined fighting force, based on unitary, and not single, combat.

The Romans had honed the tactics of laying siege to a fortress, such as a hillfort or oppidum, down to a fine art, and had a number of fixed and, more terrifyingly, mobile siege-engines from which the defences could be attacked. The Iron Age Britons were thus faced with something completely different, and one has to say, without giving too much away, that although not without their successes, the task was both beyond the warriors and their defences.

In many parts of the South and South-East, hillforts had been falling into disuse before Caesar invaded, and this position had changed still further by the Claudian invasion. The Roman army under Caesar had been busy campaigning in Gaul and Northern Europe before coming to England, and had notched up some noteworthy successes. These have been recorded for posterity, fortunately, and though the authors might well have exaggerated the number of opposing forces, it soon becomes apparent that warfare involving the Romans was in a different league altogether from the English tribal raid.

At an oppidum near Namur in Belgium, Caesar had a siege-mound built and used a movable tower. This latter so alarmed the defenders that ultimately 4,000 were killed and the remaining 53,000 sold into slavery. In the same year, at Martigny near the Franco-Swiss border, the Romans killed 10,000 out of 30,000 opponents. A year later, at a hillfort of the Vocates and Tarusates tribes in France, the Romans trounced an army of 50,000. Alongside such figures, and those of the early 50's B.C. when Caesar's army was able to overcome forces estimated at 250,000 at Alesia in France, the English opposition was fairly small-fry. True, the 55 B.C. landing came to nought, but the following year Caesar's forces took Bigbury* hillfort within hours of debarking. Once they crossed the River Thames the opposing English chief, Cassivellaunus, disbanded his army, save for 4,000 charioteers. This gives an indication of both the nature of English warfare, which troubled Caesar's men, and the numbers involved.

Nonetheless, within a few weeks, the Romans had beaten the English forces, taken the large oppidum capital of the Catuvellauni at Wheathampstead, exacted an annual tribute, and were on their way for more fighting in Gaul. The Bigbury* gazetteer entry, shows that English hillfort resistance was on a much smaller scale than the Romans encountered in Europe, and was all over within a day; a lot of building effort for no benefit.

Roman Legionary soldier.

When the Romans decided to come again, and this time to stay, in 43 A.D., it was on an altogether much greater scale. Four Legions crossed the Channel, and there may have been three points of landing; at Richborough in Kent, with a possibility of another in 'friendly' Atrebates territory near Chichester and a third, also in Kent. The II Augusta, IX Hispana, XIV Germana and XX Valeria Legions took part, totalling about 20,000 men, with Auxilliaries (cavalry) bringing the total to about 24,000. These figures might not seem very large in comparison to those quoted earlier, but the English tribes were far from united in their opposition to Rome, which in the South and East mainly involved the Catuvellauni tribe and its allies.

After defeating the native forces at the two day Battle of Medway, the Romans crossed the River Thames and sent for the Emperor Claudius. He duly arrived from Rome, and was involved in organising the assault on the Catuvellauni oppidum at Camulodunum (Colchester). Although Claudius was only in England sixteen days, eleven native kings submitted to him at Camulodunum, and the Romans were well on their way to victory.

None of the above has, thus far, involved hillforts, but these native bastions were to be put to the test when Vespasian, a future emperor, was despatched with the

II Augusta Legion to subdue the tribes in the South and South-West. Details of the campaign of 43-44 A.D. remain scant, but Vespasian reputedly fought thirty battles and captured twenty 'oppida' (hillforts) and the Isle of Wight in his advance in the South-West, as far as Exeter. This resistance was undertaken by members of the Durotriges tribe and those in the south Dobunni tribal area, and although the battle sites remain un-located, some hillforts have produced evidence of the Roman arrival.

Successful attacks were made against Maiden Castle* and Hod Hill*, while Spettisbury Rings* has also produced a mass grave, thought to be from an encounter with the Romans. Compared to figures quoted for Caesar's campaigns in mainland Europe, nearly a century before, the English resistance seems to have been slight; over a hundred bodies at Spettisbury Rings, thirty odd at Maiden Castle and none at Hod Hill. More bodies could easily be awaiting discovery near these hillforts, or indeed might have been cremated, while none of the other seventeen hillforts have been located with any certainty; who knows what gruesome sights are waiting to be uncovered? This does not hide the fact that English hillforts, when faced with a thoroughly organised, well trained fighting unit, failed just as surely as did the mediaeval castles confronted by cannon.

Siege techniques used by the Romans in Europe, such as circumvallation of the hillfort, siege mounds, under-mining the defences and filling in the ditches seem to have been unnecessary, or at least there is no evidence of such actions. From ballista-bolts found at Maiden Castle* and Hod Hill* though, it seems that the Romans were quite prepared to use their siege engines if necessary, while the accurate firing of these at Hod Hill leaves a possibility of a wooden siege tower being erected. One might assume that the presence of an apparently well disciplined, large fighting force, complete with weapons far superior to the hillfort defenders, not forgetting the reputation of the II Legion as it swept from hillfort to hillfort, would have been enough to undermine the confidence of the defenders.

It did not take the Romans long to establish an area of control which ran from the River Exe to the River Humber. Generally speaking, hillforts within this area were abandoned, or at least had the defences slighted, but this only really affected the hillforts of the South, for many areas, such as East Anglia and the Midlands, had few hillforts anyway, while most in Sussex, Hampshire and The Chilterns had long been abandoned. Those hillforts in the Welsh Marches fell outside this area of immediate Roman control, and once they began to invade this area, and push on into Wales, these hillforts generally went the same way as the others, for example Midsummer Hill* was taken in 48 A.D.

It would be wrong to suggest that all hillforts were abandoned after the Romans arrived. For one thing, they do not appear to have indulged in a mass slaughter of the defenders, as the 'locals' might well have done; partly because some would have made valuable slaves, while once the hillfort was rendered defensively useless, further destruction would only have embittered feelings further. Quite a large number of hillforts have produced evidence of Roman pottery and coins, including many in the gazetteer of this book, which suggests that, at least, some people lived within the defences of the old hillforts in the days of the *pax Romana*. Maiden Castle*, for example, may have remained occupied until the new town of Durnovaria (Dorchester) was built three decades after the possible conflict with Vespasian.

Following the putting down of the revolt led by Boudicca and the Iceni tribe, but including many others, in 60-61 A.D., the Romans began a short-lived purge against tribes who had either supported the revolt, or were sympathetic towards it. Thus we find that a massacre took place at South Cadbury Castle*, and that the victims were left unburied, to rot. We could assume that the hillfort was forcibly abandoned, but the Romans returned later to set up a temporary camp while they dismantled the defences. Hod Hill* is one of the few other hillforts that was certainly cleared by the Romans, in 43-44 A.D., but that was to allow the invaders to build their own fort within the hillfort; another example of this was at the massive, but now badly quarried, hillfort of Ham Hill (Somerset).

Once the volatile situation in the Roman-governed area of England and Wales, and the rest of the Empire, had stabilised, the Romans began to move northwards against the divided, warring conglomeration of peoples known as the Brigantes tribe. The great encounter of this campaign was at the huge hillfort of Stanwick*, in 71 A.D. It goes without saying that the Romans were successful, while the few other hillforts, such as Ingleborough*, were also cleared of inhabitants, or at least made indefensible.

The Romans pushed further north, through country containing few hillforts, until they arrived in what are now the Scottish Borders. There, the countryside was packed with many small hillforts, a far lesser number of medium-sized hillforts and still fewer large ones. This was hostile territory, which eventually fell beyond the later official frontier of the empire, Hadrian's Wall. We know all too well how the border zone between two warring countries can become engulfed in slaughter and other inhumane acts, such as in the former Yugoslavia and in Africa. That the Romans saw fit to exclude this area from their Empire, and were never in complete control, even when pushing right up to the North of Scotland, suggests that to permanently conquer it was not worth the effort required.

Hillforts in the Scottish Borders thus continued to remain inhabited, although not in a defensive manner. Yeavering Bell*, for example, seems to have been occupied well after the Romans were thought to have pulled down the stone ramparts. The same could also be said of certain hillforts in Wales, and the tribal area of the Dumnonii, in Cornwall and Devon, where their rounds hillforts often continued to be occupied into the second century A.D., or later.

The first 250 years of Roman rule thus saw most hillforts abandoned, while those that retained inhabitants probably only did so on a temporary and/or small scale basis, without effective defences. Some, such as Yarnbury Castle* and even Stanwick*, had Roman-dated enclosures added to their former defences. However, a glance through gazetteer will show that almost half of the hillforts produced some evidence of use in Roman times; this would probably over-state the position on a national scale, and should not be regarded as a statistical sample.

Later on, from the fourth century A.D., if not earlier, some hillforts had Romano-Celtic temples built within the interior, or nearby. Examples include Maiden Castle*, Chanctonbury Ring*, Cadbury Congresbury and Worlebury (both Somerset) and Lydney (Gloucestershire). Perhaps others are awaiting discovery, for they were all pretty small-scale affairs, at least in comparison to the size of the interior. In some, the temple was accompanied by other buildings, possibly including a residence for the priest.

Still, like the fabled former champion boxer, hillforts refused to lie down, even when badly beaten and seemingly out-classed. Times, and warfare, change and what was seemingly outmoded in one era can make a comeback in another. During World War II the Germans were able to hold up the Allied forces for several months by defending the pre-mediaeval, fortified hill-top monastery of Monte Cassino, in Italy. Once the Romans had departed, early in the fifth century, mercenaries were recruited to defend England against incursions of Angles, Saxons and Jutes from Europe, Picts from Scotland and possibly even the Irish. Some of these mercenaries liked what they saw of the country, and decided to stay.

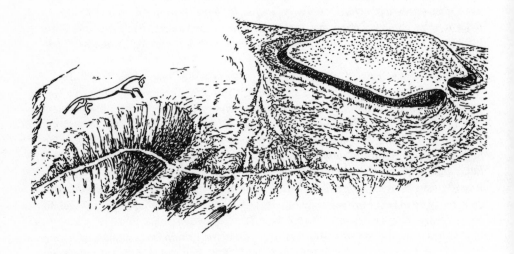

Uffington Castle and the white horse.

Thus we entered the Dark Ages, and with that time some hillforts were re-fortified, such as Chun Castle*, while there is a possibility that new hillforts were built, like Clare Camp (Suffolk) or High Peak (Devon). Defences that could not withstand the organised might of the Roman military fighting machine, were more readily suited to the tactics of these barbaric mercenaries. If the defences could be brought back into use, they might have served a useful purpose again, as they did against tribal raids of the Iron Age.

Research has shown that 20% of Iron Age hillforts in Somerset were used in the late Roman/post Roman period. So far, the best known example is that of South Cadbury Castle*, a possible site for the fortress known as Camelot. It is most unlikely that there was ever a character known as King Arthur, still less one who was a king of England. There is no doubt, however, that South Cadbury Castle had its inner defences completely, and massively, rebuilt by c.500 A.D., and was probably the fortified camp of a chief of more than immediate local importance. The comeback did not last long though, and by the mid-sixth century South Cadbury, and probably others, had been abandoned again, or were no longer defensible.

South Cadbury Castle was still not finished though, and in the late pre-Norman times it was a Saxon burh, although this did not denote its standing as a town. The arrival of the Normans after the Battle of Hastings saw the introduction of the motte and bailey castle, as a means of controlling the surrounding countryside. The motte was, usually, a large earth mound, constructed to take a wooden keep which commanded the locality. There has been a long history of the use of hill-tops and high ground to command an area, and many acropolis' were used in Greece until the days of Turkish rule. Hillforts, with their often naturally dominant position, suddenly came back into strategic reckoning, or at least some did.

Old Sarum (Wiltshire) hillfort had served as a Roman posting station, before being abandoned again. The Normans not only built a motte in the centre, using the re-fortified hillfort defences, as the bailey, but later built a cathedral in the bailey, as it became a town. It was only in the thirteenth century that the new town of Salisbury was begun, with its cathedral, on the low ground by the River Avon, two miles to the south. Almondbury Castle* hillfort, abandoned in the fifth century B.C., and Herefordshire Beacon* hillfort were both re-fortified by the Normans as motte and bailey castles.

These were obvious exceptions to the general rule of hillfort abandonment, at least as a place to live, although the often flat, enclosed interiors were ideal for the keeping of cattle, or as a ready-made corn field. Many interiors have suffered as a result. On the other hand, the post-mediaeval period has seen some hillforts converted for a variety of uses. The massive Brigantes hillfort of Stanwick*, like the Neolithic henge at Avebury, now houses a village, two in fact. The growth of the country house/mansion in the seventeenth and eighteenth centuries also saw some hillforts once again coming back into use. Wandlebury* even had a country house built within its ramparts, while West Wycombe* had a church and the family mausoleum of the nearby mansion owners built within it. St Catherine's Hill (Hampshire) not only had a church, now demolished, but has a maze cut into its turf.

The building of follies or monuments also became popular in the post-Civil War period, and the location of certain hillforts virtually ensured they would not be forgotten. Bredon Hill* found itself on the receiving end of a folly castle, while Oldbury Castle* has been graced by the presence of a large obelisk, with a white horse nearby, as has Bratton Castle (Wiltshire) and Uffington Castle*. More recently, Almondbury Castle*, which boasts the ultimate attraction, a pub, had a tower built on its Norman motte in 1897, to commemorate Queen Victoria's Diamond Jubilee.

Perhaps the most common development of the last three centuries, for hillforts, has been their use as a landmark by the planting of trees. Some, of course, were already overgrown, but deliberate planting was often undertaken by a landowner to 'beautify' the countryside. Chanctonbury Ring* has become internationally known through its Beech trees, while St Catherine's Hill (Hampshire), Clearbury Ring (Wiltshire) and Badbury Rings (Dorset), among others, have also been similarly adorned. You will notice that none of these, except Chanctonbury, have been included in the gazetteer. That is because, although attractive from a distance, the trees just about cover all of the hillfort. Many hillforts are completely tree covered, and have been for centuries, but others, like Boddington Camp (Buckinghamshire), Aconbury (Herefordshire) and even the very important Croft Ambrey (Herefordshire), have been recently planted with trees, which make a visit a waste of time.

Almost all hillforts are now national historical monuments, and the defences are at least afforded a degree of protection. That does not mean that a hillfort is public property, and if in doubt one should get permission to visit from the local landowner; I have never had such permission refused. Quite a number are owned by English Heritage, for the state, or the National Trust, but we in the twentieth century have perpetrated some of the worst excesses, allowed by the 'chance' (market forces), government policies, or pure ignorance.

Chilworth Ring (Southampton) has been decimated by having, in the main, characterless, modern houses, built on its defences. St. Catherine's Hill near Winchester is currently being severed from the neighbouring Twyford Down by the M3 extension. This destruction of an Iron Age village and several sites of special scientific interest, is currently underway despite assurances given to the public enquiry by the government over the damage that would be caused. The site in question was left to Winchester College, in perpetuity, decades ago, for public recreation, not to be sold and destroyed, while the headmaster refused to put the issue of the sale of the land before the College's board of governors.

Perhaps the saddest example of the destruction of an English hillfort is that of Ham Hill (Somerset). For centuries this great hill has been quarried for its highly distinctive stone. This could easily be stopped by the government, of any party, as the land is owned by the Duchy of Lancaster, but still the destruction goes on. The worst of it is, that the beautiful stone is not used to build worthy buildings, but modern characterless houses in the villages below the hill, that would not look out of place on the blandest of housing estates.

Inevitably, some hillforts were used in Word War II but, unlike many country houses, have not been damaged beyond belief. In the South, many served as 'lookouts', and do not seem any the worse for the experience, while the two pill-boxes at Old Berwick*, in the North, add a link over time. The radio masts at The Trundle* might not be the easiest things to miss, but at least they have not greatly damaged the defences. In any case, with due care, modern use ought not to be precluded, provided damage is minimal and, preferably, the hillfort is enhanced; like the house in Berkhampstead (Norman) Castle, which adds to the overall scene.

Like any other ancient, or historic monument, hillforts are there to enjoy and appreciate. A good understanding of hillforts and the age they came from will increase the enjoyment factor and interest. It is intended that this book will enhance your enjoyment of what is probably the Iron Age equivalent of ruined castles or cathedrals to the Middle Ages or, heaven forbid, multi-storey tower buildings to post-war Britain. Just imagine, in 4,000 A.D. archaeologists will possibly be digging up the foundations of your house, and trying to fit your material remains into an image of the National Westminster Bank tower building, in London. No wonder archaeologists today are still coming up with conflicting evidence about Iron Age Britain. Fortunately, '. . . they don't build them like they used to . . . ' and one suspects that the post-war equivalent of Maiden Castle will have long since disappeared by 4,000 A.D.

Now it is time to cast historical fact, theory and innuendo to the wind, and to get out and see the great Iron Age hillforts for yourself. Remember, as a book, this 'visitors' guide' is only an introduction to the subject, one to get you to visit the hillforts, rather than to become bogged down in all the archaeological minutae of the Iron Age. That, and joining an archaeological dig (for which you should contact the various university archaeology departments), is the next step along the road. So, armed to the teeth with all the knowledge of the Iron Age you did not want to know, take this book and off you go to your selected hillfort, and do not forget to close your eyes and try and imagine yourself back in the Iron Age. Tread carefully though, as you might find yourself in something a little more sticky than a storage pit.

Part 2

GAZETTEER

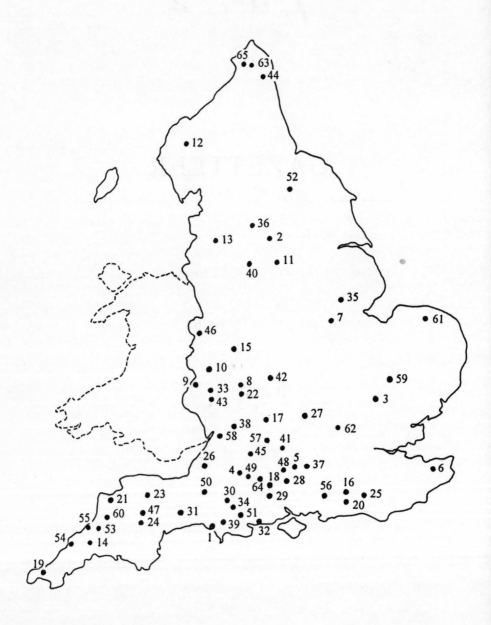

1.	Abbotsbury Castle	34.	Hod Hill
2.	Almondbury	35.	Honnington
3.	Arbury Banks	36.	Ingleborough
4.	Battlesbury Camp	37.	Ladle Hill
5.	Beacon Hill	38.	Leckhampton Hill
6.	Bigbury	39.	Maiden Castle
7.	Burrough Hill	40.	Mam Tor
8.	Bredon Hill	41.	Martinsell/Giant's Grave
9.	Caer Caradoc (Clun)	42.	Meon Hill
10.	Caer Caradoc (Ch.Str.)	43.	Midsummer Hill
11.	Carlwark	44.	Old Berwick
12.	Carrock Fell	45.	Oldbury Camp
13.	Castercliff	46.	Old Oswestry
14.	Castle an Dinas	47.	Prestonbury Castle
15.	Castle Ring	48.	Quarley Hill
16.	Chanctonbury Ring	49.	Scratchbury Camp
17.	Cherbury Camp	50.	South Cadbury Castle
18.	Chiselbury Camp	51.	Spettisbury Ring
19.	Chun Castle	52.	Stanwick
20.	Cissbury Ring	53.	Tregeare Rounds
21.	Clovelly Dykes	54.	Trevelgue Head
22.	Conderton Camp	55.	The Rumps
23.	Cow Castle	56.	The Trundle
24.	Cranbrook Castle	57.	Uffington Castle
25.	Devil's Dyke	58.	Uleybury
26.	Dolebury Camp	59.	Wandlebury
27.	Dyke Hills	60.	Warbstow Bury
28.	Figsbury Ring	61.	Warham Camp
29.	Godmanescamp	62.	West Wycombe
30.	Hambledon Hill	63.	Wooler
31.	Hembury Castle	64.	Yarnbury Castle
32.	Hengistbury Head	65.	Yeavering Bell
33.	Herefordshire Beacon		

SYMBOLS USED THROUGHOUT PART 2 ON THE PLANS

⌁⌁⌁⌁	Rampart, usually with ditch	◢	Point of arrival
ııırıᵗııʳ	Ditch	⌁⌁⌁⌁	Counterscarp bank
· ·.· · · · · · ·	Traces of banks	⌒⌒⌒⌒	Escarpment
◎	Round barrow	⬭	Long barrow
⌒⌣.⌒⌣.	Coutours of either 50, or 100 feet intervals	△	Triangulation point
		═══	Road
═ ═ ═ ═ ═ ═	Footpath	⌁⌁⌁	Brook
▬▬▬▬	River	♱	Church
■	Buildings		

List of Hillforts in Part 2

COUNTY	HILLFORT	O/S MAP No.	MAP Ref	PAGE No.
Berkshire	Cherbury Camp	164	373963	99
Berkshire	Uffington Castle	174	298863	100
Buckinghamshire	West Wycombe	175	827949	104
Cambridgeshire	Wandlebury	154	493533	106
Cornwall	Castle an Dinas	200	945623	109
Cornwall	Chun Castle	203	405339	110
Cornwall	The Rumps	200	933811	112
Cornwall	Tregeare Rounds	200	032800	113
Cornwall	Trevelgue Head	200	825630	114
Cornwall	Warbstow Bury	190	202908	115
Cumberland	Carrock Fell	90	344336	117
Derbyshire	Mam Tor	110	127837	119
Devon	Clovelly Dykes	190	312235	122
Devon	Cranbrook Castle	191	739890	124
Devon	Hembury Castle	192/193	112031	125
Devon	Prestonbury Castle	191	747900	127
Dorset	Abbotsbury Castle	194	555865.	129
Dorset	Hambledon Hill	194	841126	130
Dorset	Hod Hill	194	855105	135
Dorset	Maiden Castle	194	669885	139
Dorset	Spettisbury Rings	195	915020	144
Gloucestershire	Leckhampton Hill	163	948185	146
Gloucestershire	Uleybury	162	785990	148
Hampshire	Beacon Hill	174	458572	150
Hampshire	Godmanescamp	184	167152	152
Hampshire	Hengistbury Head	195	165910	154
Hampshire	Ladle Hill	174	478568	157
Hampshire	Quarley Hill	184	262423	160
Herefordshire	Herefordshire Beacon	150	760398	162
Herefordshire	Midsummer Hill	150	760375	165
Hertfordshire	Arbury Banks	153	262387	168
Kent	Bigbury	179	117575	170
Lancashire	Castercliff	103	885384	172
Leicestershire	Burrough Hill	129	762119	174
Lincolnshire	Honnington	130	954424	176
Norfolk	Warham Camp	132	944409	178
Northumberland	Old Berwick	75	075216	180
Northumberland	Wooler	75	984273	182
Northumberland	Yeavering Bell	74/75	928293	183

Oxfordshire	Dyke Hills	164	575938	186
Shropshire	Caer Caradoc (Ch.Str.)	137/138	478952	188
Shropshire	Caer Caradoc (Clun)	137/148	310758	189
Shropshire	Old Oswestry	126	295310	190
Somerset	Cow Castle	180	794374	194
Somerset	Dolebury Camp	182	450590	195
Somerset	South Cadbury Castle	183	629253	196
Staffordshire	Castle Ring	128	045128	200
Sussex	Chanctonbury Ring	198	139120	202
Sussex	Cissbury Ring	198	140080	204
Sussex	Devil's Dyke	198	260110	206
Sussex	The Trundle	197	877110	208
Warwickshire	Meon Hill	151	177455	211
Wiltshire	Battlesbury Camp	183	894456	213
Wiltshire	Chiselbury Camp	184	018281	216
Wiltshire	Figsbury Ring	184	188338	217
Wiltshire	Martinsell/ Giant's Grave	173	177639/166632	219
Wiltshire	Oldbury Castle	173	049692	221
Wiltshire	Scratchbury Camp	184	913443	223
Wiltshire	Yarnbury Castle	184	035403	225
Worcs./Glos.	Bredon Hill	150	957401	228
Worcestershire	Conderton Camp	150	972383	231
Yorkshire	Almondbury	110	153142	233
Yorkshire	Carlwark	110	258815	235
Yorkshire	Ingleborough	98	742745	236
Yorkshire	Stanwick	92	178123	237

Cherbury Camp

Directions. O/S 1:50,000 map 164 ref. 373963. Leave Oxford on the A420 towards Swindon. This road by-passes Kingston Bagpuize where it crosses the A415. A minor road leaves the A420, after the end of the by-pass, to Charney Bassett. Three quarters of a mile after this turning, park on the grass verge on the left, just after the drive to Lovell's Court Farm. Walk to the farm, and pass through it, following the yellow arrows, and then the Public Footpath sign that directs you across a field, bringing you to a track at the east side of the hillfort. Ask permission to visit at Pusey Lodge Farm, just to the north.

Few counties can have suffered more than Berkshire has as a result of the local Government Act of 1974 with its setting up of new administrative areas, at the expense of certain counties. The traditional county town of Abingdon has been taken away, as has much of the north of the county, and along with that has gone the county's only multivallate hillfort.

Cherbury Camp is the most readily visible of that rare category of hillforts, the valley fort. Risbury Camp (Herefordshire) is a much better example of this type of hillfort, but its ramparts are covered in trees, and its interior is an orchard. If you are familiar with the Upper Thames area, you will not expect this hillfort to sit nestling on the valley bottom, with steep hills on all sides. Situated between the River Thames to the north, and the River Ofk to the south, and on land surrounded by tributaries of the latter, Cherbury lies on a plateau just above the 200 feet mark. The land rises to over 300 feet in the north, before falling to the River Thames, but is fairly level in all other directions. During the Iron Age Cherbury's ditches were prone to flooding, while much of the surrounding land afforded the extra protection of marshes.

Three ramparts and ditches enclose nine acres in an oval shape, although only the inner rampart is now complete for the whole circuit. No doubt, the effects of periodic flooding have had an additional wearing effect on the disused defences, over the years. J.S.P. Bradford undertook an excavation in 1939, but World War II terminated this, though not before certain details were found. As with all these earlier excavations, the dating of the hillfort was rather late, but as no further excavation has taken place, there is no real evidence to give an alternative set of dates.

It was thought to have been built in one go, despite the scale of the defences, and was not a univallate hillfort that had been upgraded. All three ramparts were of the glacis type, but the inner one was partly revetted with a dry-stone wall. The inner ditch was also found to be very broad in comparison to its depth, while the outer ramparts and ditches are quite closely spaced. These are best seen to the north, south and west sides today, although a small wood impinges on the outer defences at the west. A trackway now covers the outer defences at the east side.

The entrance was in the centre of the east defences and, in its final form, comprised of a long stone revetted passage, in which two large posts were thought to have supported the gates. Several layers of track re-metalling were found, which suggests that the fort might well have been occupied over a long period, while it was quite rutted in its final state. Pottery of the middle Iron Age was also found, but none from the Belgic tribes. That could mean that the hillfort was abandoned before the Catuvellauni moved into the Upper Thames area, in the mid-first century B.C.

It is possible that Cherbury was built quite a bit before the excavators thought, perhaps in the third or fourth centuries B.C., as a univallate hillfort; the outer defences being added later. However, excavations elsewhere, particularly at Rainsborough (Northamptonshire) and Blewburton (Berkshire), have shown that a multivallate hillfort could have been built in the fifth century B.C., and had its defences refurbished at a later date, say when the Catuvellauni tribe began to spread their wings. A further extensive excavation at Cherbury is required to determine its Iron Age past, as we can only speculate at the moment.

Being a shallow valley, the view from the defences is quite restricted, although the Berkshire Downs can be seen to the south. An ancient settlement existed to the east, and this might well have been connected to the hillfort; perhaps even being occupied instead of Cherbury during the years that the Belgic Catuvellauni occupied the area. That is speculation, but perhaps has a little more foundation than the possibility that Cherbury served as a stronghold of the future King Cnut, in the war against Ethelred the Unready, in the eleventh century A.D. Well, if so, it will probably need a great deal of luck to prove.

The interior is now used by grazing cattle, so there is not much to see in that quarter. Cherbury's main assets are its defences, which although not complete are still of a considerable size, and its peaceful, rural location. The walk from the main road certainly takes you slowly out of the modern world of rushing around, through a quiet rural, yet industrious, farm to the peace of a pre-historic oasis amidst the countryside. Once there, you can begin to feel the transformation back to another time, and another place.

Uffington Castle

Directions. O/S 1:50,000 series map 174 ref. 298863. Uffington is situated next to The Ridgeway long distance path, between the B4000 and B4001. Alternatively, leave Swindon heading east on the A420. Turn right on the B4000 at Shrivenham, and turn left on the B4507 at Ashbury. The third turning on the right, opposite that for Uffington village, leads up to the hillfort car park.

Berkshire is a county famed for its downland which has examples of just about every type of pre-Roman relic, often several of each kind. Iron Age hillforts are no exception, there being at least seventeen to my knowledge, many of which are in good condition, even today. When it came to selecting some for inclusion in the gazetteer, I opted for two from the county, but then found out that both Uffington and Cherbury, are now regarded as being within Oxfordshire. So, as with the 'little piggie', Berkshire 'has none', but then with all the lies that come from our 'careerist' politicians, and their 'yes men', we never take any notice of them anyway, and quite rightly so. Berkshire, the county and not the 'administrative area' still has its downs and seventeen hillforts.

Uffington Castle is surrounded with ancient antiquities, many of which have associated legends. It is one of four decent sized hillforts that lie next to the ancient track known as The Ridgeway, within a mere 15 mile length. Although very well known among hillforts, it is, of course, the adjacent white horse which has attracted much interest to the area. The two may well have been linked, as the white horse (which has also been interpreted as a dragon) was possibly cut in the first century B.C., while it is thought that the hillfort dates from a century, or so, before.

A single rampart and ditch, with a significant sized counterscarp bank, enclose 8 acres on the plateau which rises to 856 feet at the triangulation point, sited on the east rampart. Surprisingly, for such a well known site, and one in the care of English Heritage, it had only been excavated in the middle of the last century, until the recent White Horse Hill Project, of which the hillfort's excavation (1989) was only a part thereof.

The pioneering excavation showed that the rampart was of the glacis type, probably faced with sarsen stones which, as on Fyfield Down today, were possibly spread all over the nearby downs. Post holes suggested that the rampart had been timber-laced, but it was also considered possible that a timber palisade had preceded the hillfort proper.

The recent, partial excavations showed that the nineteenth century excavators were not far wrong, and that the hillfort was constructed in three stages. The first of these was on open grassland, while it might have been connected with Hardwell Camp, less than a mile to the north-west, beside the B4507. Uffington fell within the area of the Dobunni tribe, although was uncomfortably close to the Atrebates and Catuvellauni tribal areas. A silver coin of the former tribe has been found in the interior, which, like the defences, is now grass-covered. For a site that must have been of some importance due to its proximity to the Ridgeway, and its commanding position over the Vale of the White Horse, that is a fairly poor return, but then, its use did not end with the demise of its permanent occupation.

The entrance is on the west, and is quite unusual as the rampart wraps round back on itself, to displace the counterscarp bank. This is particularly evident to the north, but is also visible to the south of the entrance. None of the defences look especially formidable though, even after allowing for 2,000 years of weathering, so perhaps the hillfort was more of a trading centre for the people who worked the vast acreage of fields on the downs to the south, many of which can still be seen. Perhaps it was the very proximity to the Ridgeway that ensured a peaceful existence.

One cannot possibly view Uffington Castle in isolation though, for the area positively exudes ancient history. The white horse has already been mentioned, with its probable late Iron Age date. It is similar to the design on some Belgic coins, but its association as a marker for flying saucers to land on the flat-topped hill below, known as Dragon Hill, can be discounted; after all, if beings from another solar system can navigate all the way to planet Earth, they are not going to need help from hill-figures to locate a particular area.

On the other hand, the white horse is not visible as a horse, or dragon, from immediately below, and must have been difficult to cut. It is very clear from the valley, particularly from a train, so perhaps an ancient semaphore system was used in its creation.

Dragon Hill, with its patch where the dragon's blood is supposed to have spilt when it was slain by St George, is another site of mystery, and grass has not grown on that patch for several centuries, at least. The Manger, between Dragon Hill and the hillfort, was used for rolling cheeses down and chasing after them, during days of sport and contests held when the nearby villagers gathered to clear the white horse. This event lasted until about a century ago, many of the contests taking place within the confines of the hillfort. That probably explains the lack of surface finds, or hut circles, and so on as for the white horse to have survived it must have been cleared regularly, thus offering many opportunities for events on the hillfort, and the removal of finds.

In any case, the Ridgeway continues to be used by farm traffic, and was used until recent centuries as a cross-country route. The hillforts beside it would have provided ideal places to rest for the night, if sleeping rough or with livestock, especially the further back in time one goes. Besides, one of the two mounds above the white horse was excavated last century and was found to contain 46 Roman bodies. It is possible they were victims of a battle, but were buried by their fellow men, as five had coins placed between their teeth, to pay for the ferry ride across the River Styx. Are those Roman bodies connected with the clearing of the hillfort? At present that is the only clue as to the demise of the hillfort as a population centre.

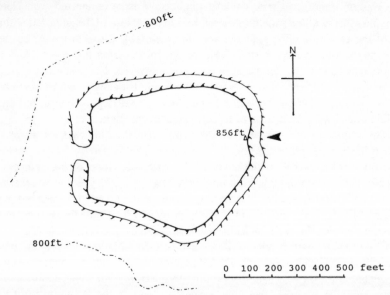

From Uffington Castle you have a magnificent view over the Vale of the White Horse. This would probably have been of much importance during the active life of the hillfort, although much of the area might have been clothed in forest. That was probably why the Ridgeway path followed the high ground, which in turn caused the hillforts to be built nearby. With Wayland's Smithy long barrow a mile to the west, the downs to the south covered in celtic fields, strip-lynchets, burial mounds and ditches, and a disused canal and main line railway down below, our time on this earth seems very short. Better keep your money handy for that ferry crossing of the Styx in the after-life.

Directions. O/S 1:50,000 map 175 ref. 827949. Pass through High Wycombe on the A40 and turn first right after the A4010 junction. Park in the car park on the left, just over the West Wycombe Garden Centre, also used for the mediaeval caves. The hillfort is at the top of the hill across the road.

As those of you who have visited many of the hillforts in this book, plus the many others not included, will have gathered, not too many served any useful purpose once they had been abandoned. Several continued to be occupied in Roman times, in one form or another, while a surprising number were used in World War II, usually as lookout posts for enemy aircraft. Fewer still have been built on, fortunately, but West Wycombe hillfort defences now serve as the boundary for the local churchyard. It is not unique in this respect, although I cannot think of another hillfort that also houses a mausoleum.

That is rather jumping the gun a bit, and we need to go back in time by two millennium. Buckinghamshire, traversed by the Icknield Way, and the later Lower Icknield Way, has quite a number of hillforts, both large and small, some of which date back to the very earliest Iron Age days, not far into the first millennium B.C. Unfortunately, few have escaped damage, or being planted with trees, although Cholesbury Camp also encloses the village church. West Wycombe has been built on, partly destroyed and the remaining defences planted with trees, yet it is certainly worth a visit.

Built, probably, in the second century B.C., three acres were enclosed by a rampart, ditch and counterscarp bank, although the natural steepness of the hill on the south-west side allowed two terraces to suffice. The rampart still rises up to 11 feet in height, in the north, and generally forms the boundary for the churchyard. As the hillfort lies on the southern tip of a line of hills, about 500 feet high, it is likely that the original entrance was along the narrow ridge adjoining the hills, perhaps where the churchyard entrance is today.

However, no person from the Iron Age would recognise West Wycombe hillfort today, as it was drastically altered in the eighteenth century. Sir Francis Dashwood had initiated the enlargement of West Wycombe House, and even involved himself in the design work. He was just as active in the landscaping of the parkland, and the hillfort did not escape his attention. It was not unusual for hillforts to be landscaped in the golden age of the 'designer parkland', as Badbury Rings (Dorset), Clearbury Rings (Wiltshire) and others, were similarly dealt with. It was likely that the landowners did not know when the ancient camp dated from, and simply incorporated what was seen as a mound into the great plans. Wandlebury* even had a house built within its defences.

Sir Francis Dashwood caused the building of the church, within the hillfort, while the real damage was done to the south defences, which were obliterated to make way for the family mausoleum. In its own way, this makes for a uniquely interesting development of a hillfort, although the likelihood of there being a future excavation is remote.

West Wycombe was probably built in the middle Iron Age, although it cannot have been of anything other than local importance. Perhaps it served to oversee a route through the Chilterns, as indeed it overlooks the A40 today, or maybe it was a refuge for the people farming in the valley below, or along the ridge to the north. These are things that will probably never be known, but you can enjoy some good walks along the ridge, beyond the woods to the Icknield Way at Lodge Hill, on the north edge of the Chiltern Hills.

One would not wish to visit West Wycombe hillfort by itself, and to get the real benefit of making the journey, it is best to combine a visit to the mediaeval caves, the house or simply a walk to the Icknield Way. That way you will appreciate that the hillfort is not, unlike most, isolated from its modern surroundings, but serves an important function for both our modern world, and that of our not-too-far-off ancestors.

Directions. O/S 1:50,000 map 154 ref. 493533. Leave Cambridge on the A1307 heading south-east. Three miles from the centre, as you climb the Gog Magog Hills, the road becomes a dual carriageway. A signpost points left to Wandlebury, and the hillfort is at the end of the car park.

Although the land of East Anglia is generally thought of as being flat, this is far from the truth. Obviously, the fen-lands are indeed flat, but much of the rest is gently rolling countryside, which rises, in places, to several hundred feet. Yet, there are very few hillforts in East Anglia, about 24 at a pinch in the six counties, if you include the Isle of Ely and Huntingdonshire, and of these a mere third could possibly be construed as being within the area of the famed Iceni tribe, of which Boudicca was latterly the queen.

The area was well populated, and chariots were in use by the late Iron Age. Was it this very mobility which enabled the rulers of the tribes within the area, the Iceni to the north and the Trinovantes to the south, to prevent small-scale raiding, keep order among their own people and yet be able to rally support against an external foe, like the Romans? It certainly seems that the ruling organisation in the region, differed from that elsewhere in England.

Nobody built a hillfort for fun, so why build Wandlebury? It lies on top of the Gog Magog hills, which although they rise to only 240 feet command extensive views in all directions, including the higher land to the east. To the south ran the ancient trackway the Icknield Way, which the hillfort overlooked, and this might have been the main reason behind its initial construction.

Wandlebury has been subjected to two excavations, only one of which was of the hillfort itself, back in the mid-1950s. This showed that the hillfort was developed over three phases, spanning several centuries, the first of which dated back to about 400 B.C., or perhaps even earlier. A simple box rampart enclosed the site, being about 14 feet wide; the rampart was revetted with timber front and rear, and had a 14 feet deep and wide flat bottomed ditch. It was thought that Wandlebury might have been a stronghold with the nearby War Ditches site being a fortified village. The inhabitants produced a distinctive type of black pottery, with a flared lip and zig-zag patterns. Some bone combs were also found, which probably came from this period.

These defences decayed, as wood is likely to, and the box rampart was rebuilt, possibly a little larger, in Phase 2. It is likely that the hillfort remained inhabited by the same people throughout these times, although the later defences decayed too.

Phase 3 saw a major re-development of the site, in an unusual way. It may not have remained permanently occupied, but with War Ditches nearby, it was possibly never completely abandoned. About 0 B.C., the Trinovantes were over-run by the Belgic Catuvellauni tribe, and Wandlebury was re-fortified at this time. Whether this was carried out by the Iceni to stem any advance by the Catuvellauni tribe into their area, or the latter to keep an eye on the Iceni, or even the Trinovantes as a 'forward position', fearing an ingression by their Belgic neighbours, is not known. However, as it overlooks the low-lying land and trackways to the west, it may well have been an outpost of the Iceni.

Apart from refurbishing the old defences, new ones were added to create a position of great strength. Inside the original defences, a new rampart and ditch were constructed, the former being a wide timber revetted rampart, with a slope to the rear. The ditch was of 'V' shape, 35 feet across and 18 feet deep. The original rampart was also re-furbished, possibly being timber revetted at the top, while its ditch was re-dug to twice the former width, the extra earth forming a counterscarp bank, beyond. There was an entrance in the south-east, with a possibility of another.

The hillfort had certainly been intensively occupied, as many rubbish pits were found, while post holes of buildings, and possibly granaries, showed that these were of timber. Pottery from the later period was found to be related to that of the early type, but was less distinctive and decorative. Skulls were also found, possibly of this later period, which might have been from bodies suspended on poles, until the flesh decayed; this could have been a normal means of disposing of the dead, and would explain the lack of graves in the area. Moving forward a little, a coin of Cunobelin and other Belgic debris has been found at the site, as have Roman coins, which suggests that it served as a place of residence, although un-fortified, well into the period of Roman rule.

There is another, fascinating aspect probably directly related to the hillfort, yet distinct from it. This concerns the hill-figures that reputedly existed at the site. Evidence for these was to be found from various sources, although nothing could be seen. In the mid-1950s T.C. Lethbridge began to search by using a simple, ingenious system of knocking a steel pole into the turf, and through a combination of assessing the vibration and the ease and depth of the pole going in, was able to locate and uncover part of the figures.

Lethbridge did not just knock his pole in willy-nilly, and used what evidence he could to determine its likely position. The figures were last reported as being seen from Sawston c.1850, before being obscured by the planting of the beech trees, so he knew they would be on the south-facing slope, below the hillfort. The figures had last been noted by an antiquary c.1725, while scholars from the university had been forbidden from attending festivities and games held on the hillfort, possibly in connection with the regular clearing of the figures, as at Uffington Castle*, c.1600.

By this method, Lethbridge uncovered part of Magog, the goddess, and plotted the existence of two more figures, a man with a sword and the sun god with a horse and chariot. Magog was thought to have been cut about 200 B.C., well before the major extension of the hillfort, while the other figures were thought to have been added c.50 B.C., or later, possibly by the Catuvellauni. Like so much of the Wandlebury site, the goddess has become overgrown again.

Unlike so many hillforts, Wandlebury's past is both relatively well known, and fascinatingly varied. When you arrive in the car park though, with woods all over, you might be wondering if you are at the right place. That is because in the late seventeenth/early eighteenth centuries Lord Godolphin decided to build himself a mansion at the hillfort, and it was while digging the cellars that the aforementioned Roman coins were found. The largest, internal rampart and ditch were flattened, while the outer rampart, ditch and counterscarp bank were rounded down. In, c.1730 the interior was walled in, and what you can see today, as you follow the path round, among the trees, is two ramparts, rising up to 6 feet, with a ditch up to 10 feet deep in-between.

The interior, now grass-covered, was ploughed in both the Napoleonic War and World War II, while a carriage drive made its way to the house through the only certain original entrance. Rather perversely, history has got is own back for the mutilation of the fort three hundred years ago, for the mansion itself was demolished in 1955, and all that remains now are the stable blocks.

Thus Wandlebury has less to see than its distinguished and varied past might suggest. The hillfort remains can easily be seen among the encircling trees, while a walk through the woods to the north and east give extensive northward views over Cambridge and beyond. It remains a popular place for visitors, and is administered by the Cambridge Preservation Society, which should at least safeguard its future. You will need a bit of imagination to make the most of your visit, but time can be spent in locating the positions of both the destroyed defences and the overgrown hill figures, as you appreciate this East Anglian rarity.

Castle an Dinas

Directions. O/S 1:50,000 map 200 ref. 945623. The hillfort is off the A30 heading west from Bodmin. After crossing the Par-Newquay railway line, you will cross a junction with the B3274. The railway again crosses the road, and within a mile take the next turning right. Turn left at the 'T' junction, and in half a mile the hillfort is signposted on the right. The bridlepath leads to a car park, and the hillfort is a quarter mile away at the top of the hill.

Cornwall and its people have so many aspects of life that are peculiar, if not unique, to the county, ranging from place names, tin mines, a wide variety of ancient relics, food and their own ('dead') language. It will come as no surprise to find Cornwall no different when it comes to hillforts; there being a good many promontory cliff-castles, and in particular the multiple enclosure rounds hillfort. Crowning a hill between the north and south coasts, Castle an Dinas is of the latter type, and its defences would have graced many a hillfort of far greater size than its six acres. By Cornish, non-cliff-castle hillfort, standards, Castle an Dinas is one of the largest.

The word dinas means a stone wall in Cornish, but you will be disappointed if you expect to find exposed stone-faced ramparts. These, and much of the interior, are covered in bracken, but the defences remain impressive. Although there are a number of gaps, the original entrance is at the south-west. You will arrive from the south, and from here it is quite obvious that the camp is mainly formed of two concentric ramparts, each with a ditch and counterscarp bank. This latter is increased in size, and a second ditch added along part of the line of the inner defences.

In the enclosure between the two main ramparts, the flattened remains of a further rampart, with incomplete ditch, can also be seen. It seems that, in places, Castle an Dinas was defended by four ramparts and ditches, but it is unlikely that this rampart was contemporary with the main defences. Whether or not this pre-dates the main defences is unknown, but it is clear that, although undoubtedly a multiple enclosure, rounds hillfort, like Tregeare Rounds*, defence was its primary function.

That being the case, and considering both the camp's proximity to ancient tin workings, and its outstandingly prominent position, Castle an Dinas was probably a major stronghold for the local chief. So many Cornish hillforts combine daily activities and the need for defence, with an emphasis on the former, that Castle an Dinas stands out for this very reason.

As is the norm, the inner rampart and ditch are bigger than the outer ones. The ramparts were presumably stone-faced, and would have been strengthened at different times, the entrance included. Huts were built within the inner rampart, and some can still be traced, with a few stones still lying around. Water was provided from a spring, and a pond can be seen in the north of the interior.

The diminutive growth of the odd thorn tree suggests that the camp stands right in the path of the westerly winds. This is not surprising when you consider that, at 765 feet high, Castle an Dinas has outstanding views to every point of the compass. True, the whole prospect to the south is dominated by the china clay mines but, of course, these did not exist in the Iron Age. To the east, Bodmin Moor forms the next barrier, while to the west and north the views are prodigious. One assumes that its strategic position must have been taken into account when contemplating its building.

Built perhaps in the second century B.C., like so many of Cornwall's relics, Castle an Dinas had its legendary associations. Tador, the Duke of Cornwall, was supposed to have been killed here, while Thodoric, the King of Cornwall c.460 A.D., is also associated with the camp. Legendary figures they might be, but they hint at the perceived importance of the site to our forebears, and indeed one cannot imagine a much better site from which a local chief might wish to control his domain. Certainly, today, there is no better place from which to oversee central Cornwall.

ANOTHER ANCIENT SITE
Nine Maidens: Bronze Age line of stones. O/S map 200 ref. 937675.

Chun Castle

Directions. O/S 1:50,000 203 ref. 405339. Leave Penzance heading west on the A3071. Turn right at Tremethick Cross, and turn left at the crossroads in Madron, towards Morvah. After 3.5 miles, turn left to Great Bosullow, and when this road turns sharp left, go straight on and park beyond the farmyard at Trehylly's Farm. A path leads up the hill to the hillfort.

In a country of many ancient historical remains, and a wide variety of types of Iron Age hillforts, Chun Castle is both outstanding and perhaps the premier example of these. Yet the bare facts seem to conceal much of the splendour, as does the walk up from the farm. Chun is a circular hillfort of only half an acre in size, about 700 feet above the sea.

The most interesting feature of Chun Castle is that its two stone walls are both visible, although the lower, outer one is covered in heather in the summer. The inner wall is in a much healthier state of preservation though, and stands over eight feet high in places. Both walls are faced with granite stones, which gives a good impression of what certain hillforts looked like in the Iron Age, rather than being overgrown with grass, as we so often see them today.

The outer wall is protected by possibly two ditches, and has an entrance in the south-west, with a single gatepost still standing. Once through this, the passage turns left for about fifty feet, before the inner entrance, facing west and with both gateposts standing, is reached. The staggered entrances would thus have left any unwanted guests exposed to attack from the defenders manning both ramparts. The inner gateway is only five feet wide, with both sides in-turned, to give a narrow entrance passage. Unfortunately, the in-turns are now mostly lost.

That Chun Castle has survived for such a length of time is quite remarkable, given the value of its stone for building purposes. Only two centuries ago the inner rampart was recorded as being over twelve feet high, so much has been lost in relatively recent times. Once inside this hillfort there is still much to be seen, despite the removal of stones and the growth of bracken. All the way around the inside of the rampart is a number of rectangular and circular huts; the stone footings of many of these can still be seen, although some resemble piles of rubble. Indeed, the rectangular ones show that Chun was in use well beyond the Iron Age, and they actually overlay circular huts from the earliest period.

Some excavations were carried out over sixty years ago, and these revealed not only the circular huts beneath the later rectangular ones, but something of the activities carried out within the hillfort over many centuries. Not unnaturally, given the locality, Chun had long been connected with tin mining and working, and lumps of tin and iron slag were found in the interior, while a furnace stood near the well, which is in the north-west close to the rampart. Hearths were found to have been used for the smelting of metals in some huts, while pottery fragments from the middle Iron Age, Roman period, Dark Ages and possibly as recently as the tenth century A.D., were also found, along with wine amphorae, not unknown at Cornish hillforts, from the Mediterranean region. These finds, the length of occupation and the small size of the fort, all point to Chun being anything but a typical hillfort.

It is quite possible that Chun Castle was the residence of a local chief and his immediate family during the Iron Age, and that an arrangement of some sort allowed this to be carried on into, and possibly through, the Roman period. It is probable, although not certain, that occupation was disrupted during the Dark Ages, as the destruction of the circular buildings, and their replacement by rectangular ones, suggests a change of ownership took place. There are no visible signs of any battle, so perhaps it was abandoned. Otherwise, with the intricate defensive arrangements for such a small fort, the attackers would have been given a nasty surprise or two.

Another possibility is that, with a number of small settlements in the immediate vicinity, Chun Castle might have served as a refuge for the people from these in troubled times. Certainly the occupants could command the area for far enough. Much of the north and north-west coastline of the Land's End peninsula can be seen, and if the view due south is restricted by hills just over a mile away, to the south-east one can see Penzance and Mount's Bay beyond. Over to the east, a couple of derelict tin mine pumping engine houses sit on the horizon, and one might assume that the local Iron Age chief would easily be able to survey his domain, by simply walking round his 'house'.

We are fortunate that, in this area of South-West Cornwall, Chun Castle, along with Carn Euny and Chysauster (see below), have survived to the present day. One suspects that they are all fairly representative of the small-scale Iron Age settlement typical of this part of the county. An area which escaped the attention afforded elsewhere by the Romans, and in which the earlier settlements continued to be occupied. Chun Castle is quite probably England's best surviving example of an exposed stone walled hillfort to be seen today, and it enjoys one of the best locations to boot.

A path leads from the main entrance west to the Neolithic Chun Quoit burial chamber, less than a quarter of a mile away.

OTHER ANCIENT SITES
Carn Euny Iron Age village. O/S map 203 ref. 402289.
Chysauster Iron Age and Romano-British village. O/S map 203 ref. 473350.

The Rumps

Directions. O/S 1:50,000 map 200, ref. 933811. Leave Wadebridge heading north on the A39, and turn left on the B3314. After 4.5 miles turn left, actually going straight on, up the minor road towards Polzeath. Turn first left, and continue towards New Polzeath. Turn right at a crossroads, and turn left along the rough track to the National Trust car park at Pentire Farm. Leave the car park by the notice board/map, and turn right along the path which leads to The Rumps from the cliff top; a walk of about three quarters of a mile. An extended, circular walk back from The Rumps can be made via Pentire Point.

Of the many, often spectacular, promontory forts, or cliff-castles, in Cornwall, none have a more dramatic setting than The Rumps. The best sight of it is when you first see it, along the South-West Coastal Path on the cliff-top, at the junction with the footpath from Pentire Farm. The twin heads of The Rumps give the impression of two monsters rising out of the sea, while the seemingly incessant winds make you wonder why on earth anyone ever wanted to live in such an exposed spot. Rumps Point is the left one of the two headlands.

The triple ramparts across the neck of the promontory become more distinct the nearer you get, and you approach these defences downhill. The outer rampart and ditch is the least outstanding of the defences, and has a central entrance. The middle rampart and ditch is the strongest, the rampart made up of slate and the ditch being fifteen feet deep. The inner rampart, unusually, does not have a ditch, and is built on a ridge of slate. The two inner ramparts have entrances offset to the west of that of the outer rampart, but in line with each other. These entrance passages were lined with timber and dry-stone walling, and would have been quite formidable.

Once through these defences, as with most cliff-castles, there is not much in the way of Iron Age remains to see. A number of huts were found in the dip between the two points, a surprisingly sheltered spot from the winds; while pottery fragments have also been found behind the ramparts, which suggest that huts might have existed there. The pottery fragments have proved to be quite revealing, and included Mediterranean wine amphorae and other pottery similar to that found in North-West France. The finds mostly date from the first centuries B.C. and A.D., although The Rumps was occupied a century earlier.

It is possible that The Rumps, as with other cliff-castles, was built as a defensive measure against refugees fleeing from the Roman advance in Europe, in the first century B.C. Indeed, it is also possible that The Rumps was taken over by refugees, but the pottery finds rather suggest that peaceful trading with Europe, at least until the Romans intervened, was more likely.

The most magnificent aspect of The Rumps, and presumably a major reason for fortifying the headland, is the commanding views of the coastline. To the north, the whole of the coast to Tintagel Head would have come under the close scrutiny of the inhabitants, and not much would have gone on without their knowledge. From Rumps Point one can see Trevose Head to the south, but not much in-between. Presumably the Iron Age occupants would have observed happenings in the Camel estuary from the hill-top between The Rumps and Pentire Point. You can follow the coastal path from the ramparts round Pentire Point and along the estuary until you get to Pentireglaze Haven, where the path detours inland, and another path leads back to Pentire Farm. The beautiful views, and walk, will make this most rewarding.

Archaeological finds have not shown what became of the inhabitants of The Rumps, or any previous occupants. However, at least the headland, with The Rumps and Pentire Point at its extremities, would have precluded the landing of any boats during the Iron Age, so any possible landing would have been near New Polzeath, where there are some Bronze Age barrows. The Camel estuary would have been an obvious place for landing goods or refugees, if open to attack, so perhaps The Rumps was the fortified home for a community with overseas trading links in this vicinity. The ease of defending such a site is shown by the three short ramparts at the entrance.

Tregeare Rounds

Directions. O/S map 200 ref. 032800. Leave The Rumps* and join the B3314, heading north, at Plain Street. The B3267 from Port Isaac is passed after three miles, and after Pendoggett there is one more turning on the left to pass; the gateway leading to the hillfort is on the right 250 yards beyond. Parking is only available by pulling onto the grass verge.

It is difficult to justify the including of Tregeare Rounds in this book, at the expense of another, for a visit can be completed in a short time. As its name implies, Tregeare is a concentric rounds, multiple enclosure hill-slope fort, and is a magnificent example of this type. The larger outer rampart and ditch, which is covered in a thick, almost impenetrable, layer of bushes, encloses five acres, with a smaller rampart and ditch enclosing two acres within. The main entrance is at the south-east, with gaps in both ramparts, while it is possible that the gaps at the south-west, where you will arrive, might also be original.

Outside the main entrance is a later crescent-shaped enclosure, the rampart marked by bushes, as before. The north end of this is missing, presumably ploughed down. A 'covered track' leads through here, due east, to a stream. An excavation in 1902 revealed some sling-stones, rusty iron and pottery from the first or second centuries B.C., but no Roman finds, in the outer enclosure. This suggests that it was the inner enclosure that was used for keeping the cattle in.

Indeed, this seems to have been the primary use for this hill-slope fort, and not as a defensive enclosure. That is not surprising, as Tregeare is overlooked by the ground to the north-west, although there is an outstanding view to be had of Bodmin Moor, and especially Rough Tor, site of a Bronze Age/Iron Age settlement. Tregeare is still used as grazing land today, and as such retains a link with its ancient past that probably was never intended to withstand force, beyond that of a bit of cattle rustling.

Trevelgue Head

Directions. O/S 1:50,000 map 200 ref. 825630. Leave Newquay on the A392, and turn left onto the B3276. Descend to, and cross, an inlet and the car park is up the second turning on the right. Cross the B3276, and follow the footpath to the south of the pitch and putt course which leads to the ramparts. Alternatively, continue up the B3276 from the inlet, and pass the Castaway Beach Hotel on the left. You can park in the roads on the right. A footpath leads behind the hotel, north of the pitch and putt course, to the ramparts.

It was not my original intention to include Trevelgue Head in this book, as I consider The Rumps* to be the most spectacular of Cornwall's cliff-castles. That may be the case, but few of these coastal promontory forts have such a long history as Trevelgue Head, and none can boast such a complex system of defences.

The ever-present Atlantic winds, and the trample of feet over the years, have taken their toll on the defences, but they still remain impressive. The first rampart and ditch cuts diagonally across the headland, and thus forms a large outer enclosure, not unlike the outer bailey of a Norman castle. Inside this, at the north is the first of two large Bronze Age round barrows, which suggests that the site might have been occupied before 1,000 B.C.

As the headland narrows, you meet the three sets of banks and ditches which form the first line of defences of the promontory fort itself. The entrance through the outer ramparts is to the south, while that through the inner rampart, which may be a counterscarp bank, is in the centre. The middle rampart is the largest, rising to nine feet, with a ditch twelve feet deep. Next comes a gully, crossed by a bridge, formed by years of battering by the waves. It is not known if the fort was an island in the Iron Age, as it is effectively now, but the gully was possibly the ditch to the first rampart of the inner defences. Assuming the gully did exist in those days, I wonder what sort of ingenious contraption served as a bridge.

The inner defences enclose six acres and consist of a rampart immediately after the gully, followed by a further, longer rampart with flat-bottomed ditch and traces of a counterscarp bank, forty yards further on. Beyond that, the island stretches 250 yards out into the sea, with a second Bronze Age burial mound forming the highest point. From here, the Atlantic rollers can be seen pounding up the estuary

114

immediately to the south, and into the cliffs of the coastline to the north. On such occasions, with the wind blowing wildly, it is positively exhilarating, but not an ideal place to live.

Trevelgue Head may well have been occupied for a period of well over 1,000 years, although not necessarily continuously. An excavation was undertaken on the eve of the Second World War, and this revealed evidence of Bronze Age smelting. More importantly, a number of Iron Age, Roman and even Dark Age huts were found in the enclosure between the inner rampart and the gully. These had a dry-stone facing, while some had foundations cut into the rock, and others had post holes around a hearth. Finds from the excavation included an Iron Age bronze horse harness, with pottery, glass and fragments of Mediterranean wine amphorae, from the Roman and Dark Age huts. In addition, a bronze foundry was also discovered, to the south.

If such a wild wind-swept place seems an inhospitable place to live, there must have been a reason for it. Apart from its use for metal manufacture, it is probable that the camp protected a harbour used for trading in local tin. The estuary to the south would have provided a sheltered anchorage, while the wine amphorae suggests that trading in 'luxuries' was undertaken. That it seems to have been permanently inhabited from c.250+ B.C. until the fifth century A.D. at least, quite apart from possible Bronze Age occupation, shows the importance of the camp to the locality, especially with the harbour, or anchorage.

Today, Trevelgue Head is a popular place for a breezy walk, with views along the front at Newquay. It is all a far cry from 2,000 years ago, when a watch would have been kept out for the next trading ship, or worse, unwelcome visitors. An ancient hive of industry now rests silently, at the mercy of the winds.

Warbstow Bury

Directions. O/S 1:50,000 map 190 ref. 202908. East of the A39 between Camelford and Bude. Heading north, from Camelford on the A39, turn right onto the A395, and turn left up the minor road immediately beyond the junction with the B3262. Follow this for two miles, and as you descend a hill the car park is on the left, opposite the house 'Hillside'.

One of the many beauties of Cornwall is its wide and diverse range of antiquities, quite apart from more recent historical sites. Almost every parish/village seems to have some visible feature of the Celtic world, and one feels more of an empathy with our ancient descendants than is possible elsewhere. In fact, it is possibly due to Cornwall's relative isolation, at least until the coming of the railways, that many of these antiquities have survived, whereas in most of England similar ancient monuments have been destroyed or replaced, under the aegis of progress. This, in the main, does not apply to hillforts, and while Cornwall is home to a fairly unique type, and has a large number of hillforts, their total acreage, in comparison to the total land area of the county, is no greater than for many other counties in the south.

Warbstow Bury falls into the concentric, multiple enclosure, rounds, hill-slope fort peculiar to the far South-West England, and South-West Wales. It is one of the biggest rounds hillforts in Cornwall, and is undoubtedly one of the best. As with other multiple enclosure hillforts, it is likely that the inner enclosure was for the inhabitants, while the outer was for cattle and stock.

Two wide-spaced ramparts and ditches enclose eight acres, of which the innermost enclosure comprises three acres. Counterscarp banks front both ditches, being of a considerable size at the vulnerable south and west sides. In addition, the inner rampart is also strengthened to the south by a crescent shaped bank with slight counterscarp. This is thought to have been a later, unfinished defence as the outer ditch was widened at this point, but this is not certain.

There are two entrances in both ramparts; those to the east, through which you will enter, being in line, while those to the west are slightly offset. The outer entrances are of the simple straight-through type, while both inner ones have the ramparts in-turned between 15-30 feet, which suggests that defence was of considerable importance. Even today the inner rampart stands twenty feet above the bottom of the ditch in places, while the outer rampart rises up to fifteen feet. This was probably not just a simple 'cattle ranch', but, like Castle an Dinas*, more of a stronghold for the local chief.

Apart from the scale of the defences, and the size of the fort, its location adds credence to this suggestion. There are wonderful, extensive views to be had in every direction, except to the south-west, from this 790 feet high vantage point. Warbstow is some 50 feet below the round summit less than a quarter of a mile away, and gradually slopes from west to east. This begs the question of the reasoning behind such hill-slope forts; why not build them on the summit and enjoy the security of overseeing all the surrounding country? Perhaps it was to do with water supply, or possibly that the whole of the summit area could be used to graze cattle, with the inhabitants still able to keep an eye on them. An even less likely possibility is that some protection was gained from the prevailing south-westerly winds.

There is no doubting the safety afforded by the extensive views. Dartmoor can be seen to the south and east, while it is the natural curvature of the earth that restricts views to the north and north-west. This alone must have enabled the inhabitants to sleep easily at night. Little else of note is known of this hillfort, but of course something would be amiss if any Cornish ancient site was without its legend. Warbstow is not to be found wanting in this department either. The slight long barrow within the fort is reputed to be the grave of none other than King Arthur. Unfortunately, long barrows are known to be of Neolithic origin, and as for King Arthur's grave, well I am afraid that Warbstow is one of many places holding such a claim. In any case, Warbstow has no need of mere legends, there is more than enough to appreciate from a visit to this impressive site.

Carrock Fell

Directions. O/S 1:50,000 map 90 ref. 344336. The hillfort is 1,300 feet above the road; a stiff walk is required whatever route is taken. Leave Penrith on the A66 heading west. After twelve miles, opposite the turning for Hutton Moor End, turn right through Mosedale and stop at Calebreck. A Bridlepath on the left, by the right hand bend, leads up to the ridge-top. This is reached a mile west of the hillfort, beyond Meon Hill, to your left as you reach the ridge. Alternatively, after leaving Mosedale, park near the road to Stone Ends farm. The hillfort is right at the top of the hill immediately to the west.

The hills of the Lake District, like those of The Pennines, look inhospitable places to live on, but no more so than the hills of Wales, nor those of the Scottish Borders and central Scotland. Thus, it is strange to find that the former two ranges of hills have very few Iron Age hillforts or settlements, and few relics from the Bronze Age either. One must assume, from the lack of evidence, that the Lake District was sparsely populated for those times, although why this should be so, especially considering the very high number of hillforts in the equally exposed Cheviot Hills, I do not know.

It could have much to do with the organisation, if any, of the tribes, and the large, confederation that made up the Brigantes tribe to the east, seemed to be somewhat backward when compared to tribes of the South. Carrock Fell was in the domain of the Carvetii tribe, who were either very small in number, and/or probably not very far removed from what would be recognised as being Bronze Age, and were probably a mobile, cattle herding people at that.

Carrock Fell, at five acres, is the biggest hillfort for miles around and, if such a place existed, was possibly a tribal capital of the Carvetii. In plan, it bears a striking resemblance to Yeavering Bell*, with which it has many, coincidental(?), similarities. These include the elongated rampart enclosing the 2,174 feet summit to the west, a lower summit, also with a stone cairn on it, to the east, while both are situated on the summit of a hill at the edge of a range of hills and both are very difficult to reach, as you will find out.

The camp is enclosed by a single, well built stone wall, up to 8 feet wide, and with the stone facing exposed in places. There are many gaps, but the original entrances are probably those at the west end and in the centre of the south rampart. Most of the interior slopes gently to the east, but becomes steeper nearer that end. Quite unlike Yeavering Bell, there is no visible sign of any hut platforms, and while it has not been properly excavated, brief archaeological surveys have not brought any to light. This does not mean, of course, that Carrock Fell was not permanently settled.

It would seem unlikely that Carrock Fell was built, as has been suggested by archaeologists for certain hillforts, as the equivalent of an ancient air-raid shelter, i.e. to be used only in times of danger. Hillforts which lend themselves to such a potential use are usually sited near a settlement(s), or connected to a heavily farmed, and thus populous, region. Carrock Fell does not fit either of these requirements, nor would it be the easiest of tasks to retreat to its ramparts, with any cattle, from the land to the east. Given that some considerable effort was made in its construction, and its rarity in the Lake District, it was probably the settlement of a local chief and his retainers, probably along the lines of some of the Cornish hillforts.

As you will see, when you get there, the rampart has several gaps in it, and it may be that this deliberate damage was caused by the Romans, either in combat, as revenge, or perhaps as a training exercise. One would not have thought that the inhabitants would have caused the Romans too much of a problem when they arrived in the vicinity, given the experience they had gained in dealing with the native Britons. A decent sized Roman settlement and fort can be seen along the minor road that runs parallel to the A66, just before you turned off it, at the north, while another fort can be seen just east of Penrith at map ref. 538289, so there was a fair presence in the area.

With its outstanding view across Eden Vale to The Pennines in the east, and across the Solway Firth to the north, one would assume it might have served a lookout purpose against marauding invaders. At least, on a clear day, these will give you an added bonus, while contemplating your descent.

Directions. O/S 1:50,000 map 110 ref. 127837. Take the A625 from Sheffield to Castleton, and continue through the town towards Chapel en le Frith. Turn right at the top of the narrow Winnats Valley, and after passing the turning for the Blue John Mines, the National Trust car park is on the right. A steep footpath leads to the fort half a mile to the north-east.

Without a doubt, this is one of the most spectacular hillforts anywhere. Situated on the east end of Rushup Edge, rising to 1,696 feet and overlooking both the Hope and Edale valleys, its location alone is enough to stir the blood in one's veins. Celia Fiennes, the traveller of days gone by with an eye for detail, described Mam Tor as, " . . . very dangerous to ascend and none does attempt it . . .' Well, all that has changed now as you can virtually drive up to it, while not only does man ascend it, but you will seldom find a time when people are not trying to descend from it on hang-gliders and para-gliders. Yet three thousand years ago, people were living up there.

From the car park, you face an ever increasingly stiff climb until you enter through the obliquely angled, deeply in-turned south-west gateway. Almost immediately to your right is the smaller of two Bronze Age round barrows, the other being one hundred yards further north-east. The most obvious feature on entering the hillfort is the steepness of the interior, which rises over 100 feet to the summit. Yet, on this most inhospitable of sites, hut platforms can be seen throughout, cut into the sides of the hill. Mam Tor was excavated in the 1960s by students from Manchester University, and huts in the north-east revealed an extraordinary amount of pottery fragments; this was most surprising in that much of it dated from between 1,000-1,200 B.C., the Bronze Age.

The single glacis rampart, revetted by an unseen stone wall on the outside and stepped stones inside, with ditch and counterscarp bank, enclose sixteen acres, although successive landslips at the south-east and south-west corners, have eaten away at the rampart. Nature's actions, although damaging parts of the hillfort, do not detract from the overall picture, indeed that on the east seems to emphasise the exposed location. Apart from the south entrance, there is another in the north, which is also in-turned, facing the easiest approach, along the ridge from Loose Hill.

The defences are of typical Iron Age construction, probably the last of three phases of building. A post hole, discovered during the excavations, raised the possibility that a timber pallisade might have enclosed the site before the first earthworks were built. This would have been at the beginning of the first millennium B.C., as the site was definitely occupied at that time. The hill was later enclosed by a rampart which was later levelled and used to build the final defences, the ruins of which are now visible. The main problem with Mam Tor lies in the dating of the camp.

A walk up the summit will give you a good idea of the dispersal of hut platforms. The excavators concentrated on a few in the north-east, and it was these that produced the mass of pottery fragments which dated from the late Bronze Age. The pottery was quite plain, poorly made, and unlike any other in the Peak District, both in style and quantity. In addition, bronze axe fragments and a polished stone axe were found, neither of which proved to be similar to others found in Britain.

The various finds do not necessarily mean that all of the hut platforms date from the Bronze Age, nor that the defences are from that period either. The finds clearly pre-date the final stage of the defences, yet no Iron Age pottery came to light. It could be that an excavation of some other of the many hut platforms would provide evidence of Iron Age occupation, but the relationship between the hut platforms and the defences is, at present, not certain.

None of that ought to detract from your visit though, for which all your efforts to get to Mam Tor will be amply rewarded, provided it is not foggy. Once you have been to the summit, and surveyed the interior of the fort, descend to the western rampart. The former flat bottomed ditch is considerably shallower than it once was, but the defences still present a formidable obstacle even in their present ruined state. From here, you overlook the Vale of Edale with the great mass of Kinder Scout rising to the north-west, beyond. It is all quite breathtaking, as the valley sweeps before you, and even Mam Tor itself, so dominating from down by the car park, begins to shrink before your eyes.

Further along, before the north entrance, a spring rises within the hillfort and cuts through the rampart on its rapid descent to Edale. This, of course, would have been invaluable to the ancient occupants. You can leave the hillfort by the north entrance, its fifty feet long in-turns suggesting a build date well into the Iron Age, and walk along the ridge, before descending to either Castleton or Hope.

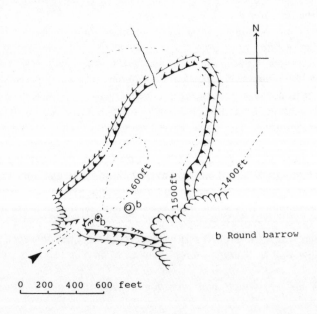

b Round barrow

0   200   400   600 feet

The eastern defences, though on the same scale as those elsewhere, seem to be superfluous, given the steep approach from that side. The landslips, one of which blocked the A625 so completely it was abandoned in the 1970s, add to the dramatic effect. The huts that were excavated, as elsewhere, are now covered in grass again and only the platforms cut into the hillside remain visible.

My own lasting impressing of Mam Tor, visited on a late December day, of beautiful weather, was what on earth possessed Bronze Age/Iron Age man to live on such an exposed, wild hill. True, it must have been virtually impregnable, at least in its final form, and it had running water, but how did they live and survive the cold and snow, having so little shelter?

Magnificent is the only word suitable to describe Mam Tor. If you visit all of the hillforts featured in this book, and any which are not included, you will find that some have equally fine and extensive views, others are just as exposed, several have much better defences, a few have a greater total of hut platforms and quite a number have a more comprehensive history. Add that little lot together though, and Mam Tor becomes one of the finest of all English hillforts, perhaps even the most memorable.

Directions. O/S 1:50,000 map 190 ref. 312235. Leave Barnstaple on the A39 heading west, beyond Bideford. Turn right at Clovelly Cross roundabout on the B3237. Permission to visit the site is required, and granted, from the East Dyke Farm, the second farm on the left, and they will indicate where you can park.

I have an unforgettable memory of my visit to this hillfort. My right leg has quite a bit of 'ironwork' holding it together, the legacy of an ancient accident. There was no answer when I knocked at the farm, so I followed the sound of a tractor away in the hillfort. I had a bit of a 'charge' to shake off the stiffness from driving, and while running into an enclosure I was suddenly brought to an abrupt halt by the waist, flung backwards and then given a nasty clout in the right leg. I was briefly dazed, but then realised that I had run into an un-marked electric fence strung across the enclosure entrance. Of course, it was a bit of a laugh, and the farmer enjoyed the story even more, but the wires are at face level for small children; so beware.

The term hillfort is a good catch-all name for any seemingly fortified Iron Age settlement. It is not, of course, entirely accurate, but has become the accepted term, and a number of sub-divisions exist to describe a particular type of hillfort. Clovelly Dykes is neither on a hill, nor was it likely to have been a fort. Nevertheless, a hillfort it is, while it falls into the concentric, multiple enclosure, plateau categories of hillfort.

There are many 'ifs and buts' associated with hillforts, but it is generally accepted that a multiple enclosure hillfort, like Clovelly Dykes, would have been used for the keeping, and separating, of livestock. The plan will give you an idea of the general layout, and if you leave the farmyard heading up the slope, you will come to the entrances to the two outer enclosures on the west side. These, as with all the defences, have their ramparts and ditches crowned with bushes. Although this makes walking on the ramparts impossible, and in fact the density of the bushes is not unlike the bocage of Normandy, it makes them easy to see, while the outer enclosures are still used for separating cattle.

The three outer enclosures are probably later additions to the earlier concentric inner pair of enclosures, or the rounds type of hillfort. The third enclosure virtually forms two separate enclosures, as its rampart is almost aligned with the rampart and ditches of the second enclosure, at the north and south sides. On the east and west sides, the third enclosure is extended well beyond the defences of the second enclosure to form separate enclosures, the east of which extends beyond the B3237. The south rampart runs beside the edge of the A39 along its length.

The original hillfort is defended by a single rampart and ditch of considerable size, with smaller, similar defences within. Access can be gained by either walking to the south end of the west side of the third enclosure, where a modern gateway gives entry, or by going to the east side of that enclosure, and entering through the original entrance. This is offset by about 60 feet to the south of the entrance through the inner defences, but is in line with the entrance through the third rampart. None of these entrances, nor those in the north-east, are of any great strength. This supports the theory that Clovelly Dykes was rather less of a fort, and more of a ranching settlement.

Clovelly Dykes was probably built in the second century B.C., with the outer enclosures being added later. It stands on a large plateau about 700 feet above the sea a mile away at Clovelly, at a junction of three ancient trackways. The inner-most enclosure is of 2.5 acres, with a further 2 acres enclosed by the second rampart. Thus the original rounds hillfort would have been similar in both size and build to several others in the South-West, although there are few other hillforts in the locality. It is the additional outer enclosures that have given Clovelly Dykes its distinction, although it is still not unique; Milber Down near Torquay is very similar. The whole site covers 23 acres and is thus one of the very largest in the South-West.

Originally, Clovelly Dykes was, like any rounds hillfort, probably home for cattle rearing people. Being at a useful junction, and near to the coast, probably led to the expansion of Clovelly Dykes into something of a 'clearing house' for the export of cattle from Devon and North Cornwall. If so, a high degree of organisation and co-operation would have been necessary, probably lasting into Roman times. Certainly such trade would be dependent on a peaceful environment, both in the South-West, and on the recipient shores.

The defences of the second enclosure are the most impressive. From the south-east or south-west corners you can get to the top of the rampart to obtain a good view of the plan of the whole site, although it is unlikely that the hedgerows existed back in the Iron Age. From one of these vantage points you can see the impressive views of the West Devon coast, and across Bideford Bay, although, being on a plateau, the views inland are restricted. The place for herding the cattle onto the boats was probably at, or near, Clovelly quayside, so a visit to that most picturesque of coastal villages is essential.

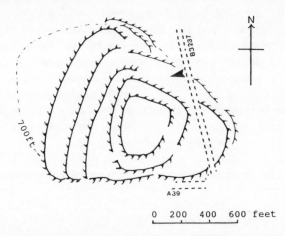

Clovelly Dykes is unusual among hillforts in that it still retains its original use, to a certain extent, with farm animals being occasionally kept in its enclosures. That it has not been damaged too much over the last 2,000 years is not surprising, as its ramparts make ideal field boundaries. Many hillforts are used nowadays as enclosures for keeping animals in, or as a ready-made arable field, but of course their primary use was for defending the inhabitants. Clovelly Dykes has two farms and several houses within its boundaries, as well. Indeed, the three outer enclosures look as well kept now as they would have done during the Iron Age. As such, not a great deal has changed over the centuries, except that the ramparts are no longer used for defence; mind you, an electric fence is a pretty good alternative.

Cranbrook Castle

Directions. O/S 1:50,000 map 191 ref. 739890. Leave Prestonbury Castle* past Drewsteignton continuing back towards Whiddon Down. Turn first left after Drewsteignton, past Castle Drogo, and turn left on the A382. Cross the River Teign and turn left in Easton, continuing along this road for 1.5 miles, ignoring three right turnings, the final one being at Uppacot. After this, park at the next junction with a stone standing beside the signpost. A Public Footpath signpost points the way to the hillfort a quarter of a mile away.

Cranbrook sits at the summit of a 1,110 feet high hill, over 300 feet above Prestonbury Castle* hillfort on the opposite side of the River Teign. It does not, however, command the river valley to the same extent, although is one of the highest points around. As mentioned in the Prestonbury Castle entry, it is possible that the two hillforts, and the now tree-covered Wooston Castle, 1.5 miles to the east, were outposts of opposing tribes, at least prior to the first century B.C.

In its present condition, Cranbrook appears to be an unfinished hillfort, for although the single, stone-faced rampart and ditch are both still of a considerable size on three sides, the north-facing defences only comprise a low mound to mark the intended line. In fact, looked at in this way, Cranbrook hides rather more than it reveals, for the northern defences, and what appears to be a counterscarp bank on the south sides, and for part of the east and west sides, are the remains of an earlier fort.

Unfortunately, nature takes over the defences during the summer and obscures them, but at other times of the year the line of the original glacis rampart, with its external ditch, can be easily seen. This enclosed about ten acres, though the defences were not particularly powerful, being about thirty feet across at ground level, and this presumably had something to do with the rebuilding.

The second, much more impressive, hillfort was built inside the line of the earlier one, with the original south rampart serving as a counterscarp bank. The rampart was probably about ten feet high, and although lower today, it still rises impressively, and encloses about seven acres. In places, the tumbled remains of the stone revetment can be seen, while part of the rampart is currently (1993) being 'sectioned', to reveal its formation. Beyond the rampart is a berm of varying width, with a flat-bottomed, silted up ditch, that was about eight feet deep, beyond that and the original bank still further out. Neither entrance, in the east nor south-west, seems to have been completed, but both have rounded rampart ends.

Cranbrook has been fortunate as it has had a number of minor excavations undertaken. The first was in 1900, which considered it to be an incomplete bi-vallate hillfort, with two ramparts. Mistaken though this might ultimately have been, a hoard of sling-stones and pottery from the middle Iron Age was found. A second survey was undertaken seventy years later, which revealed the existence of the earlier fort, while another small excavation is underway at present. Funding, or lack of it, obviously limits the extent of the work carried out.

There is little to be seen on the surface of the interior, and the later defences, and location, are the main attractions. Was the second fort uncompleted because the two possible tribes joined forces, or did one over-run the other? Another possibility could centre on the nearby Wooston Castle, which not only appears to be of a similar date, but received a later strengthening of the defences. Prestonbury Castle also appears to have been extended after Cranbrook was occupied, and possibly abandoned. Perhaps significantly, both Prestonbury and Wooston hillforts have a better view along the river.

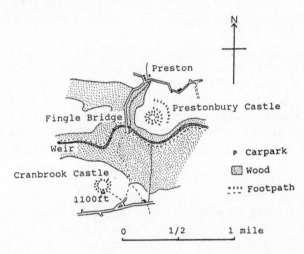

It is not unique to have a number of hillforts close together facing each other across a river. There are others in the Avon Gorge at Bristol, Cornwall, the Welsh Marches and the South, and one must assume these were mostly located for strategic purposes. Fortunately for us today, this makes a visit to both Cranbrook and Prestonbury a fairly simple, and rewarding task.

Hembury Castle

Directions. O/S 1:50,000 map 192/193 ref. 112031. Take the A30 east from Exeter to Honiton. Turn left onto the A373 and after 3 miles you will pass Hembury Fort Farm on the left. Immediately after the left hand bend, park in the lay-by on the left. Walk along the road, heading north, for 100 yards, and there is a Public Footpath on the right that leads to the south of the fort.

Here is a most impressive hillfort, which overlays a Neolithic causewayed camp. Having benefited from a well planned, and executed excavation, in the 1930s, with a further major one in the 1980s, the site is now overgrown with bracken and other scrub. That is a pity, because even the ramparts are becoming increasingly inaccessible, while the interior is quite wild in the summer. Nevertheless, the Beech and Oak clothed ramparts are both impressive in size and visual impact.

Hembury is a triangular shaped hillfort at the south tip of a ridge of hills. As such, it stands out and is easily seen from all directions, except the north, and it is the south point that you will arrive at, having followed the directions. Two large ramparts and ditches enclose seven acres, with the steep approach from the west, and the almost level approach along the ridge to the north, having an additional counterscarp bank; this is unfinished at the north. The outer defences have a covering of trees, but can be walked round, if not exactly with ease. Most impressive is the scale of the defences, especially so considering both the relatively small size of the hillfort, and the steepness of the approach from two sides. This can be best appreciated by walking up the long, steep and narrowing approach of the west and north-east entrances.

Across the centre of the hillfort are two ramparts and ditches, of a smaller size than the main defences. There is an offset gap in the centre of the outer bank and ditch, but not the inner one. These were built in the first century B.C., possibly by occupants using Belgic-type pottery, on the periphery of the Dumnonii tribal area. A reason for dividing the hillfort is not readily apparent, but the south enclosure, with slighter defences, could have been a cattle compound, while that to the north was for the inhabitants. Alternatively, the northern half could have been for the 'warrior' and his entourage, and the south for ordinary people. Whatever the use, huts from this late Iron Age period have not been found.

Both entrances had long, timber revetted passages through the ramparts, that at the north-east not having the additional counterscarp bank. These were both found to have been re-built on numerous occasions, both having stout gates, a cobbled track and probably an over-bridge as well. Despite their main defensive adornments no longer being visible, they are both still impressive. The outer defences, and long entrances, were probably built c.200 B.C.

Prior to that, a smaller single rampart, with timber and turf facing, enclosed the hill-top, on the line of the present inner rampart. This was constructed in the third century B.C., and there does not appear to have been a break in occupation between the two phases. The most recent excavations found that a palisade enclosure, whose entrances were almost aligned with those of the later earthwork, existed prior to that hillfort. This had been abandoned before the building of the hillfort proper, but not for too long a period of time.

Even so, what makes Hembury most interesting is that a Neolithic causewayed camp, dating to c.4,000 B.C., was found to have occupied an area in the south half of the fort. Two ditches and banks were discovered near both Iron Age entrances, that at the west showing the only certain site of habitation to be found, in a Neolithic wattle and daub hut. None of this would normally be visible, and today there is no chance at all, given the bracken covering.

At the other end of the pre-historic period, Hembury is thought to have been temporarily occupied by the Roman II Legion, under Vespasian, during the mid-40s A.D. campaign in the West; a Roman rectangular hut was also discovered. This only came to light during the 1980s excavations, and is further evidence of Iron Age hillforts being used by the invaders. This was not surprising, given that the Romans were invading hostile territory, and the use of a native fort as a temporary base saved a good deal of hard labour. As the Romans utilised hillforts for their own purposes at South Cadbury*, Hod Hill*, Ham Hill (Somerset) and possibly Maiden Castle*, as well as Hembury, it seems that the South-West remained an area of concern for them, even when conquered.

As a result of its vegetation cover, Hembury is a little disappointing, given its past, and its location, and this is not entirely off-set by either the scale of the defences, or the fine views. A visit in spring is best, when the bluebells add a bit of colour to what is an overpowering sea of bracken. Can you imagine St George's Chapel, at Windsor, being allowed to deteriorate so, after its fire?

Prestonbury Castle

Directions. O/S 1:50,000 map 191 ref. 747900. Leave Exeter heading west on the A30. Turn left onto the A382, going round the village of Whiddon Down, and turn left to Drewsteignton. Turn right immediately before the village square and descend the narrow hill. Turn left at the bottom, and a half a mile on the left is Preston Farm. Ask permission to visit the hillfort here. Cross the road, walk up the farm track, and the hillfort is at the top of the hill. (*see* Cranbrook Castle*).

Three hillforts sit astride the steep slopes of the River Teign valley, within 1.5 miles of each other, in the northern reaches of Dartmoor. Cranbrook Castle* is just across the valley, while the tree-covered Wooston Castle is also on the south bank, to the east. Quite why three hillforts should be so close together is not certain, but it could be that the River Teign marked a tribal boundary, and the hillforts in question were outposts of the two tribes; those on the south belonging to one tribe, and Prestonbury to another.

If the above hypothesis is correct, then each seems to have adapted the hillforts to a specific environment and use. Wooston is triangular shaped and utilises natural inclines on one side, having ramparts on the other two. Cranbrook was unfinished, while Prestonbury was extended at a later date, probably in more peaceful times, the extensions being used for cattle ranching.

A single rampart encloses the 790 feet high, oval, 3.5 acre summit, without an external ditch. The rampart is continuous, with a simple straight-through entrance in the east, and is now grass-covered, as is the interior. The south is naturally protected by a steep slope up from the river, several hundred feet below and, being situated on a spur, some very attractive views along the river valley are to be had. It is from the south rampart that Cranbrook Castle can be seen, almost 300 feet higher, but without the dominating views over the valley.

It might seem unlikely that these two, probable opposing tribes could contest each other, from such a height, but the river is readily crossed immediately below, just by Fingle's Bridge. As the Iron Age progressed it could be that these two tribes joined forces, for just as Cranbrook was incomplete, so Prestonbury was extended. About 200 feet beyond the original rampart, another one, with an external ditch, was built which enclosed a further two acres, on the north and east sides. This annexe also had a simple, straight-through entrance in line with that of the earlier hillfort. Again, this can be clearly seen today, although the ditch is quite silted up.

Finally, it is thought, in the second or first centuries B.C., the third rampart was added to the east and north sides, about 400 feet further out. This is more akin to a typical cross-bank than a normal rampart, and is crowned by a hedge for much of its length. There is quite a deeply in-turned entrance in the north-east, near the field boundary, which suggests that it was probably well defended. This additional annexe adds a further 12 acres to the total, and was probably used, as with many multiple-enclosure hillforts of the South-West, for cattle ranching purposes. The original hillfort encircles the summit, but the third rampart is almost 100 feet lower down the hill.

Although Prestonbury has not been excavated, it would probably have lasted well into the first century A.D., if not later, in its final format. It is still used for grazing cattle, and the ramparts are all now worn down, but clearly visible. More than anything, it is the outstanding location that makes Prestonbury so attractive to visit, while its somewhat unusual shape gives it a very real interest as a hillfort.

A visit to Cranbrook Castle* is highly recommended; it can be reached either by following the directions given for that hillfort, or by returning to Preston Farm, and going back along the minor road. Instead of turning right to Drewsteignton, go straight on to Fingle's Bridge, where you can park. Cross the river by the bridge, and follow the track south, before turning right and following the track for one mile up through the woods, away from the river. The hill on your right is Cranbrook Castle, and can be reached from a number of tracks across the field.

Directions. O/S 1:50,000 map 194 ref. 555865. Leave Abbotsbury village heading west, on the B3157. After about 1.5 miles take the turning on the right, signposted 'Abbey Chase only', and park in the little quarry on the left, just after the brow of the hill. The modern beacon marks the point of entry.

Compared to the many large hillforts in Wessex, Abbotsbury is very small beer indeed. In its heyday it obviously played a very minor economic and administrative role, and there is no evidence of any significant historical event having taken place within its walls. Abbotsbury merits inclusion in this book on two counts though: its unusual ramparts, and the outstanding views from the fort, no doubt of strategic importance over the centuries.

As you make the short walk up to the beacon you will come to the most stoutly defended part of the fort, the south-east corner, with four ramparts and deep ditches. A long entrance passage makes its way to the main entrance, part way along the north-east ramparts.

Abbotsbury, as you will soon notice, is a triangular hillfort, of approximately 4.5 acres, situated over 650 feet above the sea, which is less than a mile away. The defences to the north-east and north-west sides comprise double ramparts separated by a single ditch, the inner rampart having a ledge about 6 feet above ground level running round the inside, possibly to serve guard/watch purposes. The single, south-facing rampart was presumably considered sufficient in view of the steep approach from that side. There is also what is thought to be a postern gate mid-way along the north-west ramparts.

Towards the centre of the fort can be seen traces of about ten huts, gathered close together in the eastern half. To the south of these, and close to the rampart, is a Bronze Age round barrow. This is more obviously seen than the huts, but some of them can be made out easily enough. One theory has been put forward that the hillfort, built c.250 B.C., was the permanent home for the local chief and his family, but only occupied by others during troubled times. It may well have been one such occasion that caused the defences to be enlarged, particularly in the south-east corner.

A walk around the ramparts will soon show how well sited the hillfort is. Good views inland are to be had for several miles in all directions. However, it is the coastal views, and particularly that along the natural phenomenon of Chesil Beach to the east, which are both the most spectacular and probably of more relevance to the original inhabitants. This may well have been the case towards the end of its more active years. The south-western corner has been formed into a small enclosure by the addition of a rampart and ditch, which cuts into the main ditch. It is thought that this could have served as a Roman signal station, its prominent position being ideal for such a function. The siting of the modern beacon in the south-east corner, though totally unrelated, enhances this point of view.

As with so many hillforts, Abbotsbury Castle is not exactly forthcoming about its past. Despite its prominent position, and elaborate defences, it more than likely led a fairly mundane and peaceful existence. If the theory about the Roman signal station is correct, then this might well have been its most important function, on a regional basis, but do not allow this to detract from your visit. Consider this; would a hillfort be so well sited, and have such elaborate defences, if it were to be little more than a fortified village, at best? Perhaps so, after all, this has occurred elsewhere but, considering its prominent location, could not Abbotsbury have had a more strategic significance, right from the start?

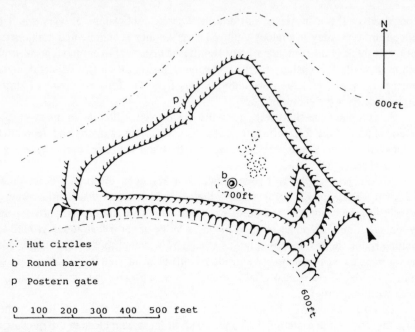

N

600ft

700ft

600ft

∴ Hut circles
b Round barrow
p Postern gate

0 100 200 300 400 500 feet

OTHER ANCIENT MONUMENTS
Within a three mile radius of the hillfort you have just about the full set of ancient remains: long barrows, round barrows, stone circle, earthen circle, standing stones, strip-lynchets, celtic fields, earthworks, pit dwellings, the lot . . .Look at the map and take your pick. That is apart from the many mediaeval remains in Abbotsbury village itself.

Hambledon Hill

Directions. O/S 1:50,000 map 194 ref. 841126. There are two main approaches to this hillfort. One is by following the path from the north-west corner of nearby Hod Hill* and arriving up the Steepleton (south) spur. Otherwise, head north from Blandford Forum on the A350, past the A357 junction, and take the first turning left at Iwerne Courtney, or Shroton village. You can park near the church. Turn left at the next road, and take the footpath to the left of the cricket ground. At this point, Hambledon Hill rises in front of you. Follow the footpath south, until you reach the gate and fence, then head west up the Shroton (east) spur. Follow this until you reach the plateau where the three spurs of the hill meet.

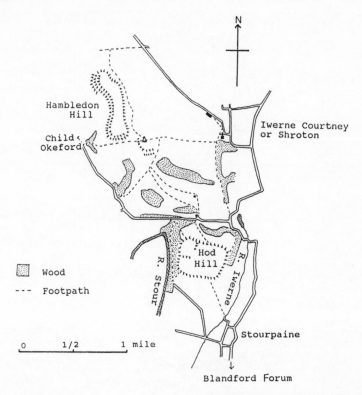

Visual impressions are very much a personal matter: 'one man's meat is another man's poison', and all that. There can, however, be few, if any, Iron Age hillforts so spectacularly sited as Hambledon Hill. Even its near, and historically more noteworthy, neighbour, Hod Hill is completely overshadowed in this respect.

If you have followed the directions given above, you should be standing on the reasonably level piece of ground which links the three spurs of the hill. A study of the plan would be of benefit at this stage, as you will be standing near the earliest permanent habitation of the hill, at least as far as can be deduced. In fact, whatever your approach, you will have passed the remains of the cross-dykes which separate the Shroton and Steepleton spurs from the central plateau. It is thought that cross-dykes also separated this plateau from the north spur, but these, if they ever existed, will be under the outer defences of Hambledon Hill hillfort. These cross dykes may well have been erected before 3,000 B.C.

At this central plateau traces of a Neolithic enclosure of five acres can be seen, for which the plan will be helpful. It was presumably the people that lived here who buried their dead in the 240 feet long long-barrow which surmounts the hump of the

Iron Age fort, and the 92 feet long long-barrow which can be seen near the Steepleton cross dykes. Before you get too excited though, those marks that can be made out within the enclosure are not ancient huts, but relatively modern flint diggings.

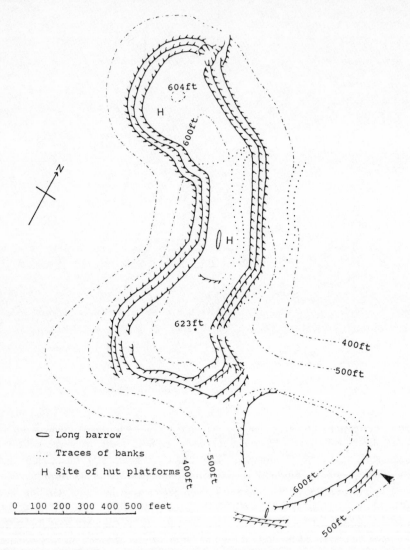

The massive ramparts which cling to the sides of the great north spur are thus pre-dated by some considerable time. In fact, it is worth noting that the hillfort as you can see it now, at 2,000 years old, is closer in time to the present day than it is to the Neolithic camp. It is, however, the Iron Age fort that we are here to see.

Approach the hillfort to the left of the two massive ramparts and ditches, and follow the main ramparts to the west. You will come to the long passage between the main ramparts that leads to the south-west gateway, thus having followed the original route to this gate. It is this entrance that is almost identical, if a mirror image, to the north-east gateway of Hod Hill, and which led to the theory that the latter fort was something of an 'overspill' town to Hambledon Hill.

As with so many multivallate hillforts, Hambledon Hill was evolved over a period of several centuries rather than built in one go. Again, the plan will be of use to understand its development. Initially, probably about 500 B.C., the north of the spur was enclosed by, almost certainly, a single glacis rampart and ditch, possibly dug from the quarry ditch running round the inside, to give an area of 7.5 acres. As you will see later, a rampart and ditch, which can just be made out, ran across between the ramparts to the north of the central 'hump' to form this hillfort.

Pressure on space must have proved too great, for this was further extended to cover the long narrow section of the spur, with a new, more visible, rampart and ditch across the width to the south of the central mound. Behind this is a raised mound, which might have served as a lookout. The enlarged hillfort covered an area of 15 acres, but it was thought at one time that this was the site of the first Iron Age camp. This theory has not been disproved, but it does beg the question of what the northern cross rampart was used for.

At a still later date, the hillfort was further extended to enclose the southern part of the spur, enlarging the fort to a full 25 acres. It is not known neither when this task was undertaken, nor when the single rampart and ditch defences were increased to their present double ramparts and ditches, with a significant counterscarp bank, virtually throughout. As the internal quarry ditch runs nearly all the way round, one might surmise this strengthening was undertaken after the hillfort underwent its final extension, perhaps during the first century B.C.

Hambledon Hill in its final form has three gateways, the south-west being perhaps the best defended, where you gained entry. All three almost certainly had wooden gates, and quite probably an over-bridge as well. It is quite likely too, that the approach passage to the south-west entrance enabled the defenders to make the 'welcoming party' as hostile as possible for any un-invited visitors. Inside this entrance, and to a lesser extent the ground inside the south-east entrance, there are numerous marks in the turf which denote the position of hut platforms. These are mostly round, although there are a few oblong-shaped ones in the central section, and are often in groups or clusters, measuring between 15-45 feet in diameter. As over 200 of these hut platforms are currently visible, it could well be that Hambledon Hill, in its final form, had a population ranging between 500-1,000 people.

Moving north along the western ramparts, it can be seen just how impregnable these must have been, with the steepness of the slope below adding considerably to their defensive capabilities. It is clear, particularly in the way the ramparts follow the contours and then change direction to follow a lower course at the north end, that they were well planned. You will soon pass the south rampart of the earlier 15 acre fort, and the long barrow on the top of the mound. We will come to these later.

As you follow the ramparts round you will be treated to breathtaking views of the Stour valley and hills to the west, with the Mendips rising in the distance.

Continue past the central mound, and the barely visible south rampart of the earliest Iron Age camp, and below is Child Okeford manor house. The ramparts drop down the hillside some way, as they make their way round the head of the spur to the badly damaged north gate. The hills to the east, that lead up to Shaftesbury, come into view, offering yet more wondrous sights in an every changing journey.

The north gate, now ruined by chalk quarrying, once had out-turned ramparts, and probably a defensive platform at the bottom of the hill. Inside the gateway, and either side of the summit of the northern section of the camp, there are numerous hut platforms which can be clearly seen. As with many hillforts built around the sides of a steep hill, these are the platforms on which the huts were built, and not the actual huts themselves, as at Hod Hill.

Return to the north-eastern ramparts, over 100 feet below the summit at this point, and make your way past the rampart of the original camp which is visible where it joins the main ramparts. It is now time to ascend the hump in the central section of the fort, with yet more hut platforms dug into the eastern side, some very close to the summit. These are very similar in form and layout to those in the north and south sections, which suggests, considering the great leaps forward made in the defences, that progress in domestic buildings was restricted.

At the south of this central hump lies the great Neolithic long barrow. This appears to have been dug into on a couple of occasions, but no records of 'finds' have been made. One thing that will have changed since this great fort was last in regular use, is the scenery from this point but, I daresay, 'spectacular' would have been just as accurate a description of the views then, as it is today. The panoramic view, in all directions, from the central hump questions the value of the 'viewing platform', if that is what it was, inside the second camp's south rampart.

Back to the main ramparts, and you soon pass the south rampart from the second camp, and more hut platforms can be made out as you near the south-east gateway. The approach to this entrance was via a steep north facing pathway which can still be seen. The outer of the three ramparts separates from the inner two to the south of this entrance and, joined by another rampart and ditch, forms an outer barrier to the most vulnerable approach, the strip of land joining the plateau with the Neolithic camp. This rampart then retreats back to join the second rampart, there being only two on the short section leading to the south-west gateway, by which you entered.

Thus ends the tour of one of the most magnificent Iron Age hillforts. It was undoubtedly inhabited by members of the Durotriges tribe, in its later years, but what caused its abandonment, and when, is unknown. Unlike the nearby Hod Hill, there is no evidence of any attack by the Romans, although one might assume that it ceased to be inhabited shortly after the events nearby. If Hambledon Hill was inhabited when the Romans arrived, did the occupants accept a similar 'treaty' to that at Hod Hill, having witnessed the likely consequences of resistance to the Romans, or was it already deserted, and the people from Hod Hill moved 'next door'? None of this is known at present, and perhaps never will be, so you are at liberty to conjure up your own theory of events, safe in the knowledge that some 'know all' is really no better informed than yourself.

Unlike so many hillforts, there is a sequel to the story of Hambledon Hill. During the summer of 1645, following the Parliamentary defeat of the Royalists at the decisive Battle of Naseby in the Civil War, certain of the King's supporters encouraged the villagers of Wiltshire and Dorset to resist the passage of *any* troops, effectively Parliamentary, in their counties. Thus began the Clubman's Rebellion.

Up to 10,000 were reputed to have pledged to resist troops, and certainly considerable numbers seem to have taken to the hills. Fairfax and Cromwell were with the Parliamentary army at Sherborne, and after the former marched his men to Dorchester he met leaders of the Clubmen, and explained the error of their ways. The Clubmen then gathered on a hill at Shaftesbury, and Cromwell's troops took 50 of their leaders prisoner. Further Clubmen then gathered to, 'rescue their leaders', and after firing on Cromwell's men who exhorted a peaceful discussion, Cromwell put them to flight, taking 300 prisoners whom he described as, 'poor silly creatures', and later, mercifully allowed them home.

Not before holding them for the night in Shroton church, whereupon the Clubmen entrenched themselves on Hambledon Hill. The next day Cromwell sent 50 dragoons to bring the Clubmen down, and it seems that a number of the latter lost their lives in the process. Hambledon's ancient ramparts, like the mediaeval castles after them, were no match for firearms. Thus ended the almost farcical Clubmen's Rebellion, and Hambledon Hill's last, brief entry in the history books.

OTHER ANCIENT SITES
Combs Ditch, Iron Age/Roman linear dyke. O/S map 194 ref. 851021-890000.
Rawlsbury Camp, hillfort, O/S map 194 ref. 767057.
Ringmoor Iron Age Settlement. O/S map 194 ref. 809085.

Hod Hill

Directions. O/S 1:50,000 map 194 ref. no. 855105. Heading north from Blandford Forum on the A350, the village of Stourpaine is half a mile beyond the junction with the A357. Turn left to the village down South Holme, and right at Manor Road. Head north up this street and then carry straight on when it turns right. This becomes first a track, and finally a footpath where a sign points in the direction of Hod Hill. This briefly follows the River Iwerne, and then heads up to the hillfort.

Of all the hillforts which overlook the River Stour, this is the largest, with the exception of Hengistbury Head at the river's mouth. It is, however, overshadowed by its immediate neighbour to the north, Hambledon Hill, and it is likely that these hillforts were closely connected. In view of this, a visit to Hambledon Hill would be advantageous on the same day. Hod Hill is virtually unique among hillforts, although not wholly for its Iron Age remains.

The Iron Age fort rests neatly around the summit of a hill between the Rivers Stour and Iwerne, half a mile north of the confluence. It is rectagonal in shape, and its ramparts roughly follow the 350 feet contour to the south and east. The interior, which rises to 471 feet, is conical, and it is not possible to see the south ramparts from the north for most of the length. It covers 54 acres of 'prime site' Iron Age building land.

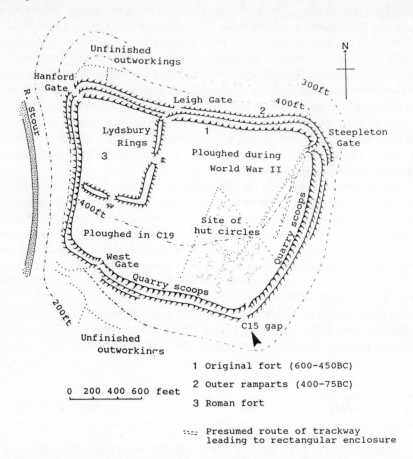

1 Original fort (600–450BC)

2 Outer ramparts (400–75BC)

3 Roman fort

0 200 400 600 feet

≈≈≈ Presumed route of trackway leading to rectangular enclosure

Prior to a series of excavations undertaken in the 1950s by Sir Ian Richmond, some later lesser 'digs' and the use of carbon-14 dating of charcoal associated with the first fort, a theory had been propounded that the inhabitants of Hambledon Hill, needing more space, had simply 'moved next door', and built Hod Hill in about 100 B.C. One reason for this was the similarity between the south-west gate of Hambledon Hill, and the north-east gate of Hod Hill, although Hambledon Hill had also been extended. Time, and historical theories, have changed, and it was later thought that Hod Hill went through several phases of construction, spanning 600 years. Now the 'removal' theory is back in fashion, once again; at least for the time being.

Phase One began with the enclosing of the hill with a univallate, timber-faced, box rampart, between 600-450 B.C. It appears that the only entrance was in the south-west corner, handy for fetching water from the river, although this is not certain. The timber ramparts were unusual in that the front timbers were dug into the ground, but the rear posts rested on the surface.

136

These defences were demolished to make way for those of Phase Two, between 400-150 B.C., when a still larger glacis-type rampart was erected, topped by a 10 feet wide walkway and stone parapet. A palisade was built outside the line of the ditch as a further defensive measure, although probably not at the west side. It was during this phase that the north-east gateway, with its long passage between the two ramparts, was built, probably with a bridge over the passageway.

During Phase Three, between 200-75 B.C., the outer palisade met a similar fate to that of Phase One, being rebuilt as a second glacis rampart, while the ditch was dug out. A second ditch was also dug, and the body of a young female was buried on the line of the second rampart, perhaps as a gift to the gods for the new rampart!

The last decades before the Roman invasion saw the main rampart reinforced and heightened on three sides, again with a walkway and parapet, although not on the western side. An outer ditch and counterscarp bank were also begun, but never completed, and have since been ploughed down.

You will arrive at the south-east corner of the fort, the entrance there being mediaeval at the earliest. The size of the two main ramparts can be clearly seen, although the counterscarp has been ploughed down at this point. Facing the interior though, you will see one of the best sites of Iron Age hut markings to be found. There are numerous hut circles in the un-ploughed section in front of you, apparently hap-hazardly spread around. Look at the plan and you will see that this was not entirely the case, although it is not certain that all of the huts existed simultaneously. We will need to return to this position a little later.

Follow the ramparts down to the south-west corner and you will see the quarry scoops alongside the inner rampart left by the extraction of spoil used to strengthen the ramparts. About half way along the south ramparts you can also see that the interior is flatter, a legacy of nineteenth century ploughing which destroyed many hut markings.

Next comes the south-western gateway with its sizeable, yet probably unfinished, outworkings. Once again, most of these have been ploughed down and remain only as soil markings. What is apparent is that although this gateway is close to the River Stour, there is a stiff climb up, and it would not be easy to carry anything heavy. Although the River Iwerne is further away, the walk to the hillfort is much easier and, one might surmise, this could also have been used.

It is the very steepness of the western approach which resulted in there being only two ramparts on this side. Economy in the use of sheer physical hard graft was certainly not lost on the inhabitants. More impressive than the ramparts along the western flank though, is the views to be had. Almost opposite, across the Stour valley, is Shillingstone Hill with its celtic fields, tumuli and ancient villages, effectively the north point of the range of hills cut through by the River Stour. Ahead is the south end of Hambledon Hill, with its even more impressively sited hillfort. Beyond, on a clear day, the Mendip Hills rise mightily on the horizon. The builders of Hod Hill were certainly no fools when it came to strategic planning, yet it is still a mystery why Hod Hill lies so close to Hambledon Hill.

Half way along the western ramparts you come to the south banks of the Roman fort known as Lydsbury Rings. This will be dealt with shortly, but it is this which makes Hod Hill unique among Iron Age hillforts, at least for being able to see it.

There are two matters of interest concerning the Roman fort which ought to be noted at this point: one is that the Romans used the original ramparts for their west and north defences, the second is that the interior of the fort was also ploughed over during the last century, thus rendering most of the internal remains invisible.

The gate in the north-west corner, the Hanford Gate, is of Roman construction. This was probably used for taking the horses down to the river for watering, and an additional enclosure can be seen outside the ramparts. Should you wish to follow it, a path leads from here to Hambledon Hill. The view north-east from these ramparts, along the range of hills, is towards Shaftesbury. You soon arrive at the Leigh Gate, also of Roman origin, at the north-east corner of Lydsbury Rings. It is worth leaving the Iron Age ramparts at this point, and following the Roman defences until the east gateway is reached.

The Roman II Legion, under Vespasian, arrived in this part of Britain in 43-44 A.D. Hod Hill is one of only three hillforts where definite evidence of a confrontation between the Durotriges and the Romans took place. It seems that the Romans arrived before an attempt to re-furbish the defences had been completed.

As ever, the Roman troops soon set about their task, but do not appear to have made a direct assault. Instead, they might well have directed a highly accurate ballista attack on a large rectangular hut and enclosure, possibly the chieftain's, not far from the south-east corner of the hillfort, where there was no gateway. Evidence for this came from the 1950s excavations which revealed a number of ballista-bolts embedded in the earth where they fell 1,900 years before.

How the Romans came to know the position of the chief's hut and compound we do not know: did they have spies or traitors in Hod Hill, or did they erect a tower outside the defences? Either way, their 'fire-power', and probably their reputation as well, seems to have been enough to persuade the defenders of the hopelessness of their cause, and to reach some form of treaty. Once this was done, the Romans cleared them off, perhaps into the valley, and destroyed their huts and stonework on the ramparts. The Romans did not feel entirely secure in this formerly hostile environment and, possibly expecting acts of revenge, built Lydsbury Rings.

The angular bank and two ditches of the Roman defences, with the south and east gateways, guarded a set of timber buildings within, which suggests that this was always intended to be temporary accommodation. Thanks to the ploughing of earlier years, it needed the 1950s excavations to reveal the plan of the fort. Both the east and south gateways had towers, as did the south-east corner, and raised, causewayed roads led to the Principia (H.Q.) in the centre. Barracks provided accommodation for up to 600 legionaires, and 250 auxiliary cavalrymen. There were also a number of 'support' buildings. The Romans, of course, soon advanced further west, and it appears that the buildings, to the south at least, were destroyed by fire in 51 A.D. Many of the Roman finds are now in the British Museum.

If you now return to the north ramparts of the Iron Age fort you will arrive at the heavily defended Steepleton Gate in the north-east corner. The approach to this gateway is through a long passageway between the second and outer ramparts, and must have seemed fairly impregnable in its day. Before Word War II, two internal trackways could be seen, both leading south between numerous huts, and one of which ended at the aforementioned rectangular hut and enclosure, possibly that of the chief's. Thanks to another thoughtless act of wanton vandalism, presumably under the guise of 'war effort', the whole of the north-eastern half of the hillfort was ploughed over, but although the trackways cannot be made out, some of the hut markings fortunately remain.

As you return along the eastern rampart, the entrance again not being original, you will come to the sole unploughed part of the interior. Exploration, with the help of the plan, might lead you to find the rectangular enclosure which so attracted the attention of the Romans. No doubt the ensuing display of Roman 'firepower' had the equivalent effect that the British armies, with their rifles and cannons, had on the natives of Africa, 'armed to the teeth' with spears, last century.

Fortunately, the surviving unploughed portion was enough to reveal some important facts about the life in a large Iron Age hillfort. Many of the huts followed a similar plan, being 25-40 feet in diameter, circular, and built with upright posts driven into the chalk, and the gaps packed with rubble. In many huts, a cupboard inside the door, possibly for storing weapons and hand tools, was found. Given an average of three persons per hut, and a density of six huts per acre, as opposed to a more common five per acre in the south, the population was possibly anywhere between 500-1,000 persons; this might have been even higher at the time of the Roman attack, due to refugees.

This brings us back to our point of arrival at the south-east corner. Hod Hill has much to offer both the serious hillfort enthusiast, and the person with a passing interest. Its strategic positioning is almost faultless and its visible remains are out of the top drawer. Tied in with a visit to Hambledon Hill, there can be no more pleasant a way to find out about Iron Age Britain, and if seeing is believing, you will have your eyes opened in more ways than one.

Maiden Castle

Directions. O/S 1:50,000 map 194 ref. 669885. Leave Dorchester centre on the A354 towards Weymouth. A minor road on the right is signposted, and leads to the hillfort. The nearest stations are Dorchester South, and Dorchester West.

As you make your way along the straight track that leads from the A354, the ancient ramparts, which rest so majestically on the hill before you, have remained little altered for nearly 2,000 years. You are approaching what was probably the greatest of all Iron Age hillforts in England.

Today, Maiden Castle gives the impression of being a 'sleeping giant', a former champion boxer, at peace with the world and his surroundings. As with a boxer, in its heyday Maiden Castle would have looked rather different, and certainly more menacing to the bystander.

The ramparts would not have been so accommodating in the Iron Age, their spoil-covering being in marked contrast to the grass covered mounds they are today. The west entrance, where you first approach the hillfort through its maze-like passages, would have appeared quite daunting when lined with wooden palisades and fighting stands, from which suspicious guards would eagerly be watching you; the east entrance was built to a similar scale and pattern, both able to deter even the fiercest predator. The all-conquering Romans were not to be denied though, and after their victory over the native occupants, Maiden Castle was slighted, and thereafter remained a highly visible, mostly silent, monument to a bygone age.

As with most things in general, and hillforts in particular, Maiden Castle did not just happen, but evolved. Indeed, the first time the hill was occupied was about 6,000 years ago. A Neolithic causewayed camp, similar to those at Windmill Hill (Wiltshire), Hambledon Hill* and The Trundle*, was constructed on what is now the eastern half of the fort. Any visible remains of this have long since been hidden under the first Iron Age camp, which is itself virtually obscured by the massive ramparts we can see today. Evidence of the earliest camp was uncovered during excavations carried out between 1934-7, by a team of archaeologists headed by Sir Mortimer Wheeler, and more recently by the Maiden Castle Project in the 1980s.

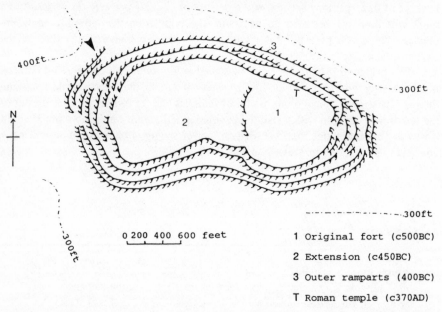

0 200 400 600 feet

1 Original fort (c500BC)

2 Extension (c450BC)

3 Outer ramparts (400BC)

T Roman temple (c370AD)

Wheeler discovered the causewayed camp in 1934 while digging in the ditches of the Iron Age hillfort. It comprised two ditches, with a bank in-between, which followed the line of the inner rampart on the eastern knoll, and then cut across what is now the centre of the hillfort. The bank that crosses the interior is the rampart of the first Iron Age hillfort; it followed the line of the causewayed camp, the bank of which would have been visible when the first hillfort was built. Wheeler's excavations showed relatively little use of the interior of the causewayed camp, but its size, and prominent position, both for seeing from and being seen, suggests that it was of considerable importance. However, the excavations of the 1980s revealed a large quantity of debris from a relatively small excavated area, especially in comparison to other causewayed camps, further enhancing its probable importance in Neolithic times.

Despite a number of causewayed camps having been excavated, the main purpose of these is still unknown, but from the evidence uncovered at Maiden Castle it is quite feasible that they served several functions. A number of burials, particularly of children, were found, which allows for the possibility of it serving as a venue for ritualistic acts. Axe heads from Cornwall, and pottery from the South-West suggests that it could have been a trade centre, while items from the immediate locality, or the coast might indicate a, highly visible, local meeting place.

A considerable quantity of domestic rubbish was found, so there may have been a settlement on the site, and with flint arrow-heads also being uncovered, a defensive purpose cannot be ruled out, although the limited area of excavation did not reveal any post holes for a wooden fence. There was also a large number of cattle bones, so perhaps they too were used in some kind of ritual sacrifice, although the site could have served as a ranch just prior to an annual slaughtering. Some of this evidence has been carbon-14 dated to 3,900-2,700 B.C.; thereafter, it probably remained unused, but there was evidence of a small settlement on the west knoll between 1,900-1,700 B.C.

Until the coming of the Iron Age, the hill was probably uninhabited, but the existence of several round barrows in the vicinity, allows for an alternative view. However, apart from background information, none of this need concern us, as the only visible residue from this 3,500 year time span is a 1,790 feet long Neolithic bank barrow, which began life as a long barrow. This is best seen from the flattened western ramparts of the first Iron Age fort. If you stand midway along, and look towards the western entrance of the present hillfort, the mound can just be made out.

The Iron Age hillfort was begun as a single rampart and ditch affair, built over the former causewayed camp, around the eastern knoll, about 500 B.C. This was a time when hillforts were being widely built, and Maiden Castle, which enclosed 16 acres, was large but not particularly distinguished. It has been estimated that the wooden revetted ramparts by the east gateway stood to a height of 10 feet, but the rest were of the glacis type.

Within a century, the fort had undergone its most dramatic change, and taken on the shape that now greets the visitor. The western knoll was enclosed, with a single glacis rampart and ditch, increasing the interior to 47 acres; and the original eastern defences were similarly rebuilt. A substantial barbican was erected at the east gateway, while a new western entrance, with two gateways and barbican, was also built. During the 1930s excavations, a female skeleton was found at the junction of the earliest Iron Age fort, and the newly extended fort, on the north side. One wonders if this was a particularly gruesome ancient equivalent of the modern 'foundation stone'?

This extension seems to have been built at the expense of the nearby Poundbury and Chalbury hillforts, along with other small settlements. It is quite possible that a number of four-post granaries and storage pits were built before the western extension, as a means of attracting labour to build the new defences, or perhaps as a sinister means of cajoling the neighbours into action.

A little later, c.400 B.C., the additional outer ramparts and ditches were added, while the inner rampart was strengthened, along with both entrances. The defences were subsequently improved on several occasions throughout the middle Iron Age, the inner rampart being heightened to 18 feet with a wooden fence added at the back of the rampart, which would not hinder the use of a sling, and a stone revetment on the inside. Both of the entrances were similarly up-graded, resulting in the layouts seen today.

The 1980s excavators described the interior at that time as being ' . . . densely occupied . . .' with a well planned layout of tracks, and with areas for huts, storage pits and granaries. As with many hillforts, the housing was quite egalitarian, with similar principles probably dictating work, at least on the land. However, evidence of manufacturing on a scale commensurate with that of the hillfort was not found, raising the possibility that Maiden Castle, in the middle Iron Age, had more of a consumer-led community than was the norm. One must assume that a hillfort of such a physical size would have served an important ruling function over its area. Its great population would have been a major attraction for whatever trade was going in those days, and perhaps trade was more important than manufacturing to its local economy.

Nevertheless, the defences were allowed to decay, and the settlement declined. There was evidence of storage pits being filled with rubbish and of roads being overgrown, and even being built over. During the first century B.C. it seems that the western half became virtually dis-used, while the settlement in the east declined in numbers, with organisation becoming lax, and even the track system being abandoned. Settlements once again sprang up in the vicinity of the hillfort, and some huts were even built just outside the east entrance. Land was becoming owned by the individual, rather than communally worked; was this the Iron Age equivalent of the 1980s 'Thatcherite individual society'? As we today will have to bear the legacy of the 'Thatcher revolution', in the form of rapidly declining social and moral standards, and especially public services, for many years to come, so too did the inhabitants of Maiden Castle carry the ultimate sacrifice for their 'individuality' revolution.

Times were certainly beginning to change, but the biggest change was to find the inhabitants, and probably members of the Durotriges tribe elsewhere, unprepared for subsequent events. As with most pre-historic events which took place in these islands, the details are not exact. After the Roman invasion of 43 A.D., Vespasian advanced westwards with the II Legion, sweeping all before them. Vespasian, a renowned military leader, is reputed to have launched a formidable assault at the eastern entrance, opening the attack by directing his ballistae weapons at the 'out-gunned' defenders. The scale of Maiden's defences was more than adequate to deter the native sling and spear weapons, but was incapable of withstanding the ancient equivalent of the 'nuclear bomb', the Roman artillery.

It was thought by Wheeler, following his 1930s excavations, that a murderous battle took place for Maiden Castle, and this was backed by the discovery of the 'war cemetery' near the east gate. Several bodies were hastily buried, some bearing sword or spear injuries, while most convincing of all was a man with a ballista-bolt embedded in his spine. Here indeed, was evidence of a Roman battle for the hillfort, and Wheeler accompanied this with his own picturesque account of the events of the battle.

Unfortunately, as with most things, 'progress' interfered with that story, and the recent excavations have thrown doubt onto the existence of the 'war cemetery, and even the scale and likelihood of the Roman assault. Recent excavators have a point though, as compared to some of the Roman assaults against hillforts in Gaul (*see* Chapter 6), during the campaigns of Julius Caesar, a grave containing 38 bodies, some of which were women, is very small beer indeed. Still, it was a good story while it lasted, while some form of action, however minuscule, does appear to have taken place.

Maiden Castle remained occupied, though not defended, for a further thirty years, until the inhabitants moved down to the new town in the valley, Durnovaria, modern Dorchester. However, it is now thought possible that the hillfort might have been temporarily occupied by the Roman army, at some time during this period. The east entrance was certainly re-built, while a large quantity of Roman finds, which included jewellery and pottery, pointed to Maiden's for use by Romans rather than Britons. Roman military occupation of a native hillfort was not unknown in the South-West, with Hod Hill*, Hembury*, South Cadbury* and Ham Hill (Somerset) all having evidence of such.

By 100 A.D., Maiden Castle was effectively abandoned and the interior ploughed, the long barrow probably being destroyed at this time. Then, about 370 A.D., a Romano-Celtic temple, with its attendant priest's house, was erected in the north-eastern part of the fort. A bronze statuette of Taurus-Trigaramus, a three-horned Celtic bull-god, was found, and this, and other finds from the hillfort, are in the Dorset County Museum, High Street West, Dorchester. The wall footings, and outline of the priest's house, can be seen in the hillfort.

Other than as useful farm land, Maiden Castle had probably served its last purpose soon after the Romans finally left the island. However, close to where the eastern end of the long burial mound was, a body of a young man, dating from about 625 A.D. was found. This may, or may not, suggest that the fort was subsequently occupied, but it remains the last evidence of the hillfort's once glorious past.

As with all hillforts, a walk around the ramparts is essential, and more so here at Maiden, if only to appreciate their vast scale. Go along the north ramparts first, as you have fine views of Dorchester, and the various scattered burial mounds. Almost half way along you will come to the juncture with the ramparts of the original Iron Age fort, where the human 'foundation stone' is buried. Then, on to the eastern entrance, perhaps the scene of the 'battle'.

From here on the enormous southern ramparts fold out before you. Here, perhaps more so than at any other hillfort, one can appreciate the sheer physical effort required to build such a fortification, never mind that it is the ruins that we see today. 'Massive' is the only word that can fully describe the scale of the ramparts and ditches, and the thought of the sheer physical graft needed to build them, with few primitive tools, is daunting.

Historians, archaeologists and others often make references to the damage caused by the tramp of feet, or hands, over our historical remains. Here, on these vast ramparts, you have your chance to range around as you wish, with care. Indeed, the best way to appreciate their size is to make your way to the bottom ditch, and then run all the way to the top. Now think of doing it with spears and sling-stones raining down on you! Rather be a defender?

It is worthwhile venturing along the earliest hillfort's western rampart, to see the bank barrow. From the centre of the rampart strike out north-east, and you will find the remains of the temple. Whenever I read of a 'Roman temple' I am always disappointed at the remains (the same goes for Roman villas, except where mosaics have been uncovered); I still expect to see colonnades, and statues. Here, at Maiden, it is no different: only the wall footings remain. Although no huts are readily visible, you can almost visualise the great interior alive with Iron Age people going about their daily tasks, but all that has now given way to pasture, which at least allows you to appreciate the remains and does not obscure them, as at many other hillforts.

So, that is it. No matter how many hillforts you visit, you will find nothing quite like Maiden Castle. This was the 'Heavyweight Champ' of hillforts, that now rests sleepily, almost benevolently over-seeing the rapid growth of modern Dorchester, and its by-pass, no doubt glad that it had its day when it did.

OTHER ANCIENT MONUMENTS
Black Down Barrows. O/S Map 194 ref. 613876.
Nine Stones Stone Circle. O/S Map 194 ref. 610904.
Poor Lot Barrow Cemetery. O/S Map 194 ref. 589907.
Poundbury hillfort. O/S Map 194 ref. 682911.
Chalbury hillfort. O/S Map 194 ref. 695838.

Spettisbury Rings *(Also known as Crawford Castle)*

Directions. O/S 1:50,000 map 195 ref. 915020. On the A350 about three miles south of Blandford Forum. Heading south through Spettisbury village, turn right up a narrow metalled road. A flight of steps leads up from the railway bridge to the remains of the station, closed in the 1950s. A short walk south, along the trackbed of the former Somerset and Dorset Railway, closed in the mid-1960s, brings you to the north-eastern rampart.

Spettisbury is one of a number of Dorset hillforts which overlooks the valley of the River Stour. During the Iron Age it was quite possibly the least important of these, as its relatively small area of less than five acres suggests.

Not a great deal is known about the early history of Spettisbury. It has been suggested that its single glacis rampart and ditch defences were constructed in the second century B.C., although compared to other hillforts in the locality that is quite late. Situated on the edge of the crown of a hill, the fort slopes gently from west to east. The entrance is at the north-west corner, with the rampart ends being out-turned slightly. The rampart on the south, west and north-western sides is protected by a flat bottomed ditch, the sides of which fall at a steeper angle to that of the rampart. The bottom of the ditch on the west side measures 22 feet across at its present depth of about 7 feet, and 55 feet across at ground level. Excavations in the 1950s have shown that the bottom of the ditch is 10 feet below the present level and was originally of 'V' shape. Suggestions that the hillfort was rebuilt, or at least partially re-fortified, are backed by the 300 feet of dump-mounds on the east side, presumably an unfinished rampart.

Throughout Britain countless historic structures have been either obliterated, or damaged, by subsequent building/developments. It is not often that any benefit is derived from such 'progress', but at Spettisbury, when its north-eastern rampart was cut through by the building of the railway in 1857, hard evidence of its past was unwittingly uncovered. A mass grave which contained about 100 Roman and British bodies, some laid full length, others with broken skulls and one skull with a four inch spear embedded in it, revealed that Spettisbury did not enjoy an entirely peaceful existence. Also unearthed at this time was a hoard of tools, ornaments and a mixture of Iron Age and Roman weapons, which included 11 swords, a short javelin, iron arrow-heads and spears. These are now kept in the British Museum.

It seems incontrovertible that the cause of this mass grave, presumably hastily dug by the victors, was the arrival of the Roman II Legion under Vespasian in late 43 A.D./early 44 A.D. Was it the impending approach of the Romans, possibly either along the River Stour, or fresh from their victories at Maiden Castle* or Hod Hill*, that caused the Durotriges peoples in this area to attempt a speedy restoration of the rampart in the north-east corner? Who knows, but the Romans were concerned enough about events encountered at Spettisbury Rings, and perhaps nearby Badbury Rings, to build their own small fort at Shapwick a mile to the east.

This one incident shines out in the known history of Spettisbury Rings, as thereafter Spettisbury has 'kept Mum' about its past. A number of Saxon coins have been found on the site, so it may have continued to be used, on and off, over a period of 600-800 years.

Despite the severity of the battle that took place for the hillfort, it is unlikely, considering the proximity of the larger Badbury Rings (Dorset) and Hod* and Hambledon* Hills, that Spettisbury was of anything other than local significance. Nevertheless, as you will find out, it commanded good views to the south and east over the Stour valley, and was one of only two hillforts on the west side of the river. That the now derelict railway caused damage to the hillfort was unfortunate, but at least it unearthed some of its past and history.

OTHER ANCIENT SITES
Badbury Rings, hillfort O/S map 195 ref. 964030
Buzbury Rings, hillfort O/S map 195 ref. 918059

Leckhampton Hill

Directions. O/S 1:50,000 map 163 ref. 948185. Leave Cheltenham on the A46 heading south, and turn left on the B4070. This skirts the steep hill to the east, and once alongside it, turn left up the minor road to the car park at the top of the hill, on the left. From here, follow the track signposed to Devil's Chimney, which brings you to the east rampart near the triangulation point.

Many hills in the Cotswolds are topped with some form of Iron Age fortification, particularly along the west escarpment, and Leckhampton is one of several that can be called a promontory hillfort. The builders knew enough about saving labour to utilise the virtual cliff as a defensive barrier for the north and west sides, and so only needed to build defences for two sides.

An excavation of the site was undertaken as early as 1925, which was quite comprehensive by contemporary standards, and concluded that the first phase of the camp was built possibly as early as c.500 B.C., an extraordinarily early date given the time-scales then used. However, the excavators considered that the camp was re-fortified at a later date, possibly by refugees from the Belgae advance in the South, an explanation used for developments at other Cotswold hillforts, like Bredon Hill*.

Many hillforts have been excavated subsequently and, particularly with the use of Carbon-14 dating techniques, a new time-scale for hillfort building pushed many further back in time. Parallels between building techniques and finds had always been used to 'date' hillforts, and certain anomalies grew. Thus, as part of a study of Cotswold hillforts, Leckhampton was excavated again in 1969-70, and the evidence challenged certain of the conclusions of the earlier excavators.

The single rampart and ditch defences enclose eight acres on this level site, 967 feet above sea level. The rampart was about six feet high, built of rubble with horizontal timbers running from front to rear, inside. These were not thought to have been visible, as the rampart was covered in earth and revetted at the front with a dry-stone wall. The 1925 excavators found that the rampart had been burned on the east side, but no certain explanation was given.

It was the structural features which led the later excavators to consider that the defences had been built in one period, together with pottery evidence from the 1925 excavation, which was found to be dated about the fifth century B.C. The lack of any finds of the later 'duck stamped' pottery familiar in the area, and also absent at the nearby promontory hillfort of Crickley Hill (Gloucestershire), led to the conclusion that Leckhampton had been abandoned by the fifth century B.C., at the latest. This exonerated the conclusion of the earlier excavators regarding the dating, if not the existence of their 'second phase', while adding to the growing bank of evidence of hillforts being built in the first half of the first millennium B.C.

Of particular interest to both sets of excavators was the entrance, at the north end of the east rampart. Unfortunately, this appears as merely a gap, but the additional bank at the south can be seen, and the in-turn of the gateway, while the bulge at the outer end of the rampart is also visible. What is not seen is the two guard chambers on either side of the entrance passage. The entrance is thus similar to certain others of about that time, being simple and yet comprehensive.

What caused the abandonment of the camp is not known, although the aforementioned fire on the east rampart, not necessarily from an attack, may well have acted as the precursor. You will find the rampart, and silted ditch, clearly visible and almost rising to its full height. The interior is grass covered, and just outside the entrance stands an enclosed Bronze Age burial mound. The bank running west from the entrance, inside the fort, is a mediaeval, or later, field boundary, and watch out for the mountain cyclists.

When you arrive at the west escarpment, in preference to the north which is overgrown, you will see why the hillfort was sited here. There was no way any serious assault would have succeeded from this side, while the inhabitants had a tremendously powerful strategic position. Nowadays, you look down over Cheltenham, with Tewkesbury and its abbey beyond, along the River Severn. Away to the north-west rise the Malvern Hills, and the hillforts of Midsummer Hill*, at the south, and Herefordshire Beacon*, the next hill along can be seen. To the north of Cheltenham, along the Cotswolds escarpment, the hillforts of Cleeve Hill and Nottingham Hill (both Gloucestershire) are to be seen and so is the outstanding Bredon Hill*, but I could not see the hillfort.

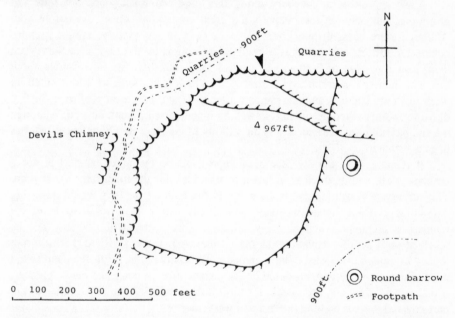

Mid-way along this west side rises the unusual Devil's Chimney. This is the reason most people visit the site, often blissfully unaware of its historical significance, and that included me in the mid 1970s. That is something which will not trouble you, and the hillfort last saw 'action' in Word War II when it was used as a radar station. Nowadays, it serves as an ideal, if breezy, place for simple recreation, one that is popular with the locals.

Uleybury Hillfort

Directions. O/S 1:50,000 map 162 ref. 785990. Leave Stroud heading towards the M5 on the A419. Turn left at the Cairncross roundabout onto the A46, cross the River Frome and turn right onto the B4066. Follow this for five miles, until past the first crossroads, and the track to the hillfort car park is on the right just before the descent to Uley village. The hillfort is not signposted, but a double Public Footpath sign marks the turning, almost straight ahead.

The Cotswolds are graced with any number of hillforts, many with outstanding prospects and all utilising nature to its best advantage. Uleybury is a well defended promontory hillfort, with the ramparts almost clinging to the contours to leave a long, flat interior. Unfortunately, this level ground has proved attractive to farmers from at least mediaeval times, and the interior continues to be ploughed today. Many are the flint implements that have been unearthed by centuries of ploughing, and even a gold coin of the Dobunni tribe, but the cost, in terms of the loss of any idea of the internal layout of the hillfort, and its past, is considerable.

Your approach to Uleybury along the tree-lined track, does not look too propitious, but once on the ramparts the great promontory opens out before you. Although there is no dispute over Uleybury being a promontory, even a pseudo-contour(!) hillfort, it is listed as a multivallate hillfort by the Ordnance Survey on their 'Iron Age Map of Southern Britain' of 1962, but there are now doubts about this. The interior is surrounded by what appears to be a low rampart, with a silted-up ditch in front. There is another rampart after this, and then a drop of over 20 feet down to another silted up ditch, followed by a counterscarp bank beyond. Although the site has not been excavated, it is the validity of the inner line of defences that has been questioned.

It remains a possibility that what appears to be the inner rampart is not a rampart at all, and its ditch is in fact a quarry-ditch for the main rampart, beyond. This arrangement would have made sense to the builders, as they would have dug out the spoil from the quarry-ditch, and simply tossed it downhill to build the rampart, a technique used at many hillforts. This matter will probably not be resolved until a full excavation has been conducted. When I visited the hillfort it looked as though there was an inner rampart, especially on the north side, and round most of the whole camp a 'lip' could be seen. Generally speaking, the inner defences, if that is what they are, are visible for the whole circuit, but the outer defences are part-covered in trees on both the east and west sides.

You enter by the north gateway, where 2,000 years ago you would have had to pass three cross-dykes, and come under the close scrutiny of guards high up on a mound. It is a lot simpler these days, but you cannot go onto the interior, and must follow the ramparts round. These enclose 32 acres, which suggests that the hillfort must have been of considerable importance, as it is one of the largest in the Cotswolds. As the interior is ploughed though, nothing can really be determined about its past, who lived there and what happened to them.

That should not spoil your visit though for Uleybury is a very attractively created, rather than built, hillfort and one which, at 730 feet high, offers the visitor much to see from its defences. The view west is over the River Severn valley and on into Wales, and this makes up for the tree-covered, lower defences. These can be seen very clearly on the south side, where there might also have been an entrance. From the south-east corner you overlook the village of Uley from which, when I visited the hillfort, the sounds of a brass band drifted pleasingly upwards. The defences to the east are more a series of sculpted gentle curves today, but back at the north side they are better defined, as if sharpened to ward off any would-be attackers.

Uleybury is large, cleverly built and quite domineering, but is not impressive in the way that say Maiden Castle* is. Its interior looks like any farm field anywhere, but its lack of authenticated history at least gives your imagination its head, and allows you to make up your own theories as to what it looked like 2,000 years ago. After all, nobody fortifies such a large site without a reason.

Beacon Hill

Directions. O/S 1:50,000 map 174 ref. 458572. Six miles south of Newbury on the west side of the A34. Beacon Hill is owned by Hampshire County Council and is very well signposted from both directions. From the parking area, signs direct you through a gateway up the steep climb to the east corner of the hillfort. Ladle Hill* is a mile due east, on the hills across the A34.

Heading south from Newbury, you are confronted by a range of hills that dramatically rise over 300 feet within a quarter of a mile. On the left is Richard Adams' *Watership Down* country, while just to the right, rises the singular Beacon Hill, identified as early as 943 A.D. as the 'watch-house'. The A34, and the former railway, gingerly thread a common path through the gap in the hills.

A single rampart and ditch, with counterscarp bank, closely hug the contours around the summit to enclose 12 acres, in a distinctive sand-timer shape. The only entrance is at the south corner. Rising to a height of 858 feet in the north-east, and therefore offering commanding views in all directions, the rampart at the west corner marks the 800 feet contour. Beacon Hill is one of those lucky hillforts in the South not to have had its interior ploughed. An obvious benefit of this lack of progress, or development, is that 21 hut circles, with diameters of between 20-30 feet, are still visible throughout the turf covered interior.

Having arrived at the east corner, you will see the first of the hut circles inside the rampart, while a quarry ditch begins just beyond and runs for the whole circumference inside the rampart. One cannot but admire the aesthetic appearance of the rampart and ditch, which if it served no other purpose would have enhanced the beauty of the hill. It is not a huge rampart, but the builders skilfully utilised the natural contours to great effect, and the hillfort can only be approached from the north and south corners, and even then any would-be attackers would have had a steep climb.

Not having been properly excavated, little of the Iron Age history is known for certain. It was thought to have been built in the first or second centuries B.C., very likely to its present plan, but in view of research elsewhere, it could easily have been built several centuries before then. Chalk is ideal for glacis ramparts, and Beacon Hill's have withstood the ravages of time and weather on this exposed spur remarkably well. Whether they were ever put to the test is not known, nor is anything about the demise of the Iron Age community, although the hut sites suggest that it was permanently occupied.

From the north-east rampart, more huts can be made out in the turf, while across the A34, the lower ground, with its villages, fields and farms, forms the backdrop for several locations in *Watership Down* and, if you remember the story, can be identified from the rampart. Despite the relatively level approach to the north corner and north-west side, the defences have not been strengthened. Down below, you have a marvellous view of the nineteenth century Highclere Castle, and its grounds. This grand house provides a link between Beacon Hill and ancient Egypt, although of fairly modern making.

You will see what I mean when you arrive at the west corner, which is fenced off, and where a monument has been erected. This is the tomb of Lord Carnarvon who not only lived in Highclere Castle, and at one time owned Beacon Hill but, with Howard Carter, discovered the tomb of Tutankhamun in 1922. Perhaps Carnarvon got his archaeological interest from the ancient site right on his doorstep.

The north-west rampart also offers fine views over the wide expanse of the River Kennet valley, with the hills rising beyond. The range of hills to the west winds its way ever higher in a north-westerly direction, the escarpment undiminished throughout, until it disappears from view. At this, the highest point, stands another hillfort, Walbury Hill (Berkshire).

To return to our present antiquity, once you have been able to rejoin the defences on the south-west side, some former fields can be seen encroaching on the hill-slope at the bottom. These are not ancient fields, but a reminder of more recent times when British isolation, and falling food imports, saw all sort of 'marginal' land being tilled. Further to the south, right at the end of the hill, is the site of ancient fields – fields moreover, which were quite possibly associated with an occupied Beacon Hill.

The level approach to the south corner points to the entrance. The rampart and counterscarp bank join together and are then in-turned by forty feet on either side to form the gateway. Defensive outworkings, of a simple bank and ditch hornwork, leave the rampart about one hundred and fifty feet from either side of the entrance, and curve out to form a gap of sixty feet in front of the gateway, about thirty feet away. What form the main gate took is not known, nor indeed whether there were any supplementary defences to the outworkings, for they do not prevent a direct approach on the gateway.

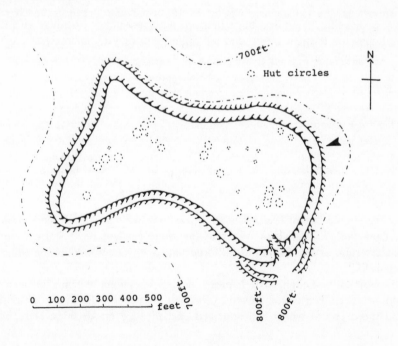

151

About fifty yards inside the entrance is another cluster of hut circles, with a number of pits towards the east corner. Three of these pits were excavated in 1927, and animal bones and Bronze Age pottery was found. Also found inside the hillfort have been two gold rings and a hoard of bronzes so the site might have also had some temporary use in the Bronze Age. From the entrance, a mile to the south beside the A34, a group of round barrows, known as the 'Seven Barrows' (although there are more across the A34) can be seen forming a linear cemetery. You can walk down to them, or there is a lay-by at the gateway. The field they are now in was the one Geoffrey de Havilland made his first flight from in 1910.

As you make your way back to the east corner there, on the hills opposite, can be seen the unfinished defences of Ladle Hill*. These are worthy of study from this vantage point, as it is unusual to have the opportunity to look down on a hillfort. The defences appear more complete from a mile distance than they really are, and you could do no better than to leave Beacon Hill and make your way over there. Still further beyond, along the escarpment, is Watership Down, complete with Beech-hangar, and 'Hazel was here' graffiti.

Beacon Hill has much to commend it: outstanding views, virtually undamaged defences, un-tilled interior with hut circles and associations with different eras. Indeed until the days of telegraphy, it was used as a beacon, being known as the "Berkshire Beacon". Even the traffic noise from the A34 does not intrude. All that is needed is a full excavation, to complete the picture.

$\mathcal{G}$odmanescamp *(Also known as Frankenbury & Godmanescap)*

Directions. O/S 1:50,000 map 184 ref. 167152. The hillfort overlooks the River Avon to the east of Fordingbridge, off the B3078 at the village of Godshill. Leave Fordingbridge on the B3078 towards Southampton. After 1.5 miles, turn left at the junction with the 'Fighting Cocks' pub on the corner, and park 100 yards down on the left, beside a Public Footpath sign, and opposite a former chapel. Follow the direction pointed by the sign, and continue with the hedge on your left. A path crosses from the right. Cross the style at this point, turn right, and continue with the hedge now on your right, crossing the style at the end of the field. Continue straight ahead up the track, and turn left at the Public Footpath sign. At this point the hillfort is to your right, as you look in the direction of the Public Footpath sign. Follow the edge of the field, keeping the hedge on your left, but do not leave the field, until you reach the south-east corner of the fort.

It is a regrettable fact of life that nearly everything we do, or find, these days has been done before. It matters not what the subject might be, historical studies, mountaineering, or the visiting of hillforts, someone, somewhere, at sometime has beaten us to it.

Occasionally though, one happens across something which, for whatever reason, has been overlooked. Several years ago my nephew discovered an obscure sailing speed record which had remained unchallenged for decades. Here, so he thought, was his chance of fame. He spent a year, and a good deal of money, designing and building his own 'record breaker'. Eventually, the great day came, and he descended on Southampton to launch his boat. Unfortunately, after only two minutes of the maiden voyage, the boat self destructed, and the obscure record remains both obscure, and intact. The wreckage, meanwhile, resides in my garden awaiting its fate.

Godmanescamp is an obscure hillfort of eleven acres. It has been neither excavated, nor received anything more than the briefest of passing comments in even the most academic of archaeological writings, although it lies at the southern end of the Salisbury Ley. The very fact that it is still known by at least three names adds to the confusion.

Do not, however, think that by visiting this hillfort, you will be breaking fresh ground; a path on the univallate, glacis, rampart top can be followed. Indeed, given the close proximity of the campsite passed on the way, to say nothing of the small sewage works, you can bet your life that the southern rampart, at least, has seen its fair share of children's 'war games' at one time or another. However, it is usually a peaceful haven, and if a quiet walk is desired, without having to trek for miles, then this is the place to go.

The best time to visit is undoubtedly May, when the bluebells are at their finest. The track along the tree covered eastern rampart winds its way through the sea of blue, and you will soon come across what is the only original entrance. Nowadays, this allows farm vehicles to enter the cultivated interior.

As you continue along the top of the rampart, with its associated ditch, you will see the flat expanse of land to the north and the east. The fort is rectangular in shape, and the north rampart is much the same, until you draw level with the western edge of the ploughed interior. At this point the exterior ground begins to fall away, and the rampart rises up to a height of twenty-one feet above the bottom of the ditch.

This is where the hillfort becomes more interesting, and was probably a major reason for its construction, yet conversely where you might, nowadays, find it a touch disappointing. As you traverse the gradual sweep of the western rampart, which sits atop a steep incline, your view is obscured by the very trees in which you walk. Two thousand years ago there was a grand vista to be had over the River Avon valley, some 200 feet below.

Every now and again you will catch a brief glimpse through the trees of what might have been, but that is all. Even the rampart, on this western side, is less obvious than hitherto, mainly due to the steep angle of the hill itself. Beneath you, a little way down the hillside, the terrace which now serves as a pathway, marks the line of the ditch which acted as a further deterrent to any would-be attackers from this side.

The southern rampart stands abreast a similarly steep incline for much of its length, but you soon leave the wood and have a clear view across the ploughed interior. From this vantage point you can appreciate the strength of the rampart facing the flatter north and east sides, and see the main entrance.

Without any excavations having been undertaken, little is known about this hillfort. A glance at the O/S map, and a little imagination, will give some ideas as to why it was built, with its commanding view. The gravelly nature of the soil suggests that it might have been an earthwork of a pastoral people, but this is merely an educated(!) guess.

Unlike so many of the hillforts featured in this book, Godmanescamp does not have spectacular views, nor does it stand imperiously before you on approach. However, as you walk around in a reflective silence, you will be able to form your own ideas as to why it was built, who used it, what its purpose was, and why it declined. The main difference between Godmanescamp and the majority of hillforts in this book is that nothing has been found, or written, to contradict you. You too can make your attempt at that 'obscure' (historical) record.

OTHER ANCIENT SITES
Gorley Camp, hillfort. O/S Map 195 Ref. 165112.
Great Woodbury, Iron Age farm. O/S Map 184 Ref. 144278.
Little Woodbury, Iron Age. O/S Map 184 Ref. 150279.
Castle Ditches, Whitsbury, hillfort. O/S Map 195 Ref. 128196.
Rockbourne Roman Villa. O/S Map 184 Ref. 120170.
Soldiers Ring, enclosure. O/S Map 184 Ref. 082176.

Hengistbury Head

Directions. O/S 1:50,000 map 195 ref. 165910. The A35 road acts as a by-pass to Christchurch. The B3059 forms a junction with the A35 just west of Christchurch centre. Turn left up the B3059 towards Southbourne and, having crossed the River Stour, the road to Hengistbury Head is on the left, sign-posted from a lamp post on the right. There are car parks along this road on the right, and an information bureau just before the ramparts.

Not surprisingly, at a promontory that forms the southern breakwater to the natural Christchurch Harbour, which is itself just downstream of the confluence of the Rivers Stour and Avon, evidence has been found of man's use of Hengistbury Head dating back to the Paleolithic Age, c.7,000 B.C. The importance of the two aforementioned rivers to the ancient Briton can be clearly seen if one follows their respective courses, and those of their many tributaries. Within a couple of miles either side, along both rivers, there is an astounding array of ancient sites, none more impressive than the numerous Iron Age hillforts.

If the above hints at the material evidence for the importance of the two rivers, they would both have served widely differing peoples, many with little knowledge of the existence of others along the waterway's winding routes. Even in the later Iron Age, it is accurate to say that the River Stour served many hillforts of the Durotriges tribe, while the River Avon and its major tributaries catered for both the Durotriges, and Belgic Atrebates peoples and also reached the fringes of the Dobunni tribe's domain. That the nearest land most suited as a port for these two invaluable arteries through the great forested valleys should be so developed, was only to be expected. The excavations and writings of Professor Barry Cunliffe have, during the last fifteen years, thrown much light not only on the internal trade network, but the scale of the Iron Age settlement at Hengistbury Head and its extensive trading network with Northern France and the Mediterranean region.

It would probably be accurate to compare Hengistbury Head, as a port of the later Iron Age, with the Port of London in the 1950s, until the days of container ships. Indeed, Hengistbury was almost certainly the major port of the south coast at that time. The promontory, which occupies about 175+ acres today, was at least 50% larger, coastal erosion having taken its toll of the two sea-facing sides. The Iron Age settlement, at its greatest, occupied the low-lying area inside the cross-dykes and stretched about half way to the present eastern side, and covered about half the current width. It was, therefore, of considerable size, although not the Durotriges 'capital'; this being more of a loose confederation of semi-independent communities than a centralised tribe.

One might well imagine that Hengistbury Head would have been a relatively cosmopolitan settlement, quite unlike most in that it relied on trade rather than a relatively self-sufficient, subsistence economy. Archaeological evidence from the site makes it plausible to suggest that the later Iron Age Hengistbury was something of an entrepot port. Apart from the import and export of raw materials and finished goods, inter-tribal trade between the Atrebates, Dobunni, Durotriges and others was possibly the port's mainstay, while imported raw materials, or semi-finished goods, were worked-up and finished 'on site' and re-exported again.

Overseas trade at that time would probably have consisted, for the most part, of the import of luxuries, such as jewellery or wine, and the export of bronze/iron products and certain raw materials, perhaps stone, clay and salt. The import of luxuries, in particular Italian/Roman wine, of which countless fragments of the two handled containers known as amphorae have been found, suggests that the local tribes may have had a fairly urbanised culture, with a warrior-class having the power, or nous to accumulate the necessary wealth to pay for such goods.

Of course, any form of Iron Age trade would have been on a relatively, and absolute, minuscule level in comparison with today, but a port of any size, and particularly one engaged in overseas trade, would have made provision for the needs of ships, sailors and trade. One assumes that, even if ships were not built at Hengistbury, repair facilities must have been available, while the need to trade and store goods would have to be catered for. As for the sailors themselves, history has shown that their more physical needs have always been well catered for in port settlements, and there is no evidence to suggest this did, or did not, occur at Hengistbury.

All the above must not be taken out of proportion. Hengistbury was not a thriving commercial city as we would expect today, with impressive civic buildings and so on, but it would have been an Iron Age equivalent. What Hengistbury undoubtedly did have though, was its own Mint. Over 3,000 bronze coins, half of which were minted locally and have come to be known as the 'Hengistbury Head' type, were found in 1911-12. This fact, perhaps more than any other, hints at the importance of the settlement at Hengistbury, although the coins date from the period between a probable decline in the ports overseas trade, and Caesar's short invasions of 55/54 B.C.

So far, I have concentrated on what might be described as the 'great days' of Hengistbury, i.e. the first two centuries B.C. Hengistbury did not just grow overnight though. There are several Bronze Age round barrows visible on the higher ground of the promontory, and also at the north end of the Iron Age ramparts. Archaeological evidence has shown that trade was conducted with Ireland, Italy and Sicily during this period, and one might assume that the port, however little used before c.550 B.C., was an obvious place to develop.

Earlier theories, which are usually discounted nowadays, contend that Hengistbury was the point of arrival for successive incoming migrations, or invasions, hence its continued importance. This possibility is supported by later events, as the Roman fleet in support of the II Legion's forays may have used the harbour, while the legendary leaders of the Jutes, Hengist and Horsa, supposedly landed at this point to establish a settlement in South Hampshire. It is also possible that the Vikings made incursions inland, having landed in the area. Finally, if William the Conqueror landed elsewhere, it is reputed that Napoleon planned to invade in the vicinity. As mentioned, the idea of the Iron Age being a period of one invasion after another is not thought to be accurate these days. The first written account of Hengistbury appears in a document from 877 A.D. as Heddinesburgh.

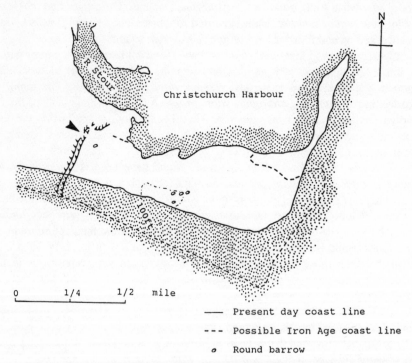

Christchurch Harbour

0   1/4   1/2   mile

——— Present day coast line

- - - Possible Iron Age coast line

o   Round barrow

Yet, the community at Hengistbury was probably in decline almost a century before the Romans arrived. In 56 B.C. the Veneti of what was then North-West Gaul, rose against the Romans. A terrible revenge was exacted by Julius Caesar, which included the destruction of the Veneti fleet. Overseas trade seems to have dropped off suddenly at this time and, following Caesar's invasions of Britain in 55 B.C. and

54 B.C., was probably concentrated more on the Kent and Essex coastline, where the Romans kept a sharp watch over events. It may be that Hengistbury was succeeded by Poole Harbour in later Roman times.

Despite all the above, there is not much to actually see on Hengistbury Head which dates to the Iron Age. Being so naturally well defended, double ramparts and ditches were erected, and subsequently rebuilt on several occasions, across the throat of the promontory, with a central entrance. The ramparts were higher and probably half as long again in their day, being swept away, along with much of the headland, through coastal erosion. They also curved east at their northern extremity to protect the harbour area.

For all that, and you pass these shortly after setting out, the walk to the coast-guard look-out at the summit, which was a gun battery during the Napoleonic Wars, offers some fairly breath-taking views. You can see from the Isle of Wight in the east, to Durston Head beyond Swanage on the Isle of Purbeck. Down below is Christchurch Harbour, now used by the pleasure boating fraternity, while the town, with its outstanding church and Norman motte and bailey castle, lies to the north. The area of the Iron Age port is clearly seen, with the junction of the two river's beyond. It is not very often one gets the chance to look down on a major Iron Age settlement. The quarried area below was used to provide the iron-ores for the ship-builders at Bucklers Hard, near Beaulieu, who, amongst other things, built four of the ships under Nelson at the Battle of Trafalgar; this of course effectively ruled out a possible Napoleonic invasion.

Hengistbury Head, thanks to its three natural advantages of the junction of the rivers, the harbour and its prominent position, has thus endured a lengthy and noteworthy history. It was in the Iron Age that it enjoyed its peak though, and even if it has not held such a prominent position since, there has probably not been a time in the last 3,000+ years when this headland did not play a part in the active life of our island.

Ladle Hill

Directions. O/S map 174 ref. 478568. One mile due east of Beacon Hill*. Leave Newbury heading south on the A34. After 5.5 miles take the left turning to Burghclere and Kingsclere. After passing through Burghclere, park near the entrance drive to Symonton Court, on the left. Ladle Hill is half a mile to the south. Follow the rutted trackway opposite up the side of the hill, and when the fence on the left ends, follow the path back on yourself. A gap in the fence leads you to the south-east corner. Should you want a circular walk, continue along the path. A trackway leads down the hill to the road, while a little further on a minor road does the same. The hill across this road is 'Watership Down'. Beacon Hill is across the A34 to the west.

'T'was ever thus'. Although not the oldest, Ladle Hill is Britain's foremost ancient construction site, and like so many up and down the country today, remains unfinished. One hopes that not too many of the ghosts of the early 1990s construction recession will remain unfinished for the 2,000 odd years Ladle Hill has silently waited. Perhaps there is a direct lesson for those who are all too ready to destroy more of our country with nasty buildings of mass produced materials and design, thrown up in the name of progress.

The work published by Stuart Piggott in 1931 originally highlighted the value to hillfort development of Ladle Hill in particular, and unfinished sites in general. Ladle Hill, had it been completed, would have been an oval shape of about seven acres, with possible entrances on the east and south-west sides. It was thought that the work was undertaken in the second or first centuries B.C., about the same time as the neighbouring Beacon Hill* was built, on the site of two earlier enclosures. The north-west and north sides roughly follow the line of one of two boundary ditches, which run from Great Litchfield Down to the south, and which in turn overlay a celtic field system on the down. At the north half of the hillfort, is the outline of a Bronze Age disc barrow, while just outside, by the solitary tree, is a much better preserved example, complete with robbers hole in the top. It is, however, the hillfort we are here to see.

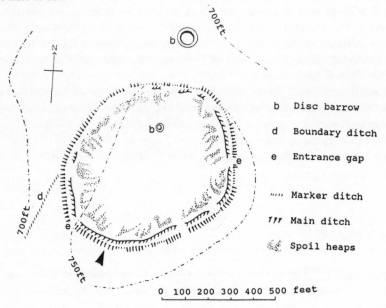

b   Disc barrow

d   Boundary ditch

e   Entrance gap

""""   Marker ditch

ʇʇʇ   Main ditch

Spoil heaps

0   100 200 300 400 500 feet

When one wishes to construct something, it is best to plan out the area of building, and this was thought to have been done at Ladle Hill with the use of a marker-ditch. This can best be seen about fifty yards north of the possible east entrance, for a length of thirty yards but is also visible elsewhere. Why pegs or stones could not have served the same, easier purpose is unclear, so perhaps it was not a marker-ditch after all.

Once this was completed, the main ditch had been started in many places, with the top-soil, turf and chalk-spoil placed inside the intended line of the rampart. This forms the little mounds that can be seen all around, which are not the beginnings of the rampart. In certain places, in particular at the south-east corner where you came in, the rampart has been started, using large chalk boulders hewn from the ditch. It could have been either a glacis or box type of rampart. Had the hillfort been completed, it is likely that the rampart would have been covered over with the top-soil, turf and spoil that had been placed for this purpose.

That is the essentials of Ladle Hill dealt with, as you can see them, but there is more to be discerned. For a start, it appears that the building was divided into sections, each built by one gang of workers. What is clear from this is that some gangs worked faster than others, while one might surmise that the project was overseen, and planned, by one individual, perhaps the local organisation, perhaps even with some division of labour: and we thought Adam Smith started this off just 200 years ago! Who knows, there might have been a kind of piecework payment, given that certain gangs worked faster than others, but there does not appear to have been an ancient form of 'work study', as double-handling of the spoil heaps would have been necessary to complete the hillfort.

The study of hillforts *per se* has shown that Iron Age society must have been fairly well organised to undertake the original building, development and enlargement of the hillforts and their surrounding areas. At Ladle Hill the detail of this organisation can be seen on the ground, with perhaps some understanding gained as to how Neolithic, Bronze Age and Iron Age man went about the building of their often spectacularly large earthworks. One thing is certain, despite the immense strides made in technology since those times, those improvements in work organisation have been rather less than meteoric, at least in the case of Ladle Hill.

Indeed, thanks to the part-finished condition of Ladle Hill, and work undertaken to build an experimental earthwork on Overton Down, it has been possible to work out an approximation for the time needed to construct a hillfort of this size. With the rampart being about 750 yards long, twelve feet high and assuming a width of twenty feet at the base and three feet at the top, its volume would be about 13,000 cubic yards. A man, with contemporary tools, would dig between 1-1.5 cubic yards of chalk per day, and along with the need to transport the chalk, and cut trees for support, about 13,000-18,000 man-days would be needed to build the fort. Given an average of about twenty people per acre, that would mean about 150 people might live in the finished fort, giving perhaps 120 man/days work each day. A hillfort of this size would take about three to four months to build, but others might expect to take refuge in the hillfort, and they would probably be expected to assist in its building, thus shortening the time needed.

There are many questions about Ladle Hill which will remain unanswered though. For one thing, who began the building, when and why? Was it in response to some real, or perceived, outside danger, or was it connected in some way with the Beacon Hill* and its inhabitants? Assuming it was built to ward off certain invaders, and given the length of time needed to build the hillfort, some form of advance warning might have existed, but this is, of course, pure conjecture, if not wild speculation. Still, why did building cease so abruptly? Did the danger pass, or did the invaders arrive early and unannounced? Such are the great mysteries of hillforts, but you will have plenty of time for speculation from the great vantage point which overlooks south Berkshire. Ladle Hill has given much towards the understanding of the building of hillforts, and to social structures in Britain in the later Iron Age. However, there are still many secrets which Ladle Hill does not intend to give away, and which we will, very likely, never know.

OTHER ANCIENT SITES
Seven Barrows. O/S map 174 ref. 462555.
Walbury Hillfort. O/S map 174 ref. 373618.
Combe Gibbet and Neolithic long barrow. O/S map 174 ref. 365623.

Quarley Hill

Directions. O/S map 184 ref. 262423. Near Grateley, five miles west of Andover. Leave the B3084 as it crosses the railway, and head through Grateley village towards Quarley village. The road turns sharp right and left, and within a quarter of a mile, on the left, there is a trackway where you can park. A public footpath leads along the trackway, then turns right to the top of the hill.

Although neither particularly well known, nor outstanding as an hillfort, Quarley Hill nevertheless has its marks of distinction, even in the South with its many hillforts. The hill on which the hillfort stands, rising to 561 feet and seen from miles around, hints that the walk will be well rewarded in visual terms. We are also fortunate that the trees which give the hill its distinction neither encroach on the hillfort, (with the odd exception), nor restrict the view from it.

Two things become apparent as you make your way up the hill that becomes steeper nearer the summit: one is that the site has distinct natural defences; the other is that there is no access to water for miles around. Chalk hills are not known for their retention of water on the surface, so perhaps the topography has changed since the Iron Age.

Despite the natural strength of the position, the defences are of a considerable size, but do not enclose the whole of the summit; to do so would have made for a considerably bigger camp. The single rampart and originally 'V' shaped ditch, with a much slighter counterscarp bank, enclose 8.5 acres, and follow the contours closely to the north-east and south-west where the original entrances are situated. As the entrances are the weakest point in the defences of an hillfort, so it is perhaps surprising that those at Quarley Hill have neither outworkings to protect the level approaches, nor were they, or the camp itself, finished.

Quarley Hill was partially excavated in 1938, and the results confirmed both the unfinished nature of the north-east entrance, and the original plan for it. The rampart on both sides of the entrance is inturned and slightly offset, perhaps to prevent a direct frontal approach. The excavators revealed the existence of post holes, thought to be for gates and an overbridge, but that the timber had never been fitted. Furthermore, it seems that a pair of hastily built makeshift gates were substituted; perhaps jerry-building has been with us for longer than we think.

A walk round the defences will also reveal a gap in both the north and south ramparts. These were shown, by the excavators, not to have been relatively recent entrances through the ramparts, as at many hillforts, but that they had never been filled in. Thus, the rampart appears not to have been completed either, but these gaps may have been left intentionally, as they open onto an even older field system.

At some time during the late Bronze Age a set of field boundaries were made which met at the top of the hill. These can best be seen passing underneath the Iron Age rampart just to the north and south of the north-east entrance, to form a right-angle inside the hillfort. It is not known whether or not the builders of the hillfort knew of their existence, but one would assume so. This is one of very few hillforts with evidence of a field system around it, but it is probable that many more were so surrounded.

It is thought that a palisade camp existed on the site from c.650 BC.–500 B.C., and that the present hillfort was built at some time thereafter, and lasted until c.350 B.C. Why the camp was built, whether it was built by the descendants of those who made the field boundaries, why it was never finished and abandoned, all remain mysteries. At least there is plenty to ponder as you admire the view from the downs in the north to the Isle of Wight in the south, and from Sussex in the east across Salisbury Plain in the west. My lasting memory though, is of a Class 50 diesel thundering up the steep incline below, filling the valley with an echoing throb; the diesels too are now but 'history'.

Herefordshire Beacon *(Also known as British Camp)*

Directions: O/S 1:50,000 series map 150 ref. 760398. Leave Ledbury heading east on the A449. At the top of the pass in the Malvern Hills, is a hotel with a National Trust car park opposite. A footpath leads to the hillfort above. An alternative route is by a one and a half mile walk from Midsummer Hill*. Leave Midsummer Hill by its north entrance and follow the path down the hill to the left. Turn right at the bottom, past the cottage, and turn right again in the dip before the fenced off parkland. Follow this path through the woods, turning right to the top of the ridge. A path runs along the ridge to the hillfort.

Herefordshire has a number of large hillforts, many of which are archaeologically important, having been fully surveyed, have a good history or have large-scale defences. Unfortunately, many of these are either covered in trees, or are in such a condition as to hardly warrant a visit. So, far from being spoilt for choice, one is reduced to scratching around to find a decent one to include in this book. Nearly, but not quite, for the two that I have included from the county, are from the very top drawer of English hillforts.

In what was probably a heavily forested part of the country during the Iron Age, whoever decided to build this hillfort chose a magnificent location. It is possible that this was a northern outpost of the Dobunni tribal area and, compared to the land to the south and west, that to the north has considerably fewer hillforts. Unlike its neighbour, Midsummer Hill*, Herefordshire Beacon has not been excavated and events in its past are not so readily forthcoming, but what you can see today is the result of at least three phases of building, spread over 1,500 years.

The first camp was possibly constructed in the third century B.C., although a full excavation might provide a different date. A single stone-revetted rampart and ditch enclosed eight acres at the centre of the ridge, in an oval. There were entrances to the north-east and south-west, but much of this camp has disappeared under later re-buildings.

In possibly the late Iron Age, although this could well be found to be much earlier, a single rampart and ditch, with counterscarp bank, was built around the 1,000 feet contour enclosing the original camp. This gave additional enclosures of five acres to the north and nine acres to the south. The new defences utilised the west rampart of the first hillfort, but ran beyond the east defences. Four entrances were added to the extensions, three to the south enclosure, and although these were normally kept to a minimum, being the weak-spot of any hillfort, the steep natural slopes were presumably considered off-putting enough.

Some Iron Age and Roman pottery fragments have been found inside the camp, while a few hut platforms can still be seen cut into the rock, particularly near the entrances. It may be the quarry-ditch to the east was also used for huts, some of which are 50 feet in diameter. Unlike some other hillforts in the Welsh Marches (*see* Midsummer Hill*), there is no obvious sign of the huts being arranged in a grid pattern, with the attendant high population density. It is possible that Herefordshire

Beacon was built prior to the third century B.C., and that it was more of a fortified 'border post', than an orthodox hillfort housing a cross section of contemporary society.

What caused the demise of the hillfort is not known. There is no sign of a fire, or battle, as at Midsummer Hill. Did the inhabitants just flee after witnessing the plight of their neighbours? The site was deemed to be too good to remain redundant forever though, and in the twelfth century A.D. the Normans used the hillfort as the basis for a motte and bailey castle. The motte stands at the very summit of the hill with its well defended inner bailey, the later Iron Age defences being adapted to form an outer bailey. This was used by the Normans against the Welsh, and was stormed by Owen Glendower's forces as recently as 1405. Thereafter, that site, like the Iron Age hillfort, fell into disuse.

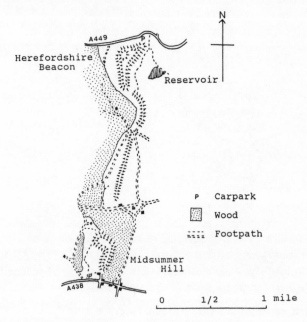

All the above conveys the history of Herefordshire Beacon, but masks the true magnificence of its position, appearance and the wondrous views to be had from its summit. The later Iron Age defences seem to cling to the contours of the hill, as if landscaped into it; an object lesson to modern architects and planners in how to enhance the surroundings. No doubt in their day, the defences were a considerable deterrent, but would have offended nobody. The first hillfort is almost crowned by the mediaeval motte, which rises to a majestic 1,114 feet high, although still lower than the hills to the north.

Perhaps of more importance was what could be seen from the summit. Bredon Hill* hillfort can be seen to the east, as can other hillforts on the western escarpment of the Cotswolds, including Leckhampton Hill*, further south. Just beyond Ledbury is the partially tree covered Wall Hills hillfort (Herefordshire), and to the south Midsummer Hill* can be easily seen. Indeed, if one had the relevant Ordnance

Survey maps, a good pair of binoculars and the time, you could quite possibly see more hillforts from the summit than from any other hillfort, and much else besides.

It will thus come as no surprise to find that on warm, clear days you will be far from alone on the hillfort. I have seen coaches disgorge fifty people at that time to the hotel and hillfort, but the Malverns are large enough to find peace and quiet, and even shelter from the wind, if that is what you seek. The walk between Midsummer Hill and Herefordshire Beacon is worth undertaking, rather than driving from one to the other, if only to get a different perspective of each hillfort on your way. It is about four miles for the round trip, but even if weary in leg, you will be up-lifted in spirit.

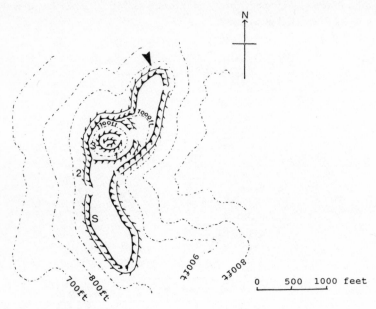

S Site of hut circles

1 Site of original fort (c3rd century BC)

2 Outer ramparts (c1st century BC)

3 Ring-motte (c11th century AD)

The relationship between these two hillforts is unknown, although it could be that the Herefordshire Beacon was more of a lookout, at least until extended. There is a parallel to the adjacent Hambledon* and Hod* hillforts, in Dorset. Both sets share a hill mass, separated by a dip, and the northern-most of each is a long contour shaped hillfort, extended in stages, each with a central mound, a long barrow in the case of Hambledon Hill. Also, the southern hillfort of each pair seems to have had a longer, more structured settlement, each of which came to an unpleasant end. A set of pure coincidences?

Directions. O/S 1:50,000 map 150 ref. 760375. This can be approached by following the path to the south from Herefordshire Beacon*, a walk of about one and a half miles, or head east from Ledbury, on the A449 and turn right onto the A438. Approximately one and a half miles after passing Eastnor there is a car park at the brow of a hill on the left. There is a very steep climb from the car park, north into the trees, where a National Trust sign denotes the south-west of the hillfort.

Unlike so many other historical monuments, even in the age of the motor car, there are few hillforts where one can drive straight up, get out, and 'do it'. As a very general rule, the more effort required in getting there, the better the fort, and the more spectacular its location. The hillfort on the adjacent Midsummer and Hollybush hills most certainly falls into this category. No matter what approach you take, short of landing by helicopter, a steep ascent has to be made.

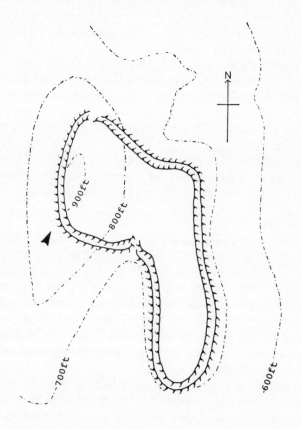

0 200 400 600 feet

Assuming that you have parked as directed, the climb will bring you sweating, to the single glacis rampart, originally with a dry-stone facing, ditch and small counterscarp bank, that defends the hills. This is an unusual hillfort in two respects: firstly its shape, dictated by the enclosing of the two hills, and secondly that the north-western rampart surrounds a summit rising to over 900 feet, while the eastern rampart generally follows the 750 feet contour. Was Midsummer Hill itself an enclosed look-out post, while the plateau of Hollybush Hill was used for the settlement? There is, however, no evidence to suggest that the fort was built in more than one stage.

As you reach the rampart, follow it to the east, downhill. The hillfort was constructed about 400 B.C., and you will soon come across the south-west entrance. This is at the head of a dry valley, and is impressively in-turned at both sides by 40 feet. Evidence from archaeological digs has shown that, although built in one go, the fort did not remain static. Indeed, the gate at which you now stand was rebuilt at least seventeen times during the 400 or so years of occupation. A timber guardroom was added c.390 B.C., this being contemporary with a similar addition at Maiden Castle*, possibly as a result of trading connections, but it could easily have been the inhabitant's own design. About 350 B.C. twin portals were added, while c.325 B.C. a stone guardroom was built. Many later refinements were carried out, which included the addition of a bridge. As with all wooden built structures from the Iron Age, none of these can be seen today.

As you follow the rampart south along the 750 feet contour you might begin to wonder if I have been playing a macabre practical joke on you, having climbed close to the summit, and descended to this plateau. This feeling may even be enhanced as you follow the rampart through a 360 degree turn, at which point the defences have been damaged by quarrying, and begin heading north, particularly as the woods to the east restrict your view.

The plateau around which you have followed the rampart thus far is Hollybush Hill. As recently as 1875 it was claimed that 11 terraces could be made out, and over 200 hut sites were visible. Nowadays, as you explore the interior, you will find some of the 36 remaining round hollows, each marking the site of a hut, but the terraces remain elusive to the eye.

Archaeological excavations carried out in 1970 have shown that these huts measured either 48 feet x 39 feet., or 39 feet x 36 feet. Being rectangular these were unlike those in most hillforts of the South and East, and unusual in being laid out to a regular grid pattern. The huts were only about 15 feet apart, and four were found to have hearth sites. Here indeed, though not visible, was a distinctive Marches pattern of social organisation. Hillforts in this area also had relatively large populations, with a density of 70-100 people per acre (which could give Midsummer Hill a population of up to 3,000), and were probably continually inhabited, with few farms lying outside the fort boundaries.

Along this plateau is a low 150 foot long barrow, with side ditches. It was thought, following excavations carried out in 1924, that it might be a 'pillow mound', but this theory seems to be discounted nowadays. Little else is known about it, but the mound probably dates from the late Neolithic Age. Approximately 60 yards to the north are three low, circular mounds, presumably round barrows, constructed between 1550-1250 B.C. Doubts remain about these, and at one time it was thought that one might have been connected with a Romano-Celtic temple. Excavations failed to confirm or deny this, but that is one of the beauties of such antiquities: nothing is certain.

You should now rejoin the rampart for the stiff climb up to Midsummer Hill itself, passing the north entrance, with only one side in-turned, on the way. This is your point of departure should you wish to continue on the lovely walk to the Herefordshire Beacon*; or indeed if you have just arrived from there, this is where you will join Midsummer Hill.

Follow the rampart as it curves south along the 900 feet contour, then leave the rampart and go to the 937 feet summit, where a glorious sight awaits you. To the north can be seen the Herefordshire Beacon*, with the bulk of the Malvern Hills behind. To the east you have extensive views of the plain traversed by the River Severn, with the Cotswolds beyond. To the south you overlook Gloucestershire, while to the west you can see Eastnor Park with the obelisk beneath you, the Brecon Beacons in the distance, and much else in between. Compared to these scenes, all but the most hardened of archaeologists would find the faint outline of a terrace, or hollow of a former hut, something of a let-down.

It is these remarkable views from Midsummer Hill that make this 30 acre hillfort so attractive. Here you are, on a pair of fortified hills that were occupied for over 400 years. A community that combined arable and cattle farming on an highly organised basis, and may well have remained relatively undisturbed throughout that time.

Then, the Romans came. Evidence suggests that almost all of the huts were destroyed by fire. This might well have occurred in 48 A.D., when Ostorius Scapula attacked. Although it is only speculation that it was the Romans who 'fired' the huts, as with so many hillforts a period of continuous history came to an abrupt, and violent end, once the Romans arrived in the vicinity. They had, by that time, five highly successful years' experience of overcoming these native fortifications behind them. As with so many hillforts, no records remain of what actually happened at Midsummer Hill, but after the Romans had arrived on the scene, it is unlikely that it remained fortified, if indeed occupied, however much Caradoc and his followers remained a thorn in the Romans' side.

OTHER ANCIENT SITES
Cadbury Bank, hillfort. O/S Map 150 ref. 793316.
Wapley Camp, hillfort. O/S maps 137/148/149 ref. 346625.
Caplar Camp, or Woldbury, hillfort. O/S map 149 ref. 593329.

Arbury Banks

Directions. O/S 1:50,000 map 153 ref. 262387. Leave the A1 (M) at its northern junction, and head south towards Baldock on the A507. Turn first left to Ashwell, take the first turning right as you enter the village, and park. Walk up the road on the Icknield Way Path, but take the Public Footpath off to the right near the top which leads to the hillfort. A circular route can be taken by walking beyond the fort and following the footpath to the road to Ashwell.

This 12.5 acre, circular plateau hillfort lies at the northern edge of the East Anglian Heights, a continuation of The Chilterns. The long distance path, and ancient trackway, the Icknield Way, passes close by on its way to the Norfolk coast. Although only about 280 feet high, Arbury Banks overlooks the low lying ground to the north and east giving prodigious views, and they are equally good to the west. Unfortunately, most of the eastern rampart was destroyed over 200 years ago, and much damage has been done to the rest since. A curved line of trees mark the line of the rampart, except on the east where it is difficult to see.

A hasty excavation was undertaken in 1856 prior to the agricultural enclosure of Ashwell, and Iron Age pottery was found in some pits, of a typical East Anglian style. Roman coins and pottery were found in and around the site, while pottery from the Saxon period was also discovered. This is not surprising given the importance of the Icknield Way, and one would assume a certain amount of trade would have taken place at such a permanent settlement.

A marking from a large circular building is visible within the fort from the air, but not from the ground, along with other rectangular enclosures. It is possible that the hillfort was home for a local chief, as the building is much bigger than a normal hut, and may even have served as a port of call for travellers on the Icknield Way. A number of skulls were dug out of the rampart in the eighteenth century, as it was being levelled, and were buried in Ashwell churchyard.

The defensive bank is very low or non-existent at the east and for part of the north, but rises to a considerable height in the west. The interior at that end is level with the top of the rampart, which is not an original feature, while the ditch and part of the counterscarp bank are also visible. The former was of 'V' shape, 15 feet deep and 20 feet wide, while both the main rampart and counterscarp bank were of the glacis type, built from chalk spoil. There were probably entrances at both the east and west ends, while an earlier plan shows double ramparts at these sides, which have a level approach.

Arbury Banks may not be as spectacular as some hillforts in the South of England, nor has it been so obviously woven into the fabric of ancient history but, as the pottery finds have shown, the site probably served man for a considerable period of time. With the arrival of the Belgic peoples, and in particular the Romans, the days of living on hills, at least in terms of important settlements, were numbered. Thus, many of the larger hillforts on high ground near long distance routes, such as the Icknield Way or Ridgeway, appear to have been abandoned, while a much lower, less isolated, hillfort like Arbury Banks continued to be inhabited well beyond Roman times, although not as anything more than a local village. This relative accessibility has, of course, led to the mutilation of the hillfort, as the level land has been ploughed for centuries, while the rampart now survives as a field boundary.

For those readers not familiar with this part of East Anglia (or is it the Home Counties?), north Hertfordshire is surprisingly pleasant, the more so considering the proximity of the A1 (M) road. Arbury Banks is equally surprising as, for all the damage of the last two centuries, there is enough left to leave an impression of what it was probably like. Its location has not changed though, and you can see why it was built, and remained in use for many centuries. The modern Icknield Way Path, the successor to the ancient Icknield Way, lies beneath the A505; this also makes for some lovely walking.

Bigbury

Directions. O/S 1:50,000 map 179 ref. 117575. Leave Canterbury heading towards London. The road (leading to the A2) becomes a dual carriageway at Harbledown, within two miles. Take the only turning left and turn immediately right. This road leads up and over the Canterbury by-pass, and immediately on the right is the *Pilgrim's* Way footpath. Park here, and in a quarter of a mile the footpath leads into the annexe. The main hillfort is up the hill to the south, in the woods. The road continues through the main hillfort enclosure.

It was not an easy task to select the hillforts for the gazetteer of this book. The problem was not in finding enough suitable hillforts, more of being spoilt for choice. In the end, I resorted to a good old 'marks out of ten' scoring system, under the following headings: visible remains, view from the hillfort, accessibility, historical interest, location and any unique features. As you arrive at Bigbury you would be forgiven for wondering just what went wrong with my scoring system.

The northern half is covered in woodland, while the southern half is a private orchard. Thus, the remains are not easy to see, while views are restricted. As for accessibility, well there are few problems, as three roads and the *Pilgrim's* Way all run through it while, when I visited it, the annexe was being used by a number of moto-cross cyclists for a bit of practice.

There is nothing particularly unique about Bigbury either, although it is an example of what has become known as an enclosed oppida, a sort of Belgic/late Iron Age development of an hillfort. It is the only hillfort within a thirty mile radius, but even that did not guarantee inclusion in the gazetteer. What tipped the balance in Bigbury's favour was its historical interest', and its part in one of the few recorded accounts of English pre-history.

Bigbury is an 'L' shaped semi-contour hillfort of about twenty-five acres, sitting on the 200 feet contour. The land falls quite steeply on all sides, except the narrow approach from the west. To the north, running down to about the 150 feet contour, is a seven acre annexe which was probably used for herding cattle. It is this, not the main fort, which the *Pilgrim's* Way passes through.

The road from Harbledown, after crossing the Canterbury by-pass, passes through the east entrance. This was defended by a bank and two ditches, the gaps being deliberately staggered to hinder intruders. There was probably an entrance to the west as well. The main defences comprise a single rampart, which rises up to ten feet in height, a ditch and a counterscap bank. Where these can be seen they are mostly covered in trees, and gravel digging has caused much damage to the interior. On the face of it, so it seems, Bigbury has little going for it.

Now we come to the interesting bit. In 54 B.C. Julius Caesar made his second invasion of Britain. The first, a year earlier, had hardly got off the ground, or at least the beaches, before the good old Channel weather came to the Britons' aid, and wrecked half of the Roman ships. The second time around, Caesar learned from his lessons, brought his army over in boats with a shallow draught and left them riding at anchor, not beached as before. Caesar landed unopposed, and marched his five legions and 2,000 cavalry through the small hours to a river about twelve miles inland. This is thought to be the River Stour, at what is now Canterbury. The natives, no doubt taken by surprise, retreated to their nearest fortified position, here at Bigbury.

Caesar described the hillfort as, 'A place well fortified by nature and strengthened by man, no doubt for their own tribal wars, with all entrances blocked by felled trees . . .' The area of Kent was under the Belgic Cantiaci tribe, not unknown to the Romans, who quickly set about mounting their first assault on a British hillfort, backed by much experience of similar attacks in the rest of Europe.

The VII Legion raised their shields above their heads, to form what was known as a 'testudo', a tortoise, and made their way to the rampart, building a ramp up to it. They then fought their way inside and drove the defenders off into the woods, but the battle had lasted all day long, and the pursuit was put off until the following morning. Then, as before, the weather on Britain's first line of defences took a hand and, before a full pursuit could be started, Caesar received the news that his fleet had been dashed to pieces once again; and Hitler thought he was unlucky with the Channel weather!

It is not absolutely certain that the above events took place at Bigbury, but an alternative place is not known. Some things are of interest though, despite the un-promising condition of Bigbury today. Caesar said that the 'entrances were blocked by felled trees', and not gates. Does this suggest that Bigbury was largely un-inhabited at the time, possibly with only a very basic maintenance of the defences? The gravel diggings, though damaging, have revealed many metal tools, horse and vehicle fittings, and chains from a cauldron and for slaves. These suggest more of a settled, perhaps fairly wealthy, farming community than one used to occasional skirmishes.

On the ground though, exploring is the most fascinating aspect of a visit to Bigbury. From the annexe there are reasonable views to the north, but by following the Pilgrim's Way either east or west, these will be considerably enhanced, once clear of the woods. Bigbury's proximity to Canterbury is an obvious attraction, and while it is possible to drive through the hillfort and not know it, the adventure of seeking out a hillfort in woods is one of the pleasures of 'hillfort hunting'.

Directions. O/S 1:50,000 series map 103 ref. 885384. Leave Nelson on the A6068 towards Colne, and turn right after passing under the railway bridge at Colne station. Follow this out of the town, up the steep hill until the gradient eases, and the hillfort is on the right at a sharpish left hand bend, by a junction. Park here, and a footpath leads from the bend to the hillfort.

Coming from Lincolnshire, almost bereft of hillforts (but *see* Honnington*), I always assumed, as the name suggests, that hilly districts would have plenty of hillforts. Thus, it was no surprise to discover that Wales, the hills of Wessex, the South-West and the Chilterns are either littered with them, or have a smaller number of large hillforts, while the 'flat' counties of the Midlands and East Anglia had very few. It was surprising to discover that northern hilly areas, in particular those in Yorkshire, Derbyshire, Cumberland and Westmorland (or Cumbria today) and Durham had so few hillforts, yet Northumberland, and the Scottish Borders were covered with them.

Lancashire too, has few hillforts, six in fact, none of which are of any great size. Castercliff is the county's best example but, if truth be told, there are many finer hillforts omitted from this gazetteer, especially in the South and West, to make room for a Palatine presence. That said, Castercliff is not without its merits, although first impressions are of a circular pile of rubble.

That in itself makes a change from the grass-clothed ruins of most hillforts, while Castercliff has an unusual appearance. On the inside a low bank forms an inner circle, which now is only about one foot high. This was the original rubble filled, wooden-laced, stone-faced rampart. Unusually, there does not appear to have been a ditch, while entry was gained in the west. A number of excavations have been undertaken on this two acre site, in 1958, 1960 and 1970-71, and it is thought that this rampart had been 'vitrified', either by design, accident or attack. This is unusual for England, but there are a great number of vitrified hillforts in Scotland, i.e. the rampart's internal timbers have been set on fire, by any of the three aforementioned methods, to weld, or 'vitrify' the stones together.

Immediately beyond the original rampart is the second timber revetted, box rampart, with a ditch up to ten feet deep in places, and a counterscarp bank to the south. This rampart is in a series of short lengths in the north, and the excavations have shown that the flat land between has not been built on. Castercliff was thus abandoned before its rebuilding was completed, and the excavators came across no finds of significance, which begs the question of it ever being permanently occupied.

The entrance to the later hillfort also appears to have been in the west, while it might have been intended to have one in the east as well. It was thought that Castercliff was built in the first century B.C., but good old Carbon-14 dating of charcoal has revised that somewhat, and it was probably constructed in either the sixth or seventh centuries B.C.

Castercliff stands on a surprising 930 feet high plateau, in the foothills of The Pennines. Although the hills rise to a considerable height to the east, they are not overpowering, while the hillfort was well situated in terms of over-seeing the land to the north, south and west, in particular the river valley. The immediate view west is not quite so endearing today, with the towns of Colne and Nelson below, and a motorway, but the valley can be followed beyond Burnley to Blackburn, all part of the once-great Lancashire industrial heartland, and itself one of the historic centres of the Industrial Revolution.

As the outskirts of Nelson reach outwards and upwards, Castercliff is increasingly threatened with engulfment, but as the area is criss-crossed with public footpaths, two of which cross the hillfort, it should be safe from 'development'. The survival of what is, in effect, an early Iron Age building site, raises as many questions as to why it was never completed, as some of the larger hillforts raise about their abandonment. Where did the builders come from and go to? – there are few other hillforts in the North-West. Some things even modern scientific methods cannot tell us, and we are left simply with what we can see.

Directions. O/S 1:50,000 map 129 ref. 762119. About 12 miles east of Leicester. Turn left off the A47, heading east, on the B6047 towards Melton Mowbray. Turn right in Twyford and pass through Burrough on the Hill village, towards Somerby. At the top of the hill, at a right hand bend, the car park is on the left. A footpath leads straight to the hillfort, a quarter of a mile away.

On initial acquaintance, it is the wonderful views that attract one's attention, particularly those to the north across the valley of the Rivers Eye and Wreake. It will not take you long to realise that the hillfort itself is equally noteworthy, especially for the east side of England, while it has had what one might describe as an 'interesting' history, even if that for the Iron Age is less than certain, for the present at least.

The single rampart and ditch, with a significant counterscarp bank that runs most of the way round, enclose about 12 acres, and are of considerable size, with the rampart having had a dry-stone-facing, now invisible beneath the turf. Not surprisingly, the defences are at their most impressive scale to the east and north-east sides, where they face relatively flat ground. They are, nonetheless, formidable at the north-west and south-west sides, where the natural incline would give further discouragement to any would-be attacker. The northern corner is heavily wooded, and the defences have seemingly vanished.

It is undoubtedly the location that gives the defences such an air of impregnability, and the most impressive of these is the gateway, situated at the south-east corner, where you will arrive. The most obvious feature of this is the 150 feet long inturned rampart ends, while there is evidence of curved outworkings, although these have, in the main, been ploughed over. An excavation undertaken in 1960 concentrated on the gateway, and revealed that there were two sizeable guard chambers at either side, each with evidence of a hearth, and large double gates, with the possibility of a second set. The entrance was found to have been re-modelled on at least three occasions, culminating in the long passage seen today, while the high level of use necessitated the road surface being re-laid on three occasions. This would have been an entrance of formidable proportions.

If the siting, size and scale of the defences, and the level of use, suggest to you that this must have been a place of particular pre-Roman importance, then you are in good company; many archaeologists think along similar lines, but there is little direct evidence, at the present, to confirm this. It is possible that Burrough Hill was the headquarters of the Corieltauvi tribe, although it is also possible that it pre-dated them, being of a more simple construction, and was upgraded to 'tribal capital' status in the first century B.C. Indeed, there is evidence to suggest that it enjoyed at least sporadic periods of occupation for up to 700 years, from the third century B.C.

As the scope of the aforementioned excavations was relatively limited, only a few storage pits have been found, and none of the larger buildings one would associate with a tribal capital. However, the interior has been much damaged by mediaeval ploughing, and it is quite possible that an excavation of the interior will reveal much more than is known at the present. A flint arrow-head, Iron Age pottery, Roman coins, a dagger, spear-head and a crouched skeleton have been found at the site, which suggests a use by a number of peoples.

One theory is that the many gaps in the rampart are the result of slighting by the Romans, and this would suggest that Burrough Hill was a place of some importance. Another, possibly less plausible, theory is that the hillfort was the scene of the defeat of the rebellious Iceni tribe, of which Boudicca was the leader, by the Romans under Osorius Scapula. In either case, however fanciful, one might well expect the victorious Romans to ensure that Burrough Hill was to be of no further defensive use in the future.

On the other hand, despite the uncertain nature of the evidence pertaining to the Iron Age, Burrough Hill does have a considerable history from the Middle Ages onwards. It was known as Miccilberuhill c.1260 and, apart from being ploughed, was the site for a fair in mediaeval days. By the sixteenth century it was used every Whit Monday as the venue for a variety of activities, which included running, dancing, wrestling and other sports. This annual meeting was later abandoned, but revived, to finally lapse in the eighteenth century.

In the nineteenth century the Melton Hunt held a race meeting at the camp on the Wednesday after the second Sunday in June, this also took place annually until 1870. The following year, on the 2nd April, a steeplechase was held while the local population was counted for the Census. Then, finally, on Whit Monday in 1955, more games were held, but the revival was short-lived, and Burrough Hill is now part of a country park. Quite apart from its lengthy, and varied, historical associations, and its defences of considerable proportions, the views from the hillfort are mighty indeed, while from the valley below the defences almost look impregnable, even in their present ruined state. However, the most lasting effect of Burrough Hill in recent times has been the adoption of its name by the village which nestles in its shadow; Burrough on the Hill was called Erdeborough until the latter half of the last century.

For all the 'ifs and buts' concerning its Iron Age past, Burrough Hill seems to have maintained a high degree of use over the centuries. Perhaps it was the rarity of such a structure in the East Midlands that encouraged this use, or maybe it was nothing unusual (see Martinsell*), just that records were kept for Burrough Hill. As you will find out when reading through the gazetteer section of this book, not many hillforts can show such a continued use, so I prefer the former option. In any case, there are few hillforts that have an official role in society today, and as the centrepiece of a country park, Burrough Hill more than justifies its continued position in the locality.

Honnington

Directions. O/S 1:50,000 map 130 ref. 954424. Situated one mile south of the village of Honnington. Leave Grantham heading north on the A607 and after four miles keep right onto the A153. Within a half a mile there is a turning for Honnington village on the left. Immediately opposite, on the right, is the trackway that leads to the hillfort. You can either park here, or drive the one mile along trackways. Follow the track to the top of the hill and turn right. Follow this until the next junction, and turn left. The hillfort is at the top on the left.

Being born and brought up in Lincolnshire, a true 'yellow-belly', I am used to the jibes of 'Lincolnshire's flat'. When you consider the dearth of hillforts in the county, and by that I mean the true county, which includes the administrative area of South Humberside, it would seem that it is indeed 'flat'. There are, however, two very noteworthy exceptions: the Lincolnshire Wolds, which rise to over 500 feet in places, and the variously named Lincoln Heath/Edge/Heights/Cliff (take your pick), which is effectively the beginning of a range of hills which ultimately became the Cotswolds. 'Flat' indeed!

The Heights are cut in several places, most notably at Lincoln itself, and again between Ancaster and Honnington. The road and railway both make use of this latter gap, while the River Slea rises in the hills to the east of the hillfort. The Roman Ermine Street, as usual, simply went along the top of the hills, irrespective of the terrain.

You quickly rise up above the village, although the walk is not too steep. Quite soon you will arrive at a plateau rising to 404 feet high, and almost before you realise it, you will be upon the hillfort It might be Lincolnshire's only plateau hillfort, but it is a real gem, if a miniature one.

There are not too many hillforts with double glacis ramparts, ditches and a counterscarp bank, which only enclose a little over an acre. Honnington gives the impression of being a dwarf version of one of the mightiest of hillforts in the South, say Hod Hill*, but its defences, being about 60 feet wide, are purposeful enough. Little is known about who lived here, or what happened to them, although as the interior only appears to have been grazed perhaps a future excavation will reveal more.

The defences are complete, almost rectangular in shape, and with an entrance in the north-east. Their complexities, although the entrance is simple enough, bereft of outworkings, suggest that Honnington was built in the middle Iron Age. What happened thereafter is anybody's guess. Much of Lincolnshire was settled in the late Iron Age, but there seems to have been little call for fortified villages. Why Honnington was different is open to question.

Let that not deter you from a visit though, for the hillfort was certainly sited with some thought given to its strategic position. A tributary of the River Witham might have passed through the gap in the hills to the north during the Iron Age, and it is likely that a trackway did. Honnington obviously overlooks this, while it commands views along the hills to the north, the Vale of Belvoir to the west, and the Trent valley to the north-west. From the hillfort, the views to the east and south are not so impressive, being on a plateau, but the inhabitants would not have had to walk far to enjoy the security of massive views over the fens to the east, with an airfield in the foreground today, while those views to the south and south-east are commanding, rather than dramatic.

It is possible that the builders of Honnington, given the influences in the style used, migrated from the South of England, and may have been the first of their kind to penetrate this part of the country, maybe fleeing from the northwards advance of the Belgic Catuvellauni tribe. Perhaps they expected, or received, a hostile reception from the locals and decided that a bit of protection would not go amiss. If this were the case, then they were soon either 'seen off', or assimilated into local life, as no further attempt at setting up fortifications in the vicinity is apparent. These days, thanks to the electric railway, people are still migrating into the area from the South, charmed by the countryside so easily appreciated from this ancient camp.

Warham Camp

Directions. O/S 1:50,000 map 132 ref. 944409. Leave Wells-next-the-Sea towards Fakenham on the B1105. Turn left at Warham and turn right at the crossroads beyond the church. Half a mile further, a Bridlepath leads to the hillfort.

Norfolk has only six sites which might be construed as being Iron Age hillforts, and three of them are near the north coast within a few miles of each other. One is actually in an adjacent field at the north-east of Warham Camp, with nothing to see, while a second is just north of the Coke family seat, at Holkham Hall. There is not a great deal to see there either, but Warham makes up for the rest, being one of the most visually impressive, small hillforts anywhere.

Warham Camp lies on a plateau, about 40 feet above the sea, and three miles inland from the high-water mark. It was probably nearer the coast in the Iron Age. It does not, therefore, command any great strategic position, and with only 3.5 acres being enclosed, could not have been a significant centre of population. However, the Iceni tribe did not build many hillforts, so Warham must have served a particular function.

As you will have discovered from this book, most hillforts have not been excavated, and thus their past remains unknown. Warham, on the other hand, has been subjected to at least three small-scale excavations, yet has still not revealed much about itself, other than what you can see. That is more than enough to reward your visit, though.

Two concentric banks and ditches encircle the camp, except on the south-west, by the River Stiffkey. A single bank was considered sufficient at that point, with the narrow river offering additional defence, but the rampart has been worn down today. That is, though, virtually the only blemish on the defences, which are of an impressively large size, measuring 150 feet overall. The flat-bottomed ditches have, not surprisingly, silted up by about six feet, but with the height of the ramparts, these substantial defences would do justice to many a larger hillfort.

There are three gaps in the defences, but it is not certain which is the original one(s). That to the south-west leads to the river, while that to the north appears to have a causeway across the ditches, but Warham probably only had the one entrance in the Iron Age.

Naturally enough, being on a low-lying plateau, there is not much in the way of views to be had, and it is the scale of the defences, relative to the size of the camp, which is the main point of interest. Be thankful for small mercies, as landscaping of the hillfort two centuries ago could easily have caused much more damage, while it was only cleared of trees one hundred years ago and, given the beautiful symmetry of the defences, quite rightly so.

The results of the above-mentioned excavations have been limited. It was probably built by the Iceni, understandably enough, in the first century B.C., or even first century A.D. This might have been as a result of the Belgic Catuvellauni expansion in the south of East Anglia, but if so, why build a strong defensive camp, so far north? Perhaps there had been a certain amount of raiding from the sea, and with Holkham camp being similarly placed, this might be seen as a possibility. Most of the few relics uncovered by the various excavators, showed a Romano-British occupation, so perhaps it was built very late in the Iron Age, and not long before the Roman invasion.

Another, totally un-proven, theory put forward for Warham, is that it might have been modified by the Danes, possibly in the tenth century A.D. This would be understandable, but then again would the Normans not have utilised its defences as well, and built a motte inside it? All that is part of the great 'ifs and buts' of history, but confirmed or not, it is the splendour of the little site that will leave you enchanted in a way no ordinary castle, or hillfort, can.

OTHER ANCIENT SITES
Holkham Camp. O/S map 132 ref. 875447.

Directions. O/S 1:50,000 map 75 ref. 075216. Leave Alnwick heading north-west on the B6346. Two miles after passing through Eglingham the B6346 turns sharp left at a junction. Go straight on, along a minor road, until you come to some houses on the right. Park at the turning near the Public Footpath sign, and follow the track up the hill through two gates. After the second gate, turn right up the steep hill through the trees; the hillfort is beyond the fenced enclosure at the top. For a less strenuous walk, after the second gate carry on along the track until beyond the little stream on the left. Turn sharp right across the pasture, due south, until the hillfort is reached at the summit of the hill.

The three hillforts included in this book from Northumberland (*see* also Wooler* and Yeavering Bell*), were among the few in England which did not remain in an area under permanent Roman occupation, until their withdrawal early in the fifth century A.D. They thus differed in a number of respects from the vast majority of English hillforts, and this is clearly evident from those hillforts included in the gazetteer.

Old Berwick came under the area of the Votadini tribe. These people were closer to the Bronze Age in many respects, although had some Iron Age features, such as the use of hillforts. Traprain Law, in Scotland, was their hillfort capital, and it is quite probable that Yeavering Bell was the leading hillfort in Old Berwick's locality. In 80 A.D., Agricola arrived with the Romans at Corbridge, and began the invasion of the border country. Presumably, as had happened elsewhere, any resistance was put down, while it is probable that the Romans took an interest in Old Berwick, as Agricola's army's military road, Devil's Causeway, is only 1.5 miles away to the west.

The Votadini were suppressed, but hillforts continued to be occupied; Traprain Law remained inhabited throughout the Roman occupation of Britain. If anything, the Votadini held a favoured position among the tribes of South Scotland, and a large Roman presence was not maintained. Between 140-142 A.D. the area beyond Hadrian's Wall was invaded again, although the Romans always patrolled beyond the wall, and the Antoinine Wall was built in 143 A.D. This was abandoned in the face of action from the tribes of the Scottish Highlands about twelve years later, re-occupied in c.160 A.D., and finally abandoned within fifty years. Thus, Old Berwick lay thirty miles north of the empire boundary, at Hadrian's Wall, but within an area covered by effective Roman rule, via treaties and permanent Roman forts in South Scotland, until late in the fourth century A.D.

This quite lengthy scene-setting is important because the dates of occupation of Old Berwick are uncertain, but it is quite probable, as with other hillforts/homesteads in the area, that it remained occupied until the abandonment of the Antoinine Wall, and possibly afterwards. As much as anything, once the Romans had arrived, the people of the Votadini tribe were probably more under threat from the barbarians of the North, but may also have supported a rebellion in c.180 A.D. In any case, there is the possibility that the border country was used by Rome as a place for giving soldiers battle action, and generals a reputation, without the likelihood of a humiliating defeat, or at least to gain a practical benefit from a volatile situation; not unlike the experience British soldiers gain in Northern Ireland today.

The reasoning behind the construction of Old Berwick seems to be peaceful enough though. It is a most unusual shape, like a pair of spectacles, situated east/west on a promontory overlooking the River Beamish valley, with the Cheviot Hills beyond. The two enclosures are quite small, each about an acre in size, and are protected by quite sophisticated defences which are probably of more than one period. The south face, with a natural steep escarpment, has a small rampart running along its length, while there is a rampart and ditch that enclose the whole hillfort, from the escarpment on the west side to the east. In addition, there may be another boundary ditch further out, which can be seen primarily in the east, and beyond the fence in the field to the north.

It is the two circular enclosures which are the heart of the hillfort, and both are protected by double ramparts and ditches, except on the south sides, which come together to give four ramparts between the enclosures. These are of a suitable size to give protection from the gentle approach from the three sides, and they all appear to be of clay, with a covering of rubble dug from the ditches. The west enclosure has entrances at the west and north-east, and the east enclosure at the south-east and probably the north-west.

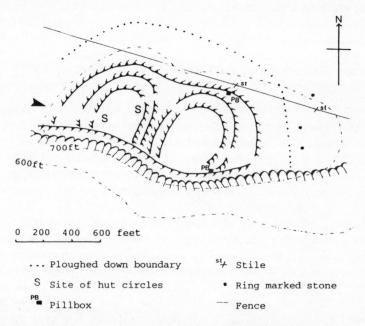

0   200   400   600 feet

··· Ploughed down boundary   ˢᵗⵏ Stile

S Site of hut circles   • Ring marked stone

PB
• Pillbox   —— Fence

Of particular interest is the apparent division of use for the two enclosures, as may be the case at Wooler*, with hut circles being clearly visible in the west enclosure, particularly near the west entrance. No traces of huts can be seen in the east enclosure, and this is divided into what are probably paddock enclosures. It may well be that the occupants were cattle ranching people, although the land to the north and east would have been suitable for crops. No evidence has been found of deliberate slighting of the ramparts, which suggests either that the Romans did not consider it to be a threat, or that it was uninhabited when they arrived. The defences appear to date from the late Iron Age in their final form.

Old Berwick is quite an outstanding little hillfort, magnificent in its ruins, and wondrous in its location. The best views are over the River Beamish valley to the Cheviot Hills, but there are good views along the valley to the north-west and south-east, to the south and, despite its 770 feet height, the hills to the north and east. Also of interest is the two World War II pill-boxes built within the hillfort. Anyone used to the often disgusting condition of the interior of these in built up areas, will be more than pleasantly surprised. Should you be caught out by rain while up here, they are fine places to shelter, and although I do not suppose it was in Hitler's masterplan to capture Old Berwick, they would have given an ideal place for surveillance.

Finally, before you make your way back, there are some 'cup and ring' markings on some large stones nearby. The reasoning behind such markings is unclear and subject to much speculation, but they probably date from Bronze Age times at the latest. Two stones which bear such markings are the one outside the farthest boundary bank to the east, and another beyond the fence to the north, near the steps. Other stones bear such markings further down the hill on the east, which can form part of a circular route back, by turning west around the bottom of the south side of the hill on which the hillfort stands.

Wooler (Also known as Maiden Castle or The Kettles)

Directions. O/S 1:50,000 map 75 ref. 984273. Enter Wooler Market Place from the A697 from the south. Turn left up Ramsey's Lane and park. Walk up the hill until near the last houses on the right, where a Public Footpath on the left goes through Waud House farm. Continue on the right hand path for a further quarter of a mile and the hillfort is on the plateau to the left. A longer circuitous walk, taking in six hillforts, is possible. For details *see* Yeavering Bell*.

Quite naturally, different areas of Britain constructed their own style(s) of hillfort during the Iron Age. The area now covered by North Northumberland and South-East Scotland seems to have favoured the small fortified farm or homestead, often of less than one acre, with the occasional hillfort of much greater proportions. Another peculiarity, is that some of the hillforts have a plan not unlike a pair of early National Health Service wire spectacles; oh how I used to hate wearing them at school, but I was always breaking them in those far-off days. Wooler is one of those 'spectacle' hillforts, and is also unusual, for the region, in being of a medium-sized four and a half acres.

Standing on almost the north-east limit of the Cheviot Hills, Wooler is overlooked not only by all the hills to the west, but the solitary hill to the east as well. Thus, it does not enjoy the classic defensive measure of virtual all-round vision. The approach from the north, which you will have taken, is the easiest, and is protected by an outer rampart, a slight bank and the inner rampart. This runs all the way round the north enclosure, which has an entrance in the north together with one in the south, and forms part of a complex system of passages between the two enclosures.

Both enclosures are joined by the rampart on the west, which forms the 'bridge' of the spectacles, but the ramparts which form the east side of each enclosure curve round in-between the two enclosures, to give triple ramparts between the enclosures. The south entrance of the north enclosure is in-turned, and leads through the triple ramparts and ditch to the south enclosure. The east and west ramparts of both enclosures are smaller in scale, as steep natural slopes protect those sides.

There is an entrance in the south-east of the south enclosure, and this may have been further protected by outworkings. All of the ramparts are clearly visible, although they have been rounded by 2,000 years of weathering. As the hillfort has not been excavated, no trace of any huts has been found, but there are some dividing walls within the south enclosure. As with Old Berwick*, this could have been used for herding the cattle, while the north enclosure was for the inhabitants. This, I am afraid, is not certain.

Undoubtedly, the most interesting part of the hillfort is the central entrance complex. Walking around the ramparts at this point is akin to following a maze, with ramparts rising and criss-crossing each other. It is a great pity we are only left with the ruins nowadays. Despite its somewhat dwarfed location, you can see for miles to the north and south. It is always enjoyable to look down on a town, and Wooler, a mediaeval settlement, makes an interesting site. The hillfort's location is still exposed enough to get the wind whistling around your ears, which adds to a feeling of isolation, despite the proximity of the town.

What became of the inhabitants is not known but, as with many of the Northumbrian hillforts, it was probably built in the late Iron Age, by people having more in common with the late Bronze Age, than the 'southerners'; nothing much changes. It probably continued to be used into Roman times although, despite being in the 'border zone' does not seem to have seen any action.

Should you not fancy the long trek mentioned for Yeavering Bell*, you can leave by the south-east gateway and either double back through the valley to the east of the hillfort, or continue down to the road, turn left and follow this back into Wooler.

Yeavering Bell

Directions. O/S. 1:50,000 map 74 or 75 ref. 928293. Head north from Wooler on the A697 and turn left on the B6351. After just over two miles, turn left on a track towards a short row of houses at Old Yeavering, and park on the grass before these. Follow the track through the farmyard and turn left through the gateway just before crossing the stream. Go diagonally across the field where there are steps over the stone wall. Head straight to the top of the steep hill.

Few areas of the British Isles, let alone England, have such a density of hillforts as this area of Northumberland/South-East Scotland. Almost every hill in the Cheviot Hills seems to have at least one hillfort or ancient settlement, while some have traces of several. These ancient places of habitation are not restricted to the high ground either, and there is much evidence of Iron Age, and earlier, settlements on the coastal plain.

As one might expect, the vast majority are little more than fortified homesteads or farms, and many of the settlements are small, but a number of hillforts are larger than five acres, while a few rival all but the biggest in the South. In addition, the ratio of hut sites per acre is quite high in comparison to hillforts in the South, which suggests, but does not confirm, a high density of population. Of course, it could be that it was the local tradition to live in fortified settlements in this northern region. Given the inhospitable weather, would one expect to find a greater population in an area where crops would not grow so well, as opposed to the warmer South? Or is it that the settlements in this region have survived better than those further south, particularly in what were possibly the heavily populated valleys of Iron Age Britain?

The twin peaks of Yeavering Bell form an easily recognisable feature for many miles around. It is not the easiest of hillforts to reach and, of course, standing at 1,182 feet, it is invariably breezy when you reach the summit, at best. Should you have followed the directions, you will have arrived at the centre of the north rampart. This tumbled stone affair is complete in its circuit; it follows the contours below the summit, and was probably 10-12 feet wide and stood about 8 feet high. Unfortunately, the stone wall, although fully exposed, lies ruined all round, but a short section of the west rampart is still standing, though not to its full height.

There were simple straight-through entrances in the north, east and south, with the latter probably being the main one, as it had a guard chamber at each side. That at the east is protected by a 400 feet long crescent shaped stone wall, also demolished, with an almost identical structure at the west end, only there is no entrance from that to the hillfort. It is probable these were cattle enclosures.

These defences enclose 13.5 acres, of well preserved ground. Inside, there are approximately 130 hut platforms cut into the hillsides, giving a relatively high ratio of 10 per acre, as opposed to 5-6 per acre in the south. All of these appear to be circular, with a diameter of 18-30 feet and are evenly spread throughout the interior. Of course, they were probably not all contemporary with one another, but this could easily be said of other hillforts. A population of about 500 is quite possible, given the density of the huts. Stone paving has been found in some of the huts, the vast majority of which, despite the abundance of stone, had wooden walls. Many of these hut platforms are easily visible and are mostly turf covered.

Surrounding the east summit is a trench, probably for a palisade and also pre-dating the huts, and thus presumably the walled fort. The small stone cairn at the summit is thought to be mediaeval or later, possibly the remains of a beacon. Thus the hillfort may have been occupied in the earlier Iron Age, if not before, and may have served a purpose until quite recent times. However, the hillfort itself probably dates from the first or second centuries B.C., while the few finds, as it has not been fully excavated, suggest that occupation lasted until the second century A.D., or later. Such a late date would seem to be at odds with the suggestion that the walls might have been destroyed by the Romans as an oppressive measure when they invaded the area, but it could have been as retribution for an up-rising, which undoubtedly occurred from time to time in such volatile 'border country'.

Yeavering Bell, although not on the same scale as some of the larger forts across the border, must have been important on a local basis. Given the number of smaller settlements in the vicinity, although not all were small, Yeavering Bell may have proved to have been a trading centre, although the Roman road, the Devil's Causeway, runs several miles away to the east. It is quite likely that the inhabitants were mostly engaged in cattle rearing, while the lower ground nearer the River Glen, to the north, might have been used for crops.

There is a great deal to see once you have made the effort to climb to the hillfort, and this is further enhanced by the truly magnificent views, particularly over the low ground to the north and east. The hillfort is overlooked by a hill to the west, but there is a good view along the valley to the north-west. Despite the rise of the Cheviot Hills to the south, and The Cheviot itself, the rather pleasant coloured hills rise gently and are not over-powering in the least.

In fact, a fine walk along the hills from Wooler hillfort* can be had. It would be eight miles long outward, with five and a half miles along the B6351 and A697 back to Wooler. The route, mostly on hills and not footpaths, takes in Wooler hillfort, Humbleton hillfort ref. 967283, Harehope hillfort ref. 956285, Gleadesglough (Akeld Hill) hillfort ref. 949290, Yeavering Bell, and West Hill Camp ref. 910295. From there, descend north and follow the track north-east to the B6351 at Kirknewton.

There is enough to keep you occupied with Yeavering Bell by itself though, especially on a fine day. The hillfort with its distinctive twin peaks, exposed stone walls, numerous hut sites and lengthy occupation overlooks the site of the Dark Age royal township of Ad Gefrin, due north near the south bank of the River Glen. Yeavering Bell continues to look down on an ever-changing environment, while it slowly decays.

Directions. O/S 1:50,000 map 164 ref. 575938. Leave Oxford on the A423 towards Wallingford. The hillfort is south of the village of Dorchester, now by-passed. Turn right onto the A415, and left through Dorchester. Turn right to a sign-posted car park, just before crossing the bridge at the south of the village. Walk south to the Catholic church, then turn right and turn left up Whittenham Lane. A Public Footpath leads to the east of the large cross-dykes.

Dorchester has had a colourful past: a noted mediaeval town; the seat of a Bishop whose see stretched beyond Lincoln in pre-Norman times; sited at the junction of important Roman roads, with the associated town to the west of the present village; and near Dyke Hills, a late Iron Age promontory fort currently of 114 acres. Dyke Hills comprises low-lying ground overlooked by nearby hills, on which a conventional hillfort stands, Sinodun Camp, and is more of an enclosed oppidum than a hillfort. The promontory is formed by cross-dykes to the north cutting off an area bounded by the River Thame to the east and the River Thames to the south and west. About sixty acres within this area were densely occupied during the Iron Age, and it is quite likely that the courses of the two rivers have altered, increasing the enclosed area.

Most of the interior is currently given over to grazing, but the path from the village passes the east end of the cross-dykes, probably at the site of the original entrance. Your route takes you to the junction of the two rivers, where you turn right and follow the River Thames round to Day's Lock. The flat land of the interior is ideal for farming, and centuries of such use have obliterated all surface signs of the numerous huts, tracks and pits visible on aerial photographs, which signify that Dyke Hills had a relatively large population.

A proper excavation has not been undertaken, so details of Dyke Hills past cannot be verified. It may have had a long period of use prior to its expansion in the late Iron Age. The large double ramparts, with central and unseen outside ditches, suggest a building date of first or second centuries B.C., while other enclosed oppida date from the first century B.C. It is quite probable that Dyke Hills commanded a junction of long distance tracks, while its position at the confluence of the two rivers would also have been important.

The ramparts are at their best in the centre, where they still rise to over ten feet in height, and which you come to on your way round from Day's Lock. All of the gaps are relatively modern, the ramparts being damaged last century. From the top of the ramparts, a good idea of the size of the enclosed oppidum can be gained, while these probably curved round at the east to reach the River Thame, but stop short now.

The demise of Dyke Hills probably came about with the arrival of the Romans, and the building of the nearby small Roman town. Whatever happened to the inhabitants is not known, but it was unlikely they were re-settled in Dorchester. Although little about Dyke Hills' history is known, it must have been quite an important trading settlement, with some form of manufacturing being undertaken, and probably served as a regional centre of the Catuvellauni tribe.

Dorchester is a pleasant village with an abbey church, grass covered remains of its Roman settlement and, of course, Dyke Hills. Footpaths follow the course of the River Thames both to the east and west of the hillfort, making for some pleasant walks in this quiet corner of Oxfordshire. The River Thames has been such a major part of our past that it seems odd that much of the history of probably the largest Iron Age settlement on its banks still remains to be discovered. Dyke Hills might have enjoyed an existence of little more than a century, but it provides further evidence of the scale of society's organisation in the Iron Age.

Caer Caradoc *(near Church Stretton)*

Directions. O/S 1:50,000 maps 137/138 ref. 478952. Head north from Church Stretton on the A49, and turn right towards Cardington. Keep right at the first junction, and turn next right to Willstone. At Willstone corner, carry straight on up the rough track and park at the small quarry on the right. A footpath from a little further along the trackway on the right hand side, leads to the hillfort at the top of the hill.

Sandwiched between the great masses of Wenlock Edge to the south-east, and The Long Mynd to the west, Caer Caradoc Hill is anything but overshadowed. Its rise of over 900 feet above the valley, traversed by both road and railway, half a mile to the west, seems to further accentuate its height, and impregnability. Given the difficulty of approach to the narrow 1,506 feet summit, it seems only natural that this hill was selected as the site for a hillfort, in the second or third centuries B.C., as opposed to the great mass of The Long Mynd which, apart from several Bronze Age round barrows, has surprisingly few signs of ancient habitation.

Make no mistake, although you can drive up to about 1,000 feet, there is still a stiff climb to be made to reach the hillfort. Should you follow the directions, you will approach via the original trackway built to serve the only entrance, at the south-east corner. The builders of this six acre hillfort, over several stages, made the utmost use of the natural advantages afforded by the site. Steep slopes offer protection on all sides, with only a relatively easy approach from the north. The whole site is surrounded by a single, grass-covered stone rampart which makes use of rocky crags on the east side. An internal quarry ditch runs round most of the north side.

Between 20-80 feet below this, again around the north side, a quarry ditch and rampart afford extra protection. The short, south side has also been given additional defences with a ditch and counterscarp bank added to the main rampart, and a quarry ditch and bank further beyond this. None of the defences are of any great height today, but the general layout is easily seen.

The entrance is via an oblique gap in the main rampart, the north part of which is slightly in-turned. There is evidence of a guard-chamber, while the whole is overlooked by the large rocky crag to the south. The interior slopes from north to south, giving a drop of about 100 feet, and is generally clothed in grass, while some hut platforms might be visible.

As with the other Shropshire Caer Caradoc*, no full excavation has been undertaken, and thus little of its past is known. A Roman road made its way up the valley to the west, and you can be sure that had the hillfort been occupied when the Romans first arrived, the inhabitants would not have escaped their attention. However, in view of the purely defensive, strategic nature of the hillfort, once the Romans had control of the area there would have been no reason for it to have been occupied, so we must assume that it was abandoned not long after their arrival, at the latest.

Once you have inspected the fortifications, there is much more to consider and feast the eyes on. Strategically, the hillfort must have been of considerable value, as this, and the defences, seem to take priority over ordinary living considerations. The ground nearby is certainly not suitable for the growing of crops, and there is precious little space anywhere on the hill for herding cattle. If defensive considerations were not of paramount importance, then one would assume that a hillfort on the huge summit of The Long Mynd would have been preferable.

Few hillforts tower over a neighbouring town in quite the fashion of Caer Caradoc, overlook such a natural phenomenon as the Wenlock Edge and yet are still dominated by a far greater mass of rock. To the north you can see across the River Severn valley beyond Shrewsbury. While to the north-east, the Wenlock Edge points to the outstanding, but smaller, Wrekin hill, with its hillfort, which looks down over Telford. The two distant Clee Hills, again with their hillforts, rise in the south, and if The Long Mynd blocks any further views to the west, there is no better place from which to appreciate it. There can be no more appropriate hillfort to adorn with the name of a great British warrior, except perhaps the other two!

Caer Caradoc (near Clun)

Directions. O/S 1:50,000 maps 137/148 ref. 310758. Take the A488 north from Knighton. Turn right at 'Five Turnings', and after passing Wax Hall Farm, park at the right hand bend with two holly trees on the left. Follow the first trackway, back on yourself, and go through two gateways, one with a sign 'To the camp', and cross the pasture land to the camp at the summit.

This is one of three camps named after the British warrior Caradoc, known later as Caractacus, who held out against the early Roman invasion until about 50 B.C., and who probably had no connection with these hillforts at all. Still, that is probably a good measure of the esteem in which Caradoc was held. Built at the summit of a 1,321 feet high hill, a full 670 feet above the River Redlake just half a mile away to the north-east, the defences are well adapted to take advantage of the natural slopes to the south and east, and follow the contours at these sides.

Although it is an uphill approach to the hillfort, you will be relieved to find that you arrive from the gently graded west side which, as a consequence, has the strongest defences. An area of about 4.5 acres is fully enclosed by a single, stone-faced glacis rampart and ditch on all sides, with a slight counterscarp to the naturally steep south side. A quarry ditch runs almost all the way round the inside of this, except in the west. Most of the north and west sides have an easy approach, and a second rampart and ditch is added from south of the west entrance all the way round to the east entrance. At the north, this is further divided to give a third rampart for about 100 yards, while there is an additional outworking to the north of the east entrance. These were both probably later additions.

The east gateway, although well defended, opens out onto a platform above the valley, and would have been virtually unapproachable as an entrance. The main entrance was in the west with a level approach, which was the potential weak-spot in the defences. This entrance, as with that in the east, is in-turned, with a shelter provided for guards, but the outer rampart and ditch have been built further away from the inner rampart, to the south, which has a counterscarp bank added. Beyond these, and about 50 feet further out, a third rampart and ditch have been added to extend beyond the line of the entrance through the inner ramparts, thus preventing a head-on approach. The grass has been worn away in places, to reveal part of the inner wall, an unusual sight.

The ramparts are still quite steep, but easy to walk on, while the interior is grass-covered, with a few gorse bushes. It was considered that there were 5 hut circles, or possibly storage pits, to be seen close to the north rampart, but these might also be part of the quarry ditch. Two huts possibly lie at the junction of the outworkings of the east entrance, and the end of the third rampart on the north side. A proper excavation is needed to determine the full history of the site.

That should not detract from your visit though, as you progress from the tranquillity of the farmland, to the semi-wild, exposed hill of the camp. Many of the hills, particularly to the east, are crowned with woods, but as all except Stow Hill, to the south, are lower, they do not obscure the view. From down below in the valley to the east, the sounds of a mixed agricultural region rise, adding to the pastoral scene you look down on. That changes when you look west where the Welsh hills rise to show their mighty remoteness. This would probably be the direction from which the inhabitants would have expected any trouble. Offa's Dyke, built to keep the Welsh out of England 500 years after the hillfort was probably abandoned, has one of its longest continuous sections in those hills, just 1½ miles away.

This is the best preserved of the three hillforts bearing the name Caer Caradoc. Built probably in the middle Iron Age, it may well have been occupied into Roman times, and the defences appear to have been extended on more than one occasion. Of all the hillforts of the Welsh Marches, this is one of the most impressive to see, as so many are now tree-covered. From its towering ramparts, you look down on what appears to be a 'working model', and not the real world. As you leave Caer Caradoc behind, the 'real world' can feel a little less appealing.

Old Oswestry (Also known as Hen Dinas)

Directions. O/S 1:50,000 map 126 ref. 295310. Assuming you have approached Oswestry on the A5 from the south, enter the town centre on the one-way system via the B4579. Head towards Wrexham, and as soon as the one-way system ends turn left up Llwyn Road, which has a signpost 'to the hillfort' opposite. Follow this up the hill into the country, and the small car park is on the left.

This is one of seven hillforts featured by English Heritage in the guide to their sites, and as such is the best documented hillfort, on-site. The notice-boards are well up to the very best English Heritage standards, both in content and interpretation, and that means setting standards which most historical organisations fail to even approach.

That said, Old Oswestry richly deserves such attention, and it is a pity that other hillforts are not provided with similar amenities; that would make this book superfluous to requirements!

You make your approach through the 350 feet long, steep west entrance, which in days gone by was an even more formidable obstacle, with its stone-lined walls from which defenders could hurl missiles down on any attackers. Once you reach the inner rampart, the immense size of the defences, particularly those facing west, are apparent. Old Oswestry stands on a plateau 500 feet high, but is overlooked by all the land to the west, hence the scale of the defences at that side.

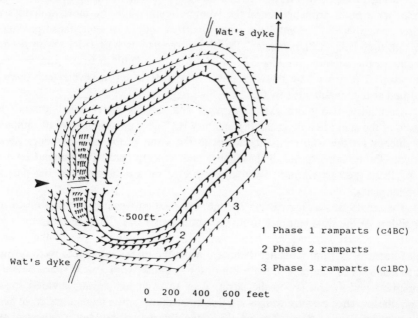

1 Phase 1 ramparts (c4BC)

2 Phase 2 ramparts

3 Phase 3 ramparts (c1BC)

0   200   400   600 feet

We are lucky to be able to see the full scale of the defences. So many hillforts, throughout the country, have their ramparts covered in trees, and many of those would have been selected for inclusion in this book were that not the case. Until the 1940s, Old Oswestry's ramparts were covered in oak trees, and much that I like woods, and in particular oak trees I, for one, am glad that the defences have now been completely cleared. English Heritage have laid out their notice-boards for you to follow round, so I will not duplicate their account of its past, but will add to it.

An idea of the scale of the defences can be gained from a few figures. The enclosed area measures about 15 acres, not a particularly large hillfort when compared to others in the Marches, but the whole area covered by the defences covers 56 acres, making it one of the greatest hillforts anywhere. Indeed, Old Oswestry must have just about the greatest defences as a ratio of the area protected by them, in England. That does not mean, of course, that all the ramparts were manned at any one time, nor that they were all built together.

Evidence of habitation of the site has been found dating back to some time before 500 B.C., although not necessarily to c.1,000 B.C. as the notices state. This was an un-fortified settlement of timber round houses, and had been abandoned for some considerable time before it was re-occupied and fortified. Phase 1 of the fortifications was begun in the fourth century B.C., or possibly earlier. These comprised the inner pair of ramparts and ditches, the inner rampart being stone revetted front and rear, and the outer one is a simple glacis type. It is likely that a timber parapet was added for further protection. There were entrances at the east and west, in their present locations, and both were in-turned and had wooden gates on the inner rampart. Intermittent excavations carried out between the 1930s-50s showed that these people lived in round, stone-built huts, while pottery similar to that in use in Wessex c.350 B.C. was also found.

During Phase 2, two further ramparts, of the box, dry-stone fronted type, and ditches were built, probably round the whole circuit, while the inner rampart was further strengthened. The entrances were modified and given stone-faced passages, although they still had inner gates. The fourth rampart was sacrificed with the re-building of the defences for Phase 3, which brought the hillfort to the plan you can see today. It may well be that this phase was undertaken in several sub-phases, modified as the inhabitants saw fit.

Essentially, two more glacis ramparts and ditches were added around the bottom of the site, possibly in the first century B.C. This gave four lines of ramparts and ditches for the whole circuit, except to the south of the east entrance, where there are three ramparts and ditches, and a counterscarp bank. The rampart ends at the south of the east entrance were all connected by a flanking bank, but not the north ramparts.

That entrance was impressive enough, but seemed weak in comparison to the re-building of the west entrance to its present massive size. To understand the final layout of the west entrance, it is best to study the plan. The outer two ramparts were built further away from the inner defences, while the Phase 2 defences were opened out to make seven ramparts to the south of the entrance, with a wide space between ramparts 3 and 4, and six to the north, with an even longer, sub-divided space. Again, the entrance passage walls were lined with stone, while there might have been three sets of wooden gates. The whole of the entrance re-building seems to have formed part of one plan.

One mystery which surrounds the re-building of the west entrance is the intended use of the wide spaces on either side, the north of which is most obviously sub-divided, and the south one might have been too. There is a certainty about the construction of these, which suggests that they served a function and were not part of some half-finished, or abandoned scheme. It has been suggested that they were for storing water, but have been found not to hold it. Another suggestion has been for the keeping of cattle, but those to the north, at least, do not have entrances. It was also considered that they might have been used for living in, but no huts have been found, and why live in these and not the hillfort? Could they have been for keeping un-invited visitors in, while their 'credentials' were checked? It may well be, of course, that they were an elaborate defensive innovation, an extra hindrance if the outer barricades, or gates were breached.

Round huts, larger than those of the earliest settlement, and one, at least, divided into two rooms, have been found from the last phase, along with pottery, armour, a pavement and a well. The population was estimated to be between 200-

350, which is quite low considering the scale of the defences, but Old Oswestry was probably the administrative, trade and religious centre for the area, and offered defensive shelter for the out-lying farms. It is quite probable that Old Oswestry was at the centre of a complex system of fields and farms, like Quarley Hill* and others, and was thus developed to serve an area, rather than the immediate population.

Most likely, Old Oswestry fell into disuse when the Romans arrived in the area. There is no evidence of a battle, so the inhabitants might have succumbed to the inevitable, having borne witness to events further south, and while little evidence has been found of occupation during Roman times, there is a slight possibility it was the site of Mediolanum. It was thought, by the excavators, that the site might have later been a Dark Age 'squat', but the pottery which suggested this is now thought to have dated from Phase 3, late in the Iron Age.

Rather more fanciful, was the legend that Gogyrfan, the father of Guinevere, later the queen of King Arthur, lived here, and it was known as Caer Ogyrfan into this century. This story remains firmly rooted somewhere between myth and legend though, and is unlikely to have any connection with the hillfort. Wat's Dyke, built in the Dark Ages to separate Wales from England, runs up to the ramparts, and from then on, Old Oswestry has lain silent.

It is often the case that the greater the scale of defences of a hillfort, the less impressive the location, and in certain respects this is true of Old Oswestry. The defences really are exceptional in their scale, even in their grass-covered state today, while long views are to be had over the low ground to the east. The opposite is true to the whole of the west side, where the hills rise, slowly at first, to a dominating level within two miles. This does not necessarily detract from the site, but what does is the ever-present roar from the traffic on the A5 Oswestry by-pass, particularly evident at the east side.

There is no need to finish this account on a downbeat note though, as the defences rank comparison with the very best of those from the Iron Age. Whenever I come to evaluate the remains of any Iron Age hillfort, one question is always borne in mind: how many of our modern day structures will survive to such a standard over 2,000 odd years? Not many, I daresay. On what is good flat land, with huge quantities of gravel, it was probably the oak woods which assisted in the survival of Old Oswestry for us today. So trees which hide Iron Age defences are not always to be cursed.

Cow Castle

Directions. O/S 1:50,000 map 180 ref. 794374. Take the A39 from Bridgewater towards Minehead, and turn left onto the A396 at Dunster. Turn right on the B3224, through Exford, and turn right on the B3223 to Simonsbath. Turn left in the village and follow the minor road for 1.5 miles before turning left on the 'no through road' signposted to Wintershead and Horsen; both are farms. This road divides just before Horsen Farm, where a signpost points to the hillfort; park here. Follow the track for one and a quarter miles through three five-bar gates, cross the River Barle by two foot-bridges, and head north. Cow Castle is the second hill on the east bank, and is easily seen from the bridges. By following this path north, you will reach Simonsbath, about two and a quarter miles away.

Depending on your sources of information, a visit to this hillfort could be considered a compete waste of time. The Arthur Mee book on Somerset says '. . . nowhere is the landscape below Simonsbath anything but monotonous . . . No form of beauty that thrills the heart at the mention of Exmoor is inspired by any scene within five miles of Simonsbath; it is the humdrum spot of this impressive world . . .' Not a particularly auspicious start.

On the other hand, James Dyer describes Cow Castle as, ' . . . one of the most beautifully situated hillforts in southern England . . . ' Can these two authors be talking about the same area, and if so who are we to believe? Taking the maxim 'seeing is believing' to be the correct course, I heartily agree with Dyer, an archaeologist with a considerable reputation. Exmoor does not have too many hillforts within its boundaries, and none are of any great size. Cow Castle is neither the biggest, at 2.5 acres, nor the strongest defended, but is a good example of the small hillforts/camps of Exmoor.

Should you have approached Cow Castle by the route given in the directions, the track from the minor road to the River Barle forms part of the Two Moors Way long distance path. The path follows a tributary of the River Barle for the last half-mile of its descent, and from the confluence, Cow Castle comes into view. A single rampart, without a ditch rests below the conical summit, rather like a coronet; simple defences maybe, but sufficient considering the sparse population, and the steepness of the approach.

There is a simple straight-through entrance in the south, on the left of which stands a small stone which is thought to have been part of the door-jamb. The interior is quite steeply sloped and covered in grass, but there are no signs of any hut platforms, although there has not been a recent excavation of the site. Follow the rampart to the west. It was revetted by a dry-stone wall, but that is now completely overgrown. The lack of an external ditch is unusual, but a ditch can be traced inside the rampart, in several places. It may well be that what huts did exist were sited in this quarry-ditch, as at other hillforts.

Water was close at hand, the river valley winding its way quite sharply in both directions. In common with many hillforts built around a steep sided hill, the rampart is not particularly large at any point, as a rise of about four feet on the inside presents a considerable obstacle when faced from the exterior. Although a date for building is not known, the occupants certainly knew a thing or two about hillforts, as the side with the easiest approach, the east, not only has the main entrance, but this has been given a second bank on either side of the gateway. It is at this point that the defences are at their most impressive, and the entrance arrangement would probably suggest a middle Iron Age building date; nothing elaborate, but a cut above a basic straight-through entrance.

Who lived here, or why it was built can only be guessed at, but the occupants also knew something about siting strategy. Apart from its accessibility to water, this hillfort commands two valleys, and while it does not dominate nearby hills, even when standing at about 1,100 feet high, its simple isolation allowed for economy of building effort. Today, it is the peaceful splendour of its location that is so attractive. It is evidence that Iron Age man gave considerable thought to his fortifications, and the effort required to build them; I can only agree with the words of Arthur Mee, if not the meaning he intended, that the location is indeed, ' . . . anything but monotonous . . . '

Dolebury Camp

Directions. O/S 1:50,000 map 182 ref. 450590. Leave Bristol heading south on the A38. After crossing the A368 at Churchill, turn left and park at the 'no through road' Dolberrow. Walk up the private road, up the hill and at the summit a path leads through a five-bar gate, on the left, with a National Trust sign. Follow the track, and a path leads to the hillfort from the left, at the top of the hill.

Fortunately, the main rampart, ditch and counterscarp bank of this 18 acre hillfort have been cleared of scrub and trees that were beginning to take-over, and obscure them from view. The defences are thus cleared, but trees in the interior, especially to the north, prevent one fully appreciating the graceful sweep of the rampart as it makes its way up the hill from the west.

The stone-built rampart, now mostly grass-covered, but with considerable sections of the collapsed wall revealed along the north and west, still rises to a lofty height. The accompanying ditch and counterscarp bank are also both of a good size, on all sides except the south. Dolebury is a rectangular shaped semi-contour hillfort, rising to nearly 600 feet high, but with an east-west interior slope of about 150 feet. It commands the north-west of the Mendip Hills and perhaps more significantly, the gap the A38 takes between the hills. As it is possible that much of Somerset was subject to tidal incursions in the Iron Age, and even later, this route would have been of considerable strategic importance.

You will make your approach through the steep climb to the well defended west entrance. The size of the rampart is very apparent from this angle, the one seen by anybody thinking of attacking the hillfort. Woods cover the west and north sides below the counterscarp bank, thus hiding the additional strength afforded by the long, steep approach from these sides. Nature has provided even greater protection on the south side, and the counterscarp bank is not so pronounced as elsewhere. From this side you look over to the main mass of the Mendips, while as the rampart makes its way up the hill to the east, the Bristol Channel comes into view.

The interior has not been cleared like the defences, and although not overgrown, a number of long, low north-south mounds within the hillfort can be made out, but they are difficult to examine. The use of these is a matter for conjecture; possibly they were mediaeval rabbit warrens, or perhaps even the site of Iron Age, or Roman wooden buildings. When you reach the summit at the east side, the counterscarp bank takes on an altogether sturdier dimension against the easiest approach.

A possible entrance may exist in the north-east corner, and the gaps in the two banks form a passage, not in-turned, of about 100 feet long. About 100 yards beyond is what remains of a probable cross-bank and ditch, with a gap in the middle. This might have run right across the summit to give additional protection to the east side, but as the north-east of the hillfort has been damaged by lead mining, it is also possible that the north-east entrance is not original.

From this point, along the north rampart and round to the west entrance, the defences are seen at their best. Long sections of the stone rampart are exposed on the inside, and although these are tumbled they make a welcome change from the normal, grass covered-ramparts. Almost due north, the tree-clothed Cadbury Congresbury hillfort (Somerset) looks down on Yatton, but the hills to the east of this hide Bristol from view. As compensation, you can see over the mouth of the River Severn to South Wales, but as you descend westwards down the rampart, this is hidden from view.

Without a doubt, despite its attractive location, it is the defences which are the main attraction of Dolebury Camp. A modern excavation is certainly needed to elicit its past, and to cast further light on what is one of the largest hillforts in Somerset, and must have been of considerable importance in the Mendip region. In the meantime, we can be thankful that the defences are now cleared and can be seen.

South Cadbury Castle

Directions. O/S 1:50,000 map 183 ref. 629253. Head west on the A303 past Mere and Wincanton. Turn left at the turning for South and North Cadbury and turn immediately left again. Turn right at the junction 300 yards away, and continue into South Cadbury, past the church. There is a lay-by on the left at the south of the village, just past Castle Lane. Walk up this lane to the hillfort.

This fine outstanding hill, which rises to 500 feet, has been home to man for a period which spans almost 4,500 years. The Iron Age settlements were the longest established, by far, but might not have been the foremost in the long history of this hill. It is known as South Cadbury Castle to distinguish it from a number of other 'Cadbury' hillforts, two of which are also in Somerset, but will be referred to as

Cadbury Castle from now on.

Cadbury's distinguished past really came to light following excavations organised by Professor Leslie Alcock, between 1966-70, for the Camelot Research Committee. Of the several publications that have emanated from these, Alcock's own *By South Cadbury is that Camelot* is well worth seeking out, not just for the hillfort's past, but also as an insight into how a 'dig' can progress. It was the policy of the excavators to concentrate on the interior, as opposed to the defences which are the usual target with hillforts. Thus, considerable parts of the summit plateau and the north-east slope were excavated, in what was a major undertaking. Even so, only about 6% of the total enclosed area of 18 acres was excavated which, more than anything, puts the limitations of excavation results into perspective. Unfortunately, as with all excavated hillforts, what has been uncovered, whether defence structures like the stone-facing of ramparts, or the post-holes or footings of any buildings, can no longer be seen by the visitor.

The first occupation of the site stems from the Neolithic Age, about 3,300 B.C. This was an un-defended settlement on the summit plateau, and pottery, pits and a ditch were found from this period. The length of time this settlement lasted, given the nomadic nature of peoples from these earlier times, is unknown. Once abandoned though, no evidence was found of any subsequent occupation, until about 1,000 B.C., if not later.

From that time, until the Pax Romana, Cadbury was possibly continuously occupied, there being a succession of modifications undertaken to the defences. Like that of the Neolithic Age, the late Bronze Age/early Iron Age community lived on the summit plateau, and did not appear to have any physical defences, although a timber stockade might have existed. There was plenty of evidence in pottery finds to suggest that this community was well established, and the first defences were begun about 500 B.C. These followed the line of the present inner rampart, and comprised a seven feet wide timber box-rampart, with a ditch outside, although not on the scale of the present ditch. It was from such modest beginnings that the mighty defences you can see today grew.

Thereafter, during the Iron Age, the defences were successively refurbished on five or six occasions, in some cases showing considerable signs of neglect. There was only one occasion when the hillfort might have been abandoned, while each refurbishment seems to have been associated with an influx of new, continental ideas. Again, whether this was through invasion or trade remains a mystery, but was probably the latter.

These first defences were replaced c.400 B.C. by a massive rubble rampart with stone-facing, and rock-cut ditch, which followed the line of the earlier defences, but were on an altogether larger scale. The following two hundred years saw the defences successively strengthened, until they reached the extent visible today. Three further glacis ramparts, two with deep rock-cut ditches, surround the inner defences, with entrances in the south-west and north-east. Even today, over 2,000 years later, they still rise over 170 feet up the hill, and are up to 400 feet wide. Without a doubt, these would have been some of the most formidable defences of any hillfort, anywhere.

As one might expect, Cadbury had developed from being a small settlement into something approaching a town; yet less than ten miles to the west, one of the biggest hillforts in England, the 200 acre Ham Hill (Somerset), was also in existence. The excavators found several rectangular and circular huts of various sizes, many of which had been rebuilt on several occasions. In addition, slight traces were found of many other huts, all of which point to a sizeable population. Cadbury also undertook its own manufacturing as well, as iron and bronze working premises were also found, while a hoard of 100 brooches was uncovered at an earlier time.

To all intent and purposes, it seems that Cadbury was something of a bustling trading centre, in receipt of new ideas and producing its own manufactured wares and, most of all, well established. The excavators found that by c.0 .A.D. the defences had been refurbished yet again; the south-west entrance was rebuilt, having become turf-covered, and thus seemingly abandoned. In addition, no buildings were found which could definitely be ascribed to this period, but there was a temple on the summit of the hill, with a processional way leading up to it, and a considerable number of animal bones, probably for sacrifice, and weapons deposited along the way. The hillfort might have thus been virtually abandoned as a 'town', and served as a religious shrine and centre. This did not last, for at about the time of the refurbishment of the defences, wheel-thrown pottery seems to have been introduced.

Prior to the arrival of Vespasian and the Roman II legion, c.43 A.D., the population seems to have been fairly high, and the defences refurbished again. This was a similar scenario to many other Durotriges hillforts, like Hod Hill* and Maiden Castle*, and the excavators found evidence of a massacre of about thirty people, including women and children, at the south-west gate. However, this was not thought to have occurred in Vespasian's time, but following Boudicca's revolt, c.60 A.D., of which the Durotriges people were at least passively supportive. Once that revolt was finally put down, Suetonius led the II and IX legions against all the tribes that supported the revolt, or were at least neutral. The fate of the Cadbury Castle inhabitants was not pleasant. The aforementioned corpses were left where they fell, with nobody to bury them, and subsequently became a 'larder' for wild animals who mauled the remains.

It seems that the remains were covered where they lay, about ten years later, when the Romans arrived and erected temporary accommodation within the hillfort, while they dismantled the defences. Cadbury Castle was not the home of a large settlement for several centuries thereafter. However, many coins dating from the third and fourth centuries A.D. were found and there is a possibility that the site served as a Romano-Celtic temple, rather than a settlement.

For most hillforts, the Roman period saw their last period of use, and they remained abandoned from that time on. That was not the case for Cadbury Castle, and on two further occasions the hillfort was re-fortified. The first began at some time after c.450 A.D., and lasted for at least a couple of generations. The inner rampart was rebuilt using copious amounts of timber framing surrounding a large bank, which included the stone from some of the ruined buildings, and had a stone revetting. A new south-west gateway was built, and the track metalled. Although the excavators only found one building from this phase, it was a 60 x 35 feet rectangular hall, and much pottery, including some from the East Mediterranean and South-West France, was found. By the scale of known settlements of the early Dark Ages, this was indeed a major site, certainly the equivalent of a town.

The evidence for this settlement, which only surfaced through Alcock's work, gives credence to the statement by John Leland, in 1542, that Cadbury Castle was the site of King Arthur's Camelot. Forget about Victorian pictures of a stone-built, many towered castle, similarly portrayed by Hollywood; Camelot, if it existed at all, would not have had mightier defences than that of the Iron Age hillfort, but in the context of the Dark Ages, they would have been a rarity, and not a better-than-average version of the norm. It would be best to say that Cadbury Castle could have been the headquarters of an Arthurian type of warrior-leader, of more than immediate local importance. That person was certainly not a king of England, and while Arthur and Camelot are the stuff of legends, the Dark Age fortified settlement on Cadbury Castle was real enough, if only for a relatively short time.

Cadbury Castle was not finished though, and like Muhammed Ali, it had yet another comeback in the offing. This did not take place until the reign of Ethelred the Unready, 978-1016, when Cadbury was created a Saxon burh, had a 20 feet thick earth rampart, with 4 feet of stone revetting, and had a mint which produced silver coins between 1009-1020. This might overstate the importance of Cadbury Castle at that time, as this was the period the 'Unready' was prepared to buy off the Danish attacks with the infamous 'danegeld'. Each Saxon burh thus had its own mint, and Cadbury was only one of a great many. Cadbury was destroyed about 1020 A.D., possibly on the orders of King Cnut.

Still it was not finished though, and during the reign of King John, 1199-1216, a sum of treasury money was spent at the site. Some pottery has been found to date from this period, along with a foundation trench, but a dry-stone wall near the rampart, possibly to herd animals, is the only other remnant from this period.

It is apt that, for a hillfort with such a distinguished past, it should enjoy a prominent present. Cadbury Castle's fortifications remain formidable to this day, even though all except the inner defences have a light, but accessible, covering of trees. You will approach through the north-east entrance, and this isolated hill offers an outstanding prospect in all directions. Glastonbury Tor can be seen to the north, while the hill on which stands the massive hillfort of Ham Hill, can be seen to the south-west. Indeed, the view over the Somerset Levels can be considerable on a clear day, as although the hills to the south and east rise even higher than Cadbury Castle, the land falls away very quickly to the west.

Whether or not Cadbury Castle is the site for the legendary Camelot, should not spoil your visit. Few hillforts of such modest size have defences on anything like this scale. The trim, grass-covered interior does not reveal any really distinguishing marks, although the summit is of interest, but any disappointment in this department is easily out-weighed by the location and defences. On the other hand, you could be visiting one of the most fabled sites in history, the only contender for the title of Camelot that can provide definite proof of a substantial occupation from the days of 'King Arthur'.

Castle Ring

Directions. O/S 1:50,000 map 128 ref. 045128. The hillfort is at the south of Cannock Chase. Leave Lichfield heading west on the A461, and turn right on the A5190. In Burntwood, turn right opposite the B5011 and continue for two miles along the straight road. Go straight on at the cross-roads, turn next left, and the car park is at the bend in this road, just to the south of the hillfort.

Despite being situated at the north end of the great West Midlands urban sprawl, and being virtually surrounded by trees, which do not obscure the wide ranging views, Castle Ring has much to commend it. Not least is the nearby pub, while its defences are both large-scale and easily seen, while for those who wish for a bit more excitement, the Hednesford stock-car stadium is only a couple of miles away, to the west.

Castle Ring rests on a promontory, with a relatively level approach from the east. It is a five sided hillfort, with an entrance in the north-east; you will approach from the south, and there is a possibility that the gap in the defences along the south-west side, might also be original. Although the hillfort has not been excavated, one look at the defences will show you that this must have been of some considerable importance.

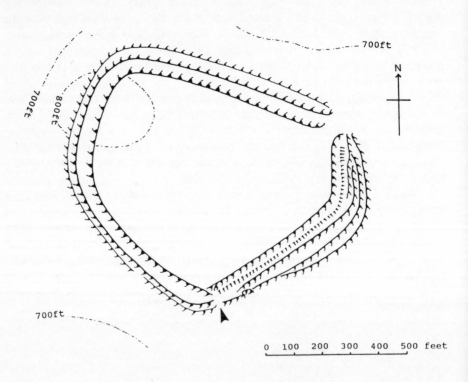

Double ramparts and ditches enclose 8.5 acres of almost level ground, but these follow an unusual format, and are increased in strength on the vulnerable east and south-east sides. An inner rampart and ditch encircles the interior, followed by a berm of up to 30 feet, and then a ditch and an outer rampart, on the north, west and south-west sides. The berm appears to be a second rampart, its height accentuated by the two ditches, and is best seen at the north and south-west sides, the outer defences being well worn at the west.

These defensive arrangements are impressive enough, but at the south-east and east sides they are widened out, and are considerably strengthened. At its greatest extent, at the east corner, the defences comprise an inner rampart, ditch, counterscarp bank (an addition), berm ditch and second rampart, almost on the same scale as the rest of the fort. Then follows a second berm and finally, a conventional rampart and ditch, the whole covering about 190 feet. Fortunately, the trees do not encroach on this.

The entrance is now well worn, but it must have been an impressive sight with all the ramparts curving round to channel visitors into the entrance passage. The sequence of building of the hillfort is not known, but as it stands today, it looks distinctly late Iron Age. It could just as easily have been an earlier univallate hillfort, with the outer defences built at a later date, for it would have been extremely well planned and thought out to have been built in its present format, although not unique in this respect.

Without a doubt, its site was carefully selected for both strategic purposes, and ease of defence. From its maximum height of 671 feet, an outstanding vista across the heart of England, in all directions, can be enjoyed. This, as much as anything, was probably the reason for its siting. These days, it is only pollution, the weather and the horizon which restricts the views, while the former probably did not enter the Iron Age equation. It may have been something of a border post for the Cornovii tribe, whose territory spread north to Cheshire, and west to Shropshire. Unlike the tribes to the south, the Cornovii were not influenced by the Belgic peoples, for good or ill and, until the arrival of the Romans under Ostorius Scapula in 48 A.D., had probably changed but slowly.

Castle Ring is a popular hillfort, as shown by the well-worn ramparts, though one wonders just how many visitors know of its past. It is within easy reach of the West Midlands, and one can see right over much of its built up area, while The Potteries can be seen to the north. Perhaps of more interest though, is the view across Lichfield and the Trent valley to the east, or the out-standing hill, The Wrekin, and much pleasant countryside to the west. Being located on the edge of Cannock Chase, it is ideal for outdoor recreation, with many walks in the vicinity. Its past might be obscure, but its present is well suited to the age of motorised leisure.

Directions. O/S 1:50,000 map 198 ref. 139120. Follow the A24 north from Worthing to Washington. Turn right on the A283 towards Steyning. After one third of a mile there is a track to Lock's Farm on the right, at a left-hand bend. Walk up the track until a Public Footpath sign directs you left, just before the farm. A Public Footpath sign directs you to the right, and follow this path past a Public Footpath 'crossroads' sign. Turn left at the next Public Footpath sign, just inside the woods, and follow the path upwards, out of the woods. The hillfort is the clump of Beech trees at the top of the hill. This is a steep climb, very slippery in wet weather. The nearest station is at Worthing, approximately five miles walk, via Cissbury Ring, which is two and a half miles to the south.

This small hillfort, with its univallate, glacis rampart enclosing 3.5 acres would not have had anything other than local significance in the Iron Age. Indeed, just two and a half miles to the south lies the mighty Cissbury Ring, which would surely have over-shadowed its little neighbour, as it did the whole of the downland between the Rivers Arun and Adur. Yet today, this small, inconsequential hillfort is one of the best. It is not through being a hillfort however, that Chanctonbury Ring found such widespread fame.

Chanctonbury, as you will find out, occupies a ridge-top position, nearly 800 feet high. The ridge-top itself is protected by a cross-dyke to the west, which you will pass on the way up, and a much longer one to the east of the summit plateau. If you continue to Cissbury Ring, you will pass the latter en route. It is likely that these cross-dykes formed a cattle enclosure for both domestic and defensive purposes. The hillfort was built about 300-B.C., probably a little after the cross-dykes. Nothing of its Iron Age history is known, but it probably fell into disuse well before the arrival of the Romans in 43 A.D., along with Cissbury Ring*.

Seventeen hundred and seventeen years after the Roman invasion, Chanctonbury underwent a metamorphosis greater than at any other time in its history. As you stand at the northern end of the rampart there, down to your right, is the initially, mediaeval Wiston House. In 1760 the young Charles Goring, son of the owner, planted the mass of Beech trees that now cover the hillfort. So it is rumoured, each day throughout his life Goring climbed this hill to tend his beloved trees, and he lived to see them become the renowned landmark they remain to this day. Given clear weather, the Beech trees of Chanctonbury Ring form an outstanding landmark from many places within a thirty mile radius, including the English Channel.

It is the trees' proximity to the latter, and their standing in the unprotected path of the prevailing south-westerly winds, that makes saplings difficult to grow. The two great storms of the late 1980s took a terrible toll, and parts of the fort are currently denuded of trees.

The Beech trees grew to a strong healthy size, yet a few in the interior remained strangely stunted, despite considerable attention. Eventually, excavations were carried out in 1908, and a Romano-Celtic temple, and associated pear shaped building, were discovered; the stunted tree roots had been unable to pierce the foundations. As with its Iron Age secrets, Chanctonbury Ring is not prepared to reveal its role in Roman Britain, although the temple is perhaps dedicated to a local Celtic deity. The name Chanctonbury is of Saxon origin, so it may be that the hillfort, and especially the enclosed plateau, found some use during the post-Roman period.

Yet, there is more. A small dew pond lies beside the hillfort on the west side, which was restored in 1970. To the east a much larger dew pond, which regularly featured in pictures of the hillfort and trees, was constructed in 1874. Regrettably, this was lost through military training in World War II.

The hillfort is oval in plan, with an entrance in the south-west, where the ditch is best seen. The rampart is relatively low, perhaps as a measure of its lowly status, as an outpost of Cissbury Ring. The interior is now surrounded by a wire fence, to protect the new trees, but an entrance can be gained at this point, over a stile. You will probably be disappointed had you hoped to see the remains of the temple as at Maiden Castle, as this has been, once again, covered over.

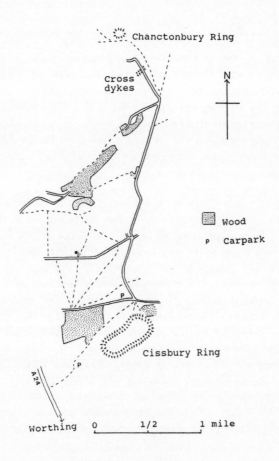

In one other respect this small hillfort, with the big reputation, remains unique. Legend has it that if you run three times round the ramparts on a moonlit night, the Devil will appear and offer you some porridge from his bowl. One has to say though, that having made the stiff climb to the hillfort you would have to be pretty fit to run around it to pass the Devil's test.

Certain hillforts are undoubtedly best visited on a relatively clear day; Chanctonbury Ring certainly falls into this category. A copy of the relevant O/S map is essential so as to identify all you can see from the rampart edge. This map will also guide you to the eastern cross-dyke and, should you wish, to the trackway to Cissbury Ring, and a circular route back. Such a walk, assuming you set out from Washington, would take in about eight miles, and last up to five hours, leaving time to appreciate both hillforts. Go prepared, and pick the right weather, for what will be a memorable trek across the South Downs.

OTHER ANCIENT SITES
Blackpatch Flint Mines. O/S Map 197 Ref. 094089.
Harrow Hill Flint mines and Enclosure. O/S Map 197 Ref. 081100.

Cissbury Ring

> **Directions.** O/S map 198 ref. 140080. Cissbury Ring lies to the north of Worthing. From here, take the A24 north, and turn right into Findon village. In a quarter of a mile, a narrow road heads east up to the hillfort, where there is a small National Trust parking area. Cissbury can also be reached from Chanctonbury Ring*, or you can walk over the downs up the trackway by the car park, heading north, to Chanctonbury. An alternative route is via the Park Brow Bronze Age/Iron Age settlement, by continuing east, and turning north onto a Public Footpath after three quarters of a mile.

There is little doubt that Cissbury Ring overshadowed the other hillforts and settlements on the downland between the Rivers Arun and Adur, during the Iron Age. With the defences enclosing 62 acres, and occupying a further 18 acres themselves, Cissbury is one of the very largest of all hillforts, and by far the biggest on the South Downs. Although it does not physically dominate the downs, in the manner Herefordshire Beacon* dominates the Welsh Marches, there is virtually no part of the land between the two aforementioned rivers that cannot be seen from Cissbury, or from where Cissbury cannot be seen. On a clear day, the coastal view stretches from Beach Head to the Isle of Wight; few hillforts have such an all-seeing, and thus all-powerful, location.

Cissbury, along with Chanctonbury Ring*, was created by the Devil as he built the Devil's Dyke* during his tussle and wager with St Dunstan. Well, that is how the legend runs, but archaeology has ruined all such stories, except for the few people with fertile, gullible imaginations, and has provided a set of reasonably accurate dates and a general picture of the society in which it existed. It was built c.250 B.C.

and was not developed to any great extent thereafter. Its defences are about a mile long and are of a considerable size. The glacis rampart rises to over 10 feet in height, and was revetted at the front with close-set wooden posts, which also served as a parapet. It has been estimated that 60,000 tons of chalk were needed for the rampart. The ditch was flat bottomed, and 25 feet wide at ground level, with a smaller counterscarp bank beyond; the whole measuring over 80 feet across. There are entrances at the east and south, although neither are of particularly great strength.

Despite its size, Cissbury appears to have led a comparatively peaceful existence, there being no evidence of any local skirmishes. It has been suggested that, given the amount of work required for its building, and the area enclosed, it might have had a population of some 1,400. If so, there is none of the usual evidence, like storage and rubbish pits, huts and so on, for anything like that number. Yet surely a hillfort of this size was not just built either as a temporary refuge, or as a personal camp for the local chief?

Along the north facing escarpment of the South Downs there is quite a number of Bronze Age burial mounds. The Park Brow celtic fields and Bronze Age/Iron Age settlement can be clearly seen from the rampart, a mile to the north-east, while Chanctonbury hillfort is marked by the clump of Beech trees to the north. There is further evidence of Iron Age settlements/farming at Steep Hill, two miles due east, near Well, two miles north-west and immediately below the south rampart. Yet Cissbury Ring shows little evidence of permanent use.

Going back to c.3,500 B.C., there is plenty of evidence of the importance of the site. Outside the defences near the south entrance, and in particular in the interior at the western end, are about 200 depressions. These are not the sites of hut circles, but one of the greatest concentrations of Neolithic flint mines in England. Certain shafts have been excavated, and apart from a couple of bodies, one of whom was thought to have fallen down accidentally, and a number of bone tools associated with flint mining, some shafts were found to be over 20 feet deep, and one, over 40 feet deep, which passed through six layers of flint. Many of those excavated shafts had galleries radiating from them. There is no evidence that the site was occupied once the mining ceased, yet the depressions can easily be seen today, let alone 2,000 years ago, but still the hillfort enclosed many of these, with no apparent attempt to re-use the land.

If much of the above is mystifying, there are at least plausible explanations for some of this intrigue. Cissbury may well have been occupied, or at least maintained to a degree of defensibility, until c.50 B.C. The area was then under the Regni tribe who were friendly towards the Romans, obviating the need to maintain defences against them. That the area was also peaceful, with regard to inter-tribal warfare, is shown by the continued occupation of the nearby settlement at Park Brow for a period of about 1,000 years.

When the Romans returned in 43 A.D., the Regni and neighbouring Atrebates were still friendly, and thus no fighting within their area seems to have taken place. Indeed, a degree of Roman gentility was possibly established, and an enlarged area, probably enclosing Sussex, parts of Surrey and east Hampshire, fell under the nominal rule of Cogidubnus, of the Atrebates, who may well have lived at Fishbourne Palace. Certainly during the Pax Romana, much of the interior was ploughed in small fields, which probably destroyed evidence of any earlier Iron Age permanent settlement. So, Cissbury's defences fell into disuse. Indeed, a hoard of smooth pebbles, probably for use as sling-shot, has been the only weaponry evidence uncovered.

At a later date though, the defences were hastily re-fortified with turf, while the counterscarp bank was removed at the entrances to facilitate their rebuilding. It may be that this was the Romano-Britons trying to fend off the invading Saxons, although there is no sign of a battle. The Park Brow settlement was destroyed by fire c.300 B.C., presumed accidental, and the site abandoned, so there are no clues to events from that quarter either.

There are, to us, many mystifying aspects to Iron Age society. That such a major hillfort as Cissbury should ever be built, and yet reveal little evidence of use, let alone a need for such a defensive site, is puzzling. What events, or fears, made such a massive undertaking essential is unknown today, but surely it was for more practical reasons than some great 'showcase' project. Perhaps it was the Milton Keynes of the Iron Age after all.

Devil's Dyke

Directions. O/S 1:50,000 map 198 ref. 260110. Leave Brighton centre heading north-west to Preston Park. After crossing the A27, the road leads straight up the South Downs to the Devil's Dyke, which is signposted, with a car park in the hillfort itself.

At the turn of the century, Devil's Dyke rivalled Box Hill in popularity, being one of Britain's favourite Sunday picnic spots, and was certainly the most visited hillfort. What other hillfort could boast its own railway station, with a branch running up from the main line, a cable railway and a funicular railway from a nearby village? In addition, there were other amusements which the crowds flocked to in the summer months, quite apart from the spectacular views. All except the latter have long since gone, but Devil's Dyke remains very popular, although most people arrive by motor car.

Still, there are not many hillforts that have an hotel-cum-pub-cum-restaurant within, and although a few can boast of a legend, not many have two, or at least two versions of the same one. After his dust-up with St Dunstan (*see* Cissbury Ring*), the Devil decided there were still too many churches in the Weald, so began to gouge out a channel to the coast to flood them. You could almost feel sorry for him as, having come off second best to St Dunstan in the first version, he loses out to an old woman this time around. Apparently, the Devil made so much noise digging his channel that he woke the lady up in the middle of the night. Realising what was going on, she lit a candle and put it to a window behind a sieve. This had the effect of diffusing the light rays and, being a creature of the night, the Devil was hoodwinked into thinking that the sun was about to rise, and left.

All great fairy tale stuff, of course, but as the Devil's Dyke hillfort has not been properly excavated the true version is not known. For a start, there is doubt over what is the dyke; is it the coomb on the south-east side of the hillfort, or is it the rampart cutting off the promontory of the south end, as for a dyke in Holland? As far as this book is concerned, Devil's Dyke is the hillfort itself.

The road breeches the south-west defences, where they are at their strongest; the only side with a relatively level approach. The single rampart rises to a considerable height, and has a ditch and counterscarp bank. This is the basic defensive arrangement for most of the circumference, common among the hillforts of the South Downs. An original entrance is at the eastern corner of the south-west defences, while the south-east defences comprise two ramparts and a ditch for much of their length. There is another gap in the rampart near the east corner of the south-east rampart, at a very oblique angle, which leads into the comb, and where the ditch might not have been finished. It is not known if this is original.

Devil's Dyke is a promontory hillfort of 40 acres, which rises up to 711 feet. It was probably used intermittently in the middle Iron Age with the main farming settlement being outside although, as with many hillforts, one wonders why so much effort was made to build defences of a considerable size, if the enclosed area was not to be permanently lived in. One circular hut, measuring 25 feet across, has been discovered near the pub, while there is evidence of a much larger settlement on the golf course outside. A late Iron Age, Belgic settlement has also been found either side of the south-west rampart, while Roman coins from the Claudian era have been found inside the fort.

There is nothing of the Iron Age left to see in the interior, and the south-west rampart has been partially damaged by military use during the war. Once on the north-west rampart, it becomes clear that the original inhabitants decided to save as much labour as possible by utilising the natural slopes. The rampart is made from the spoil cut out of the hillside and thrown downwards, and is of no great strength. The same could be said for most of the defences around the three steep sides, with the exception of some additional strengthening near the entrance.

A walk round the defences will reveal more than just the great size of the hillfort, for there are outstanding views to be had in all directions. To the west, one can see right along the north escarpment of the South Downs, including the clump of Beech trees at Chanctonbury Ring*. From the north-west side, many hang-gliders and para-gliders take off and use the uplift gained from the ridge for a good flight; they land in a field near Fulking, just below.

It seems as though there is no restriction in the view across the Weald to the north. The view defies description, except to say that it is vast. Over to the east you peer down on other hills, while to the south, especially from the south-west rampart, can be seen Brighton, the sea and much more.

Interestingly, the hillforts of the South Downs appear to be grouped in little clusters, separated by one of the north-south running rivers. Each of these clusters has one large, presumably most important, hillfort, and Devil's Dyke holds that position for the area between the Rivers Adur and Ouse. It is not known whether this arrangement was deliberate, or not, in terms of dividing up the territory, but given that Iron Age peoples were more than capable of quite intricate landscape planning, probably so. However, the lack of any sign of battles, the relatively unsophisticated

207

defences of the South Downs hillforts and the general evidence of abandonment before the arrival of the Romans, suggests the region was both peaceful and probably united under one tribe, at least during the late Iron Age.

If the above is correct, then Devil's Dyke can be seen to have held a prominent position within its territory. I am sure that, after a visit, you will concur with me that this was very likely given its size, defensibility and outstanding location.

OTHER ANCIENT SITES

Thundersbarrow Hill Hillfort. Map 198 ref. 229084.
Wolstonbury Hillfort. Map 198 ref. 284138.
Hollingbury Hillfort. Map 198. 322087.

The Trundle

Directions. O/S map 197 ref. 877110. Leave Chichester heading east on the A27, and at Westhampnett turn left up the minor road towards Goodwood. Continue past the main entrance to the horse racing course, and there is a car park just beyond the turning to Charlton, on the right hand side of the road. Cross the road, and there is a footpath heading due south up St Roche's Hill.

'Buy this book and see the races at Glorious Goodwood for FREE.' How about that for an advertising slogan for this book? No, I was not trying to 'do a Hoover' (with their aeroplane tickets incident) and bankrupt myself, but as with all such gimmicks there is a catch. The Trundle overlooks the neighbouring Goodwood race course and grandstands. You would not exactly be rubbing shoulders with the Queen Mother, but would enjoy a panoramic view of the whole course. If business and pleasure can be mixed, why not further enhance the latter side of the equation?

It is not surprising that a hill which rises to 676 feet above the nearby sea, and has extensive views in all directions, should have been of use to man for a considerable period of time. The tall masts of the radio signal station, within the hillfort, is the most easily recognisable feature from the road, and indicate its current use; while the grass covered interior shows signs of the windmill that burnt down in 1773, and the small mediaeval church dedicated to St Roche, after whom the hill on which the hillfort stands was named.

Of course, the 2,000 year-old hillfort which we are here to see pre-dates all of the above, and has been a well known feature of this highly visible hill for most of the intervening period. However, there is further evidence of man's habitation on the site that pre-dates the Iron Age hillfort by a further 2,500 years, yet did not come to light until 1925, when the R.A.F. took some aerial photographs. The 12.5 acre Iron Age camp sits on top of a Neolithic causewayed camp which dates back to about 3,000 B.C.

It is neither a particularly long, nor steep, walk to the north-east entrance of the hillfort. This is the only part of the hillfort, as opposed to the causewayed camp, that has been excavated, and showed how the hillfort had evolved.

The Trundle has often been described as an octagonal-shaped hillfort, but I prefer to think of it as an irregular, circular-shaped contour fort. Having a single rampart and ditch, with counterscarp bank, it is similar to most hillforts on the South Downs but, more unusually, has two opposing entrances. It was constructed about 300 B.C. and ended life as a tribal stronghold. As with other hillforts built on top of a Neolithic causewayed camp, like Maiden Castle*, there was no continuation of settlement, and probably no pre-knowledge of the existence of the earlier camp.

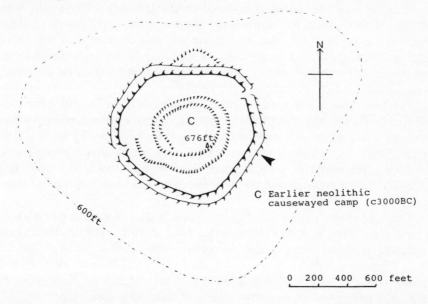

C Earlier neolithic
causewayed camp (c3000BC)

0   200   400   600 feet

The grass covered, chalk rampart is complete in its circuit and has suffered little damage, despite the radio masts. It probably had wooden revetments and would have been quite a formidable fortification in its day. As we know only too well, time does not stand still, and the defences were modified on several occasions. The north-east gateway has provided evidence of such developments, with a pair of gates closing onto a central post, the entrance passage being narrowed later, and a second pair of gates being added at the inner end. Finally, c.50 B.C., a further set of modifications were begun, which included the cutting of deep holes, possibly to carry an over-bridge, but these were never completed. Slingers platforms were also built, and a hoard of sling-stones was found.

The Belgic Atrebates and Regni peoples were spreading eastwards in Britain and their arrival in the vicinity probably caused the abandonment of the hillfort, although whether any battle was fought is not known. Unlike the earlier Celtic peoples, the Atrebates were not a hilltop race; heralding from Flanders that was not surprising, and the settlement was moved to the low ground in the south. It is likely that one of the major oppida of the Atrebates was in this area, protected by the linear earthworks now known as the Chichester Dykes. That does not mean that Chichester is the site of these, as the land has changed considerably, not least in the face of coastal erosion at Selsey.

Pending a full-scale excavation, it seems that the hillfort was then abandoned, although it might have served as a farming base. The inhabitants probably kept their cattle within easy sight of the hillfort, with crops grown beyond, so it may have remained in use for farming after its defensive days were over.

Pottery dating from about 600 B.C. has been found which suggests that the hill might have been used as an open settlement before the hillfort was built, or was the hillfort built at that time? There is, however, no doubting the use of the hill for a Neolithic causewayed camp, with the ditches crossed by causeways at regular intervals. The inner bank and ditch enclosed about three acres, with an outer bank and ditch of about 1,000 feet in diameter. In between these, and possibly joining them, was a spiral bank and ditch. As one would expect, these, or what was left of them, were flattened in the Iron Age, and the bank and ditches are best seen in the northern part of the interior, before the bushes and beyond the trackway and, more faintly, outside the Iron Age rampart to the north.

The latter shows that much of the outer bank of the Neolithic camp was destroyed by the building of the Iron Age hillfort. A skeleton of a Neolithic woman was found under stones on a ditch of the earlier camp, built over by the Iron Age rampart. Other Neolithic finds have included pottery, cattle, sheep and pig bones, with even a suggestion of possible cannibalism in those times. The overriding impression for the excavators of the Neolithic camp was of the 'squalor' of those times.

Today, of course, it is all very different. The Trundle still serves a purpose with its radio station, and is a very popular place from which to view the surrounding countryside, the horse racing course, the motor racing circuit to the south and the Isle of Wight. It is, justifiably, one of the most popular of hillforts, although will probably not be as busy as the September day in 1645 when 1,000 farmers met to complain at having to feed so many soldiers, of both sides, during the Civil War. Well, there was no Trafalgar Square in those days.

Directions. O/S 1:50,000 map 151 ref. 177455. Leave Stratford-upon-Avon towards Shipston on Stour and turn left on the B4632. Turn left to Lower Quinton, passing the church, and turn right. The second track on the right, to Meon Hall, is also a Public Footpath. Park beside the road, and follow the track past the hall and on to the summit of the hill, after the track ends.

Meon Hill, a northern outcrop of the Cotswolds, rises to over 400 feet above the Vale of Evesham, to the north, yet is only 635 feet high and therefore considerably lower than other hills of that range. It is topped by the most spectacular of Warwickshire's hillforts, a site of twenty-five acres which, like Herefordshire Beacon* and Bredon Hill*, may have formed part of a northern frontier for the Dubonni tribe. Alas, as with so many hillforts, Meon Hill has not been excavated, and so retains its past secrets, and as visitors we are left with only the ruins of a once important centre, and the majesty of its location.

Double ramparts and ditches, with a counterscarp bank, enclose the summit, although there is only a single, tree-covered rampart in the north-west. At the north, the inner defences have been ploughed down, but as compensation there is part of the, probably original, dry-stone wall revetting visible on the outer rampart. This is a rare enough sight these days, and serves to remind us that the grass covered banks and ditches we see are ruins, and not the 'real McCoy'.

You will arrive at the south-east end of the fort, and from there, around the south-west to the triangulation point, is where the defences are at their best. No original entrance can be made out, but it would probably have been in the southern half of the fort which, by and large, follows the contours. Back in 1824, a hoard of Belgic, sword shaped iron 'currency bars' were found, which served as tokens of exchange, prior to the use of coins. Most of these have now been lost, probably as they were not gold or silver, but they suggest that the fort might have been inhabited well into the first century B.C., or later, possibly by people connected with those who may have over-run Bredon Hill.

Other evidence of Meon's past is not forthcoming, but it was unlikely to have been constructed by the Belgic people who buried their currency there, and was thus built before the first century B.C. However, we can surmise why it was built, when one considers the strategic value of such a site. Today, Birmingham and the West Midlands conurbation can be seen way beyond Stratford to the north, while anything that moves in the Vale of Evesham can be seen. Translate that back 2,000 years, and it is quite clear as to just what a commanding position was held by Meon Hill. Vast though the view is to the north, it is nearly matched by that to the east, while the Malvern Hills, with Herefordshire Beacon* and Midsummer Hill* hillforts can be seen to the west. As a possible northern frontier post for the Dobunni tribe, it could hardly have been bettered.

Without doubt, it is Meon Hill's outstanding prospect which is its greatest attribute today. Whether any possible, future excavation will reveal how the Belgic currency bars came to be buried there, and who lived at the hillfort, will depend on the damage done by the ploughing of the interior. It seems as though the hillfort has much to tell, particularly through its location, but also with its defences being purposefully-built. Yet it is a big hillfort for a mere frontier post, so perhaps it served a trading function as well, which would offer a reason for the currency bars. Whatever the main purpose for building Meon Hill, it does not appear to have served for too long in a leading role.

Battlesbury Camp

Directions. O/S 1:50,000 map 183 ref. 894456 One mile east of Warminster station. From Warminster centre, head south on the A36, and after a quarter of a mile turn left onto the road leading up Sack Hill. Once at the top, a pathway leads from the right, back towards the fort. An alternative route is to follow the directions to Scratchbury Camp*. Walk the opposite direction to Scratchbury Camp either over or round Middle Hill, where you will see some well preserved strip-lynchets at the east. Once past Middle Hill, a pathway leads up to Battlesbury Camp.

The twin camps of Battlesbury and Scratchbury, no more than a mile apart, both bear the hallmarks of late Iron Age occupation, and both are large, powerfully defended fortifications. They make strange bedfellows, being so close, but within a radius of four miles there is also a further two large, and impressively sited hillforts; Bratton Castle, and Cley Hill. The number of pre-Roman sites still visible on the downs to the east of these twin forts, suggests that this was an important area in Iron Age Britain.

Unlike some large hillforts, Battlesbury is both big and impressive. It encloses 24 acres with double ramparts and ditches on all sides, including the naturally steep western side. Two extra ramparts defend the level approach to the north, from which direction you will arrive, with further outworkings and ramparts outside the eastern entrance. These defences suggest Battlesbury was occupied into the first century B.C., at the very least, possibly by the Belgae.

You will enter by the north-west gateway, formerly the scene of some form of skirmish. An excavation undertaken in 1922 revealed a number of skeletons, in a pit outside this gateway, which included those of at least one woman and child. Unlike certain hillforts in the Durotriges tribal area, it is not known whether these seemingly hasty burials were due to a visit from an advance party of Romans, or from an inter, or intra, -tribal dispute. No other Belgae settled hillfort has shown evidence of a battle with the Romans, which has led to a theory that they had abandoned their hillforts before the Romans arrived in 43 A.D.: the possibility remains that Battlesbury was occupied against the Belgae.

Once on the west ramparts you will immediately be aware of the strategic importance of Battlesbury, which rises to over 650 feet above sea level. Beneath you rests Warminster, while away to the north the Cotswolds rise beyond Bath; the Mendips form the backdrop in the west; and due west, just beyond Warminster, the hill that seems to rise out of the earth, and fall away just as quickly, is Cley Hill. Away to the south-east is Scratchbury camp, and the Wylye valley, the river making its sinuous way between the hills to Wilton.

If you think it a bit early to be describing the views, that is because the attractive beech hangar, which covers the south-western slopes of the hill, but not the ramparts, obscures the view from the ramparts in that corner, which would certainly not have been tolerated in its heyday. Inside the fort at that point, a low mound can be seen. This was once thought to have been a round barrow, but no body was found, which led to the belief that it might have been a Norman motte, the camp serving as a bailey. If this was the case, the lack of any true foundations suggests that it was very temporary accommodation, at best.

As you can clearly see, the ramparts follow the contours of the hill on the west, south and north-east sides, while good use is made of the level ground at the east to build outworkings for the entrance. Despite the natural defensive advantages, the ramparts at the west and south sides are impressive, while a quarry ditch runs inside the inner rampart for almost its whole length. Once past the beech hangar the ground levels out, and a third rampart has been built, while the outworkings for the east entrance seem pretty formidable, even today. If you have approached from Scratchbury Camp, this is where you will enter Battlesbury, and is obviously the point of departure for the return.

The eastern entrance is symmetrical, with the ramparts being out-turned to form a 110 feet long barbican passageway. It is possible that a slingers platform existed on the north side of this passageway. Wooden gates, probably with an overbridge, would very likely have been used, although no excavation has been made which shows this. The builders obviously knew what they were doing though, so it is unlikely that Battlesbury would have been without all the latest technology for its defences.

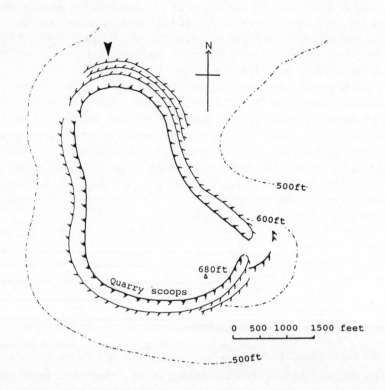

Heading back north, the ramparts revert to the original two, with the addition of a counterscarp bank, but are steeper than before. The land to the east is the site of ancient field systems and ditches, probably associated with the hillfort(s), but it is also liberally scattered with 'targets' for the Army, so it is unwise, even if there is no 'action', to go and take a closer look. Inside the fort, the aforementioned excavation revealed a number of rubbish pits which contained, amongst other things, late Iron Age pottery, a hut door latch lifter, an iron-worker's saw and a wheel hub from, what is thought to be, a chariot. These, along with the 'advanced' physical defences, suggest that the camp was occupied well into the first century B.C.

Two smaller ramparts and ditches have been built as additional protection to the flat approach from the north, leading to the north-west entrance. It is the sheer scale of the defences that lead one to think that Battlesbury Camp existed in an, at one time, hostile environment, and also that if not occupied when the Romans arrived, it had not long been abandoned. Alternatively, there was no mention of hut sites in the 1922 excavation, and it is worth speculating as to why two such powerful hillforts were built so close together.

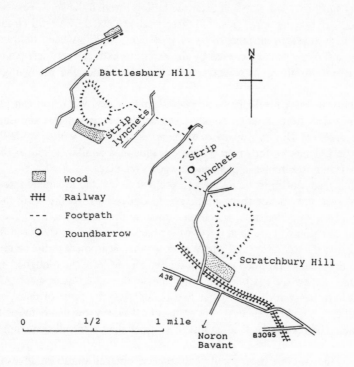

OTHER ANCIENT SITES
Cley Hill, hillfort map 183 ref. 839448
Bratton Castle, hillfort map 184 ref. 901516

Chiselbury Camp

Directions. O/S 1:50,000 map 184 ref. 018281. West of Salisbury off the A30. Chiselbury Camp is above the YMCA badge cut into the down above Fovant village. Turn left after Fovant and follow the road to the top of the hill. At this point there is a junction with an ancient trackway. The fort is just over a mile to the east along this trackway, at the north, by a bend.

Chiselbury Camp commands a narrow spur in the range of hills overlooking the River Nadder valley to the north, and the River Ebble valley to the south. Despite this prominent position, and its proximity to the ancient trackway, it does not seem as though Chiselbury Camp had any strategic significance. Indeed, in view of the paucity of relics found at the site, although like so many hillforts it has not undergone a modern excavation, it might well be something of an Iron Age white elephant.

If you follow the ancient trackway, which at one time served as the Wilton-Shaftesbury turnpike road, you will enter the hillfort through the south-east entrance. In fact, there are two entrance gaps, and these were protected by a semi-circular out-working which enclosed an area 160 feet x 70 feet. This has been obliterated by ploughing, and other damage caused by the desire to extract every last penny from the land at various times in recent centuries, and includes the ploughing of the interior.

It is best to visit Chiselbury on a bright summer's day, when you can get some magnificent views from its impressively large single, glacis rampart and ditch, 660 feet above sea level. Dinton House lies to the north, across the valley, while the even larger Castle Ditches hillfort, near Tisbury, stands at a similar height to the west. Chiselbury is almost circular in plan, and occupies ten acres.

As with many hillforts, which make excellent fields, the ploughed interior has little of interest, but outside there are a few imponderables. At the north there is a ditch with a bank on either side, which runs down to the escarpment. Go back to the south again, and you will see faint traces of the banks and ditches which run from the rampart, across the trackway, and part-way down the escarpment to the south. There was also a third bank and ditch combination, which ran from the ploughed entrance out-workings, across the road, to run down the south facing escarpment. Although there is little to be seen of these latter two boundaries, the three of them, together with the hillfort, whose defences they adjoin, cut off the narrow gap between the two escarpments. The reason for this, and even whether they were all contemporary, is unknown.

Indeed, the whole reason for its existence is open to question. Investigations undertaken in the 1920s by Dr. R.R.C. Clay, and the few 'finds' unearthed, along with the lack of wear and tear at the entrance gateways, has led to the conclusion that the hillfort, though well sited and clearly well built, served as nothing more than a temporary refuge for the inhabitants of Fifield Bavant Down village-site, nearly two miles to the south-west. This type of conclusion, from such relatively early excavations, is not uncommon though, and many have been revised in the light of subsequent excavation and analysis. We await a modern excavation of Chiselbury before this interpretation can be fully accepted, or indeed revised.

Despite its lack of hard historical facts, Chiselbury Camp remains a good example of a medium sized univallate hillfort. Like so many hillforts, it was probably not permanently settled throughout its years, if not centuries, of use. Yet, one assumes it was not built for fun, nor simply to withstand a short-term threat. This is yet another hillfort which is in need of a full excavation to determine its past, and to add to the body of knowledge for these structures.

Figsbury Ring

Directions. O/S 1:50,000 map 184 ref. 188338. Leave Salisbury on the A30 heading towards London. One and a half miles after the A338 turn off; a minor road to Pitton leaves on the right. Half a mile after this, on the left, is the signposted trackway which leads to the car park.

Figsbury Ring has not had a particularly distinguished history, and its circular single rampart and ditch, which enclose fifteen acres, is fairly commonplace for an early Iron Age hillfort in this part of the world. From an overhead plan view though, it resembles more of a 'rounds' type of hillfort, peculiar to Cornwall, and once there you will see why.

You will arrive at the east entrance, which once had a semi-circular defensive outworking, no longer visible. As you pass through the entrance you will see Figsbury's one outstanding feature, the purpose of which has been the source of much debate: an inner ditch without a bank, 100 feet inside the rampart. This ditch encloses about 6.5 acres, and has causeways through it in line with the east and west entrances.

The rampart is a simple glacis type, of a considerable size, with a 'V' shaped outer ditch which encloses a plateau about 470 feet above sea level, and which falls slightly to the west. There are two original opposing entrances, the gap to the south being fairly recent.

An excavation was undertaken in 1924 which left many questions un-answered. A relatively small number of late Bronze Age and early Iron Age potsherds were found, and one from the Roman period, but there was little to suggest that the fort was permanently occupied at any time. It was also discovered that the rampart had been strengthened on two occasions, with much of the spoil from the upper part coming from the inner ditch. A bronze sword, almost two feet long, had been accredited as being found in the rampart in 1704.

All the above suggests that Figsbury Ring was in occasional use between about 525-375 B.C., but it is the inner ditch, and in particular its location, that gives the fort its main interest. It is about 30 feet wide and up to 8 feet deep, and is quite unlike the outer ditch, which suggests that the two were dug at different times. There has never been any bank to this ditch, in its present form, so it therefore differs from a rounds type hillfort. It was thought that the ditch covered the site of a Neolithic causeway camp, but the excavations did not reveal any evidence to support this. Further suggestions have included that Figsbury Ring was some kind of ancient 'sports stadium' (unlikely), or perhaps a ritual site. The lack of domestic finds, including storage and rubbish pits, support this latter view, while animal bones (perhaps from ritual slaughter) have been found. However, the fact that the rampart had been strengthened suggests that the fort was a defensive structure to be used whenever necessary.

Without doubt though, the main question about Figsbury Ring concerns the distance the inner ditch is from the rampart. If its main use was as a quarry-ditch, why not dig from inside the rampart, as at many other hillforts, rather than have to cart the spoil over to the rampart? Perhaps the need to strengthen the rampart was also taken as an opportunity to divide the interior for cattle ranching purposes. That the ditch was never filled in, nor the idea copied at other hillforts, hints that it was dug by the final group of people taking refuge within the rampart, for a specific purpose such as ranching.

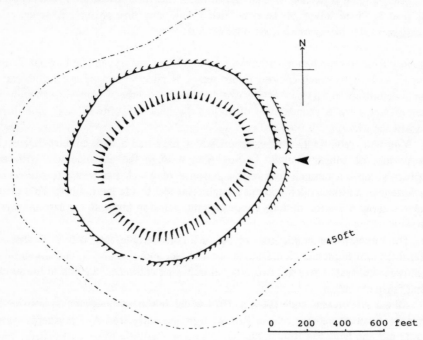

A walk round the rampart is an ideal activity while ruminating over the hillfort's use. The rampart is almost complete, with very little damage. Views are to be had in all directions, less dramatic to the high ground of the east, but invigorating elsewhere. Pepperbox Hill can be seen to the south, while from the west entrance, which also might have had an outer defence, Salisbury can be seen with its grid-like street pattern, cathedral and confluence of rivers. Almost due west over the River Bourne valley, and to the north of Salisbury, stands the even bigger hillfort of Old Sarum, now in the care of English Heritage.

If it were not for the inner ditch, Figsbury Ring would be a good example of a typical early Iron Age hillfort, and one of many at that. However, as it is, you will search in vain to find another like it, which is why it is included here. That you will also be rewarded with some splendid views as well, is a most pleasing bonus.

OTHER ANCIENT SITES
Old Sarum. O/S map 184 ref. 137327.
Ogbury Camp hillfort. O/S map 184 ref. 143383.
Stonehenge. O/S map 184 ref. 122422.

Martinsell Hill and the Giant's Grave

Directions. O/S 1:50,000 map 173 ref. 177639/166632. Leave Pewsey heading east on B3087 and take the second minor road, not farm track, left at a crossroads. Pass under the railway, then turn left at the junction and cross the canal bridge, keeping straight on towards Clench Common. Climb the steep hill and, as it eases off, you will see a trackway, which leads to the hillfort, and parking space on the left. Martinsell can be seen above the escarpment when looking west.

This pair of hillforts due to their close proximity, were almost certainly connected, in some way, during the Iron Age. Whether they were ever simultaneously, or indeed permanently, occupied is not known.

Martinsell hill, at 947 feet, is almost the highest in Wiltshire, and the large, 32 acre, univallate hillfort occupies the eastern half of the plateau. From where you parked, the eastern rampart and ditch stand out clearly on the hill, and this is the direction you should head for. Having skirted the wood, you should have arrived at the only known entrance, in the north-east, along the north rampart.

The east and south ramparts follow the contours of the hill closely and, using the natural slope, form an effective defence. Much of the interior has been ploughed, so there is little of interest there, but by following the glacis rampart round you will be treated to magnificent views over the Vale of Pewsey, with the Kennet and Avon Canal, railway and several sleepy villages below, and the hills, with the Pewsey white horse, beyond. The views alone make this worthwhile, and when you have reached the south-west corner, it is wise to go on to Giant's Grave, and return later.

Follow the field edge and head south-west. You will eventually, after about half a mile, come to pasture land which leads gently down the slope of the narrow promontory. The Giant's Grave hillfort is protected by a strong rampart and ditch which cuts across the neck of the promontory, with an entrance in the centre, and two outlying banks and ditches as additional defences.

Round the other sides a slight rampart and ditch can be seen, presumably the natural slope being deemed a sufficient deterrent by the builders. The interior is grass covered, and encloses about 2.5 acres in area; it is unlikely that this fort was abandoned to build Martinsell, due to the difference in size. It is possible that Martinsell and Giant's Grave formed a pair of hillforts; one being based on cattle farming and the other cereals. Giant's Grave was possibly built no later than 400

B.C. From pottery found at the site, it has been considered that the fort was re-used, after having been abandoned, later in the Iron Age.

Apart from its diminutive, yet neat, size, Giant's Grave overlooks Rainscombe House to the north, and across to Knap Hill, and its Neolithic camp, in the west, with yet more views over the Vale of Pewsey. It is an unusual type of hillfort for this area, being both on a promontory and so small.

Retrace your steps and return to the south-west corner of Martinsell hillfort; you will pass the remains of a deserted farm on the way, to the north. The west rampart and ditch are covered in thorns and bushes in places, and progress is not so pleasant as earlier. It is not thought that any of the gaps you pass were entrances, and the rampart and ditch, though facing the flat ground to the west, and the not-too-steep hill to the north, are no stronger than on the east and south sides.

Martinsell is one of the largest hillforts in a part of the country renowned for its large-scale hillforts. It was excavated in 1907, but this was only on a small scale and therefore little of its history is known. Withy Copse, just outside the rampart, revealed a considerable amount of Belgic rubbish, which suggests the hillfort was occupied until the latter stages of the Iron Age. However, its defences seem relatively slight when compared to other Wessex hillforts. In particular, the entrance has no outworkings, and there does not appear to have been any effort made to upgrade the defences at any time. This might seem somewhat surprising, considering its close proximity to the Atrebates tribal area, but perhaps Martinsell hillfort had indeed long been abandoned; the Belgic peoples seldom living in former hillforts.

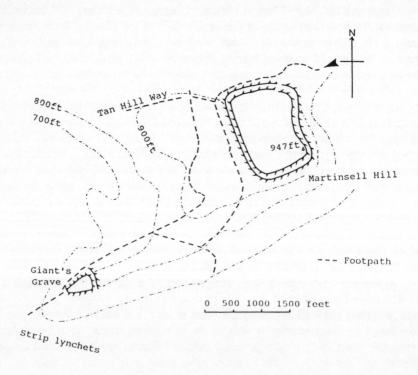

In more recent centuries, Martinsell was used as the venue for a local traditional Palm Sunday football game. Whether the hillfort marked the boundaries is not known, but despite its size, it would have been a fairly small pitch for those 'games' that took place up and down the country until well into the nineteenth century. This might seem rather a strange use for an hillfort, but Martinsell and Giant's Grave are something of an odd couple in the hillfort world.

OTHER ANCIENT SITES
Rybury camp. O/S map 184 ref. 083640.
Knap Hill Neolithic camp. O/S map 184 ref. 121636.
Gopher Wood Bronze Age barrow cemetery. O/S map 184 ref. 139639.
Giant's Grave Neolithic long barrow. O/S map 184 ref. 271563.

Oldbury Castle

Directions. O/S 1:50,000 map 173 ref. 049692. Leave Calne (Wiltshire) on the A4 towards Marlborough. After three miles, there is a lay-by just after the minor road to Yatesbury, on the left. Directly opposite, across the A4, is a footpath which leads up the edge of the quite steep hill. Aim for the prominent Lansdowne Monument, which stands in the north-west corner.

The walk up to Oldbury Castle is not easy, but there are few hillforts which have comparable views on the approach. Despite the proximity of the A4, traffic noise is soon left behind, and the tall obelisk beckons you towards it. This obelisk was undergoing repair, funded by English Heritage, when I last visited, although the north-west corner of the hillfort was damaged by its construction in the first place.

Equally visible, if not more so, from the road, and for nearly all the walk to the hillfort, is the most 'active' of all Wiltshire's hill-figures, the prancing Cherhill White Horse. This was cut in 1780 by Dr Christopher Alsop, the 'mad doctor of Calne', and it originally had a glistening eye, made from upside-down bottles. This figure stands just beyond the north-east corner of the hillfort.

Once you have reached the obelisk, follow the escarpment round. The natural slope saved the Iron Age inhabitants some work here, as only a single rampart and ditch were used to defend the north side. About 50 yards beyond the obelisk, what might have been a single rampart and ditch runs almost due south across the interior of the fort, to join the defences at the south. Archaeologists are uncertain as to whether this is the remains of a smaller, simpler hillfort which occupied the eastern part of Oldbury Castle, or whether it was an internal divide built at some stage after the hillfort was constructed. One thing appears to be certain, and that is it was not built at the same time as the present defences.

The north rampart offers outstanding views from its 850 feet vantage point, particularly over the River Avon valley and on to the Cotswolds, while the miniature cars glide past silently on the A4 below. Nearer the north-east corner, you will find that the ground inside the hillfort has been dug away. This, along with other disturbances, is not the likely site of any huts, but the result of flint-digging in the last century.

You will soon arrive at the north-east corner, with the White Horse 100 yards further along. An alternative route down and back to the lay-by can be made by following the escarpment round. At this corner the hillfort ramparts turn south, and have been considerably strengthened. For the section up to the east entrance, the inner rampart and ditch have both been increased in size, and are joined by a second rampart and ditch. This rampart is unusual as it is divided into two smaller ramparts with a level section of ground in between. This has been damaged by flint digging, and ends at the east entrance, but south of this point the two smaller ramparts are separated by a narrower gap until the normal double ramparts and ditches complete the circuit back to the north-west corner.

The east entrance is of considerable interest and is very similar to entrances at Hod Hill* and Hambledon Hill*. The outer rampart from the south widens and sweeps round to cut off a direct approach from the level ground, thus creating a long entrance passage. The inner ramparts are deeply in-turned to form an additional 100 feet long entrance passage. As no modern excavation has been undertaken, details of gates and other defensive measures are not known, but the scale of the remaining earthworks suggest that they would have been comprehensive.

Round to the south, as mentioned, the outer rampart is divided into two smaller ones, but becomes a single rampart before turning west. It may well be that the badly disturbed area at the south-east corner was an original entrance, but a full excavation is needed before anything can be confirmed. The approach is fairly level, and it would be odd, but not unique, for such a large hillfort, of twenty acres, to only have one entrance.

Just beyond this point the internal bank from the obelisk joins the inner rampart. It can be seen that the land to the west falls away, by about fifty feet, and that the area enclosed to the east is almost dead level. Whether this is significant, or not, is not known. The ramparts to the west continue round to the north-west corner, on the same scale as before, and offer good views to the west.

The interior of the fort has little of additional interest other than the internal bank. Flint-digging has caused considerable disturbance, and a full, modern excavation is much needed. Nineteenth century excavations revealed some early Iron Age pottery found in both storage pits and on the ground, while Roman pottery and coins, a bone comb and a fifth century A.D. brooch were also found.

If the site was occupied c.350 B.C., then it may have had single rampart and ditch defences. It is pure speculation, but it could be that the original camp did follow the line of the present north and east ramparts, and that the internal bank formed the western defences. Had Oldbury then been extended while simultaneously improving the defences, a similar development to other hillforts in the area, like at Scratchbury Camp*, would have taken place, perhaps for the same reasons.

For the present though, Oldbury Castle can be visited for pure enjoyment, with fine views and additional points of interest, unencumbered by historical 'facts'.

OTHER ANCIENT SITES
Oliver's Camp, hillfort. O/S map 173 ref. 001647.
Avebury Henge. O/S map 173 ref. 103698.
Silbury Hill. O/S map 173 ref. 100685.

Scratchbury Camp

Directions. O/S 1:50,000 map 184 ref. 913443. Above the A36, 1.5 miles south-east of Warminster. Can be reached from Battlesbury Camp* a mile away. Otherwise, leave Warminster centre on the A36 towards Salisbury. A mile after the turn off to the B3095, there is a track on the left up to North Farm. Follow this over the railway, up and round the hill until a junction of tracks/paths meet. You can park here. Scratchbury Camp is up to the south, while the path over Middle Hill, to the north-west, leads to Battlesbury Camp.

The twin hillforts of Scratchbury and Battlesbury have much in common. Both are large, with impressive defences which generally follow the contours of the hills; both are strategically well sited, overlooking the Wylye valley; and both have main defences which were probably constructed in the late-middle Iron Age, with a quarry ditch running most of the way round the inside of the main rampart. There are differences though, not least in the ramparts themselves, while Scratchbury Camp has solid evidence of prior use, on several occasions.

As you walk up to the ramparts, you will come to the north-west entrance, with its fine views over Middle Hill to Battlesbury Camp, over Warminster and the Wylye valley. The entrance is slightly askew, adding to its strength, and is similar to that on the north-east, although neither can compare to either of those at Battlesbury. Just inside the entrance, on the gently sloping ground, a dozen hut platforms are visible measuring 20-30 feet in diameter. These are quite rare on the heavily farmed downs of Wessex.

Once you head south along the rampart, more differences with Battlesbury arise. The most obvious is that Scratchbury has but a single, and no less massive, rampart and ditch, with a significant counterscarp bank. These run round the whole length of the camp and, unlike at Battlesbury, there is no additional strengthening, except near the eastern entrance. The other most obvious difference, most noticeable from the west and south facing ramparts, is the traffic noise from the A36.

There is more to see before you leave the western ramparts. Looking towards the slope across the interior, a slight rise and dip can be clearly seen in the turf. This marks the curved bank and ditch of an earlier camp, occupied until c.250 B.C. Within this, at the summit of the hill, and rising by about a yard, is one of four Bronze Age round barrows that can be seen; this has produced a number of bronze implements with the cremated body, including a dagger. It is, however, better to inspect the interior a little later.

Further round, where the rampart curves south-east, the largest round barrow is clearly visible on the inside. A number of animal bones were found buried here, but no human remains, which seems odd as it is a fine size. Return to the defences, and as you look across the interior, just beyond the barrow, you can see the faint traces of a bank and ditch which runs to the north-east gateway. This links up with both ends of the semi-circular rampart and ditch, at which point it is best seen. The 'D' shaped enclosure is the original, while it is probable that this was later extended by lengthening the straight side to join the main ramparts where you now stand, and at the north-east gateway. It is likely that the north and west ramparts lie over the original extension of 'camp 2'.

The south and east ramparts, which you now follow, thus appear to have been the final extension, or 'camp 3', of Scratchbury, and were probably built when the earlier ramparts were strengthened. As we have mentioned, this probably took place quite late on in the Iron Age. The eastern entrance is not the gap at the southern-most point of the ramparts, that is modern, but further round on the flat spur of ground. It shows no evidence of any additional strengthening, despite the level approach, and is a simple straight-through entrance. From this point, more round barrows can be seen away to the south-east.

Following the ramparts north will bring you to the north-east gateway which is similar to that at the north-west. The quarry ditch begins again at this point, having ended at the eastern gateway, while the straight rampart and ditch from 'camp 2' ends at the north side. It is worth venturing into the interior at this point, to see the earliest camps, or what can be made out of them. Scratchbury is certainly not unique in having been extended over a period of time, but the distinct 'D' shape of 'camp 1' is, ironically, easier to see than the later 'camp 2', and is unusual, to say the least.

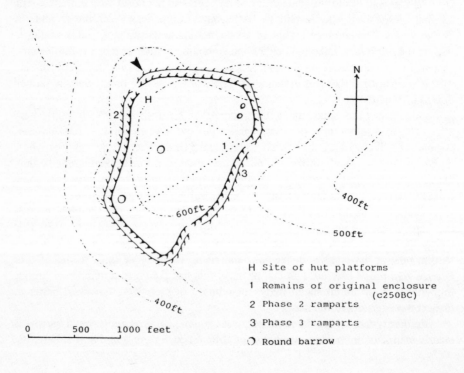

H Site of hut platforms

1 Remains of original enclosure
   (c250BC)

2 Phase 2 ramparts

3 Phase 3 ramparts

◯ Round barrow

From the north-east gateway, just inside the ramparts, are two further round barrows, the southern one of which housed a cremated burial. Once past these, the north defences overlook steeper ground, which makes them appear still bigger. From there, the ground to the north and east of Middle Hill is as visible as from Battlesbury Camp, while below is North Farm. Much more impressive though, are the strip-lynchets on the south of Middle Hill; an even better set can be seen at the eastern side of this hill. You will soon arrive back at the north-west entrance.

It is not known whether the Iron Age inhabitants of Scratchbury and Battlesbury camps tilled the same land, or indeed if they were permanently inhabited. Hut sites usually indicate a permanent settlement, and in this case Scratchbury goes 'one up' on its neighbour. How they existed side by side is still a matter for conjecture, but surely Iron Age man did not build earthworks of this size if it was not intended to live within them? I wonder if the bodies at the north-west gate of Battlesbury Camp had anything to do with a local 'bust-up'.

OTHER ANCIENT SITES
Knook Castle. O/S map 184 ref. 960440.
Ancient village. O/S map 184 ref. 968446.
White Sheet hillfort, and Neolithic camp. O/S map 183 refs. 804346, 802352.

Yarnbury Castle

Directions. O/S 1:50,000 map 184 ref. 035403. Yarnbury is situated on the north side of the A303, west of Amesbury, two miles west of the B3083 junction, or two miles east of the A36 junction. The ramparts can be seen from the road, and the 'crossroads' of trackways you need is just to the east of the fort. From the east, park by the track and cross the road. From the west, turn up the north trackway and park. This track leads just past the entrance after 100 yards.

If you have read this book from the beginning, it will be obvious that there are quite a number of different types of hillfort. Yarnbury is probably the foremost example of the type known as plateau hillforts, and certainly the best in this book.

Although an easy hillfort to find, the proximity of the main road on which you probably travelled is the least endearing feature, and the hum (or drone) of the traffic is ever present. Let not that, nor the lack of outstanding views (although at 525 feet Yarnbury overlooks most of the immediate plains) discourage you from a visit, as Yarnbury does not need such props; it can stand up easily enough on its own two ramparts.

Over the last couple of centuries there have been a number of pilot digs at Yarnbury which revealed a relatively high ratio of pits, but as yet no full scale excavation. This might seem somewhat strange for a hillfort of importance, and more so given that Roman coins have been regularly found on, or just below, the surface of the interior for over 200 years. You would be unlikely to find any on your visit and, of course, you should not go digging on historic sites.

Skeletons have been uncovered, one of which wore a bronze ring, while other bronze and iron remains have been found, along with Belgic and Roman pottery. Thus, the site might have been used intermittently from the late Bronze Age through to Romano-British days; while in another respect, Yarnbury has served a useful, if un-intended, function right into the present century. More of that later.

Once you are level with the ramparts, leave the trackway and make your way back to the only original entrance. Yarnbury is a circular fort of 26 acres, enclosed by multiple ramparts and ditches and with few natural defensive advantages. Archaeological descriptions of these have changed considerably over the years. Nowadays, the following seem to have been settled on: large inner rampart, revetted at the front, and ditch with, by normal standards, a massive counterscarp bank (this was often previously referred to as a rampart itself); 'V' shaped gap (formerly thought of as a ditch, but now recognised as the end of the counterscarp/beginning of the second rampart); and smaller second rampart and ditch. It is easy to see why it was considered that Yarnbury had three ramparts and ditches.

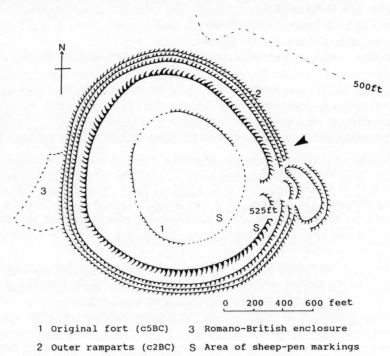

1 Original fort (c5BC)   3 Romano-British enclosure
2 Outer ramparts (c2BC)   S Area of sheep-pen markings

These defensive arrangements exist all the way round, except at the point you are standing, by the entrance. As you look back towards the trackway, an impressive 'D' shaped outworking to prevent a direct approach to the entrance itself lies before you. This would have been developed over a period of time, and it is thought that the 'D' might have latterly been joined to the main ramparts at its northern end, thus forming a long approach from the south only. The entrance itself is deeply in-turned, by 95 feet on the north side, and 80 feet on the south. The gates, of the single portal entry, are thought to have been set in line with the rear of the inner rampart, thus creating a deep, and narrowing funnel for guards to cast a wary eye over strangers.

There is more to Yarnbury than immediately catches the eye though. If you walk into the interior through the entrance, you will come across the slight, but distinct, bank of an earlier circular fort of about ten acres. This had much simpler defences, with a single rampart and 'V' ditch, and an entrance on the west side, closed with wooden gates. It was considered that this might have been a Neolithic causewayed camp, but is now thought to have been built in the fourth or fifth centuries B.C. Yarnbury is not unique in having an earlier camp obliterated by a later one, but is unusual in the later camp being concentric with an earlier Iron Age camp.

'To the ramparts', might have been the cry of defenders in the face of an attack, and that is where it is time to go, at the south-east. The A303 might not be the prettiest of sights, but some Bronze Age burial mounds can be seen on the downs beyond, along with celtic fields. Round to the south and west, the raised bank of the original fort can be clearly seen, while outside to the west, but adjoining to the main ramparts, is a Romano-British enclosure. This does not appear to have a direct entrance from the hillfort, and was probably built after the hillfort ceased to have a defensive purpose, that is after the Roman invasion.

To the north-west and north the downs rise gently above Yarnbury, but not enough to restrict views for the original inhabitants. Approximately 500 yards to the north of the hillfort, and beside the track you arrived on, a hillfort a little smaller than the original Yarnbury can be made out. This could well have been contemporary to, and associated with, the first Yarnbury hillfort. Did the two peoples amalgamate and agree to build the larger camp? Pure speculation, I am afraid.

The steepest approach to Yarnbury is from the north-east, where the hillfort sits at the head of a dry valley which has celtic fields on either side, visible in the evening shadows. The enlarged camp was probably built in the later middle Iron Age, with the outer rampart and ditch possibly being added even later. It is almost certain that the site was occupied during Roman times, and thus a history of inhabitation stretching over six centuries, at least, is likely.

Yet, until fairly recently, 4th October, 1916 to be exact, Yarnbury, although not occupied, served another useful function; the centre for a locally important annual sheep fair, which had been held for several centuries. If you go back to the area of the eastern rampart of the original camp, the grid layout of the sheep-pens can still be made out. More obviously, all the gaps in the main ramparts are probably associated with this latter-day event, along with the indentations to the inner rampart to the south of the entrance. A pond, possibly used for watering the sheep, can be seen 125 yards to the north-east of the ramparts.

Yarnbury Castle sits high, and fairly remote, on the downs, the Rivers Till and Wylye are both over two miles away. It is near a number of ancient trackways, indeed the A303 was little more than one such until a few decades ago, and in its latter form probably served as home for the people of a sizeable area. Whatever its importance at that time, like so many hillforts, once the Romans arrived that appeared to be that, although clearly it performed a farming/trading function during the early days of Roman occupation.

Bredon Hill

Directions. O/S 1:50,000 map 150 ref. 957401. Leave Worcester heading east on the A44. After Pershore, turn right on the minor road to Great Conderton, turn left in the village past the church and park. Walk to where the road turns very sharp right and follow the track through the farm, and the footpath to the top of the hill before you. See Conderton Camp* for an easier route.

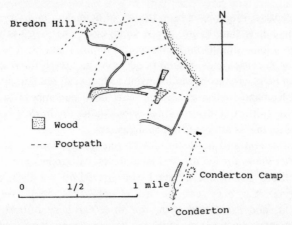

This very distinctive hill, an outcrop of the Cotswolds, is capped by an equally distinctive hillfort. It will give you some idea of the nature of the walk to it by mentioning that Bredon Hill rises to 961 feet, while Great Conderton church, about a mile away, is over 800 feet below. Add to this the fact that the hillfort does not have any defences facing the north or west, and you will gather that Bredon Hill demands its pound of flesh from visitors. Mind you, once here, by whichever route you have taken (helicopter?) I am sure you will consider all the effort worthwhile.

Bredon Hill is one of a number of hillforts which surmount the edge of the Cotswolds, and which are visible in a chain-link; Uleybury, Leckhampton and Meon Hill are just three featured in this book. It is not known whether the above is of any relevance, or part of a great strategic 'plan', but probably not, despite the forts all falling within the domain of the Dobunni tribe.

A series of excavations undertaken in the mid-1930s revealed a great deal of information concerning Bredon hillfort's past, while certain conclusions were drawn from the evidence. The natural escarpments were considered to be enough of a deterrent by the builders, on two sides, and defences were only built on the south and east. The inner rampart and ditch enclosed 10.5 acres, with an entrance in the south-east corner. The glacis rampart, probably originally with timber breastwork, still rises to 10 feet high and is 35 feet wide at the base, while the ditch was 8 feet deep. The entrance had been modified on several occasions, and in its final form comprised a 140 feet long stone-faced passage, about 8 yards wide, with double, wooden gates at the inner end and a bridge in line with the front of the rampart.

A further set of defences lie between 50-100 yards outside, and enclose twenty-two acres. These also comprise a bank and ditch, but the rampart was revetted with stone, and a berm separated it from the 6 feet deep ditch. Most unusual was the two entrances situated at the north and west escarpments, these being long passages seemingly leading over the edge. However, the land has fallen away over the intervening centuries, and neither of these survive. The gap in the outer defences, opposite the inner entrance, is of more recent origin.

That is a straight forward description of the defences, but certain pottery and metal finds caused the excavators conclusions to be challenged. It was considered that the inner defences formed the original camp, from the late second century B.C., and that the rampart may have been built over a timber-laced rampart, by invaders from the South-West. There were signs of a battle at the entrance, while the outer rampart was thought to have been built two centuries later, possibly by Celts fleeing from the Belgic advance in the South.

The above hypothesis seemed quite plausible considering that most hillforts have developed by expanding, while the dating fitted in neatly to theories compatible with those of the 1930s. As with many aspects of history, the above theories have been questioned, and while there is no doubting the physical finds, an alternative to the excavator's sequence of events has been advanced. Not only have the dates been revised backwards in time, but the phases of building have been reversed.

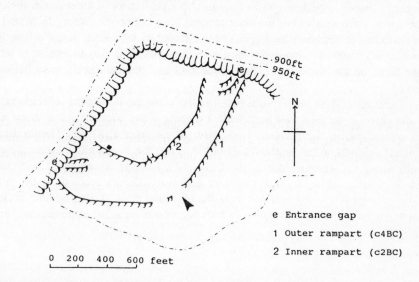

e Entrance gap
1 Outer rampart (c4BC)
2 Inner rampart (c2BC)

0 200 400 600 feet

It is now considered likely that the outer defences were built first, probably in the fifth century B.C., while the inner defences were built in the late third century B.C., and the entrance was subsequently modified on several occasions, until the fort was destroyed. This event might have taken place early in the first century A.D., but it is not thought to have been the Romans who undertook the task. Of course, it is unusual for a hillfort to contract in size over a period of time, but the reversal of the building chronology would explain the anomaly of the glacis, inner, rampart being replaced by the stone faced outer one, when at other hillforts the reverse has happened. However, although the dating of events further back in time is acceptable, until further excavations are undertaken, the new interpretation of the 1930s excavations will remain just that, and not a definitive account.

What will concern you, the visitor, is what you can see when you arrive. Both of the grass covered ramparts still rise to a considerable height, and their ditches are in place. You will soon discover why defences were only thought necessary on two sides, for although neither of the un-defended sides is impregnable, as you will probably have climbed one to get there, they would prevent a full scale attack.

That is more than the inner gateway managed to do. The excavators found that the double gates, at the inner end of the long entrance passage, had crashed down in flames, and six skulls were found close by. It was thought that these had been displayed on the gateway, and were not the beheaded remains of either the defenders or attackers; a particularly gruesome act which was carried on until recent times. Even more evidence of that battle was discovered in the form of about 65 heavily mutilated bodies, some with all their limbs hacked off, in the entrance passage. It was assumed that these were probably the bodies of the defenders, as the gates had been burned down, but the ferocity and violence of the battle perhaps suggests why people lived in defensive enclosures.

With that macabre incident came the demise of the hillfort, although evidence has been found of people living below the hill in Roman times. There are also a couple of features which are distinctly non-Iron Age, but are of interest nonetheless. The tower at the west end of the inner rampart is an eighteenth century folly, and to the north can be seen how the hill has been affected by land-slips. In the hollow lies the Banbury Stone, of supposedly mystical value, while it is also a tradition to write your name on the slopes using the stones; Gill and Sharon had done so before I arrived.

Quite apart from the physical remains, the views emphasise the strategic value of the site. To the west you have wide sweeping views over the River Avon and Severn valleys, to the Malvern Hills, with Midsummer Hill* and Herefordshire Beacon* hillforts on the southern part of these, and the Welsh hills beyond. To the south, along the western ridge of the Cotswolds, you can see beyond Cheltenham and Gloucester, while the Worcestershire and Warwickshire orchards to the north and the Cotswolds to the east complete the all round vista. It goes without saying, that you need to have clear weather to fully appreciate the effort of the ascent. What a place to live.

Conderton Camp (Also known as Danes Camp)

Directions. O/S 1:50,000 map 150 ref. 972383. *See* entry for Bredon Hill*. Leave Tewkesbury heading east on the A438. At the roundabout with the A435, turn left up the minor road to Overbury. Turn right at the junction to Conderton, turn left at the junction in the village, climbing the hill, and park. Walk up the rough track and take the track on the left beside the dry-stone wall and trees. Follow the line of trees, and the hillfort is on the right at the end.

Conderton Camp is probably the one hillfort that does not justify its entry in this book, on the grounds that it is not the best in its area. It was probably connected with nearby Bredon Hill*, a 1.5 mile walk to the north and, as such, should be combined into a joint visit. There is enough to see though, and I enjoyed my most 'exciting' visit to a hillfort. This was on account of the herd of bullocks who took more than a passing fancy to me. I kept ignoring their increasingly aggressive gestures and went about my business, until I had to put years of sports training to its sternest test and by running downhill, was able to out-sprint the most boisterous members of the herd; thank goodness I did not fall. Oh, and anyone who tells you that bullocks cannot run up and down banks and ditches at speed, well you know what to tell them, don't you . . .

The inappropriately named Danes Camp lies on a tongue-shaped spur, which slopes from north to south, on the south side of Bredon Hill. It was excavated in the late 1950s, the results of which showed there to have been two phases in the life of the hillfort. The initial camp enclosed three acres with a dry-stone revetted glacis rampart, 'V' shaped ditch, and slight counterscarp bank to the east and west sides. This covered the whole of the spur from the north rampart downwards, with a simple entrance to the south, leading to a spring, and another mid-way along the north rampart. The whole enclosure was overlooked by the land to the north, and was built about 300 B.C. This camp was considered, by the excavators, to be a cattle enclosure of the people of Bredon Hill hillfort.

The second phase began in the first century B.C., when a rampart was built across the spur from east to west, thus reducing the enclosed area to two acres and cutting off the south part. The new glacis rampart did not have a ditch, but the spoil might have come from the abandoned section of wall, while it too was faced with stone. An in--turned entrance was added in the centre of the rampart, which had wooden gates closing a passage six feet wide; this was a much stouter defensive structure, despite the lack of a ditch, than the outer rampart. It is probable that the north entrance was improved at the same time, being in-turned. At a still later stage, this entrance, always a weak spot due to the higher ground to the north, was blocked off with a dry-stone wall; it can still be made out though.

About a dozen circular huts, twenty feet in diameter, seem to have existed within the later camp, and over sixty storage pits, some lined with dry-stone wall and others, more unusually, with wicker-work, were found. Several of these had huts built over them, and were thus probably from the first phase. It may well be that by its latter days, the camp was a separate village from the hillfort on Bredon Hill, although regular ties must have been kept. Evidence of this was provided when the excavators found unfinished stew on hut floors, a sign of a rapid exit. Was this when the inhabitants fled before the advance of an enemy to the safety of Bredon Hill, only probably to be massacred there?

If the latter is correct, and it may well be, then Conderton became uninhabited at the same time as Bredon Hill. The defences at Conderton have not survived so well as at Bredon Hill, but the hut circles can be made out. Naturally, being about 300 feet below Bredon Hill hillfort, the views are nothing like as spectacular, but they are still very good to the south.

As Conderton is so close to Bredon Hill it makes for a good circular walk. Should you set off by following the Bredon Hill directions, it will involve a steep ascent to that hillfort, whereas by following Conderton's directions, and the accompanying map, the ascent is much more gentle, and a visit to both hillforts would require a walk of about four miles. But watch out for those bullocks.

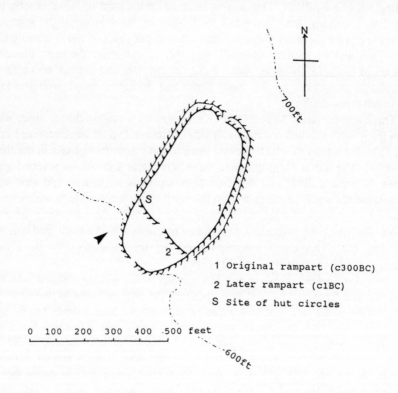

1 Original rampart (c300BC)
2 Later rampart (c1BC)
S Site of hut circles

0 100 200 300 400 500 feet

Almondbury

Directions. O/S 1:50,000 map 110 ref. 153142. Leave Huddersfield heading south on the A616. Turn left on the minor road opposite the turning for the B6108. Go under the railway bridge, keep right, go up the hill, and turn right to the top. Turn right at the next junction, signposted to 'Castle Hil'. Turn next left, at the west end of the hill, and the trackway on the left leads into a car park at the summit.

There are not too many hillforts with a pub as their centre-piece, but Almondbury has a tower, built in 1897 to commemorate Queen Victoria's Diamond Jubilee, as well. There is one other aspect of Almondbury which is quite unique, certainly as far as this book is concerned; there is virtually nothing from the Iron Age left to see. True, the banks and ditches might appear identical to those from the Iron Age which you have seen elsewhere, but all the defences you can see date from the early Middle Ages.

About 1150 A.D. Henry de Laci had a motte and bailey castle built, (Phase 7) where the tower now stands, by using the spoil from the cross-ditch between the tower and pub. The outer defences consisted of the banks that encircle the summit, plus two banks further down the hill, almost to the road on the north side. About a century later, the castle was dismantled, and the site used as a hunting lodge, (Phase 8) by the de Laci family. A house was built in the fifteenth century, (Phase 9) but that has also been demolished. Nowadays, and for many decades, Almondbury has been used as a local hostelry and viewing point, (Phase 10).

Some fourteen centuries before the de Laci family came to having their castle built, Almondbury was a well defended, multivallate hillfort, (Phase 6) home for people who probably busied themselves by keeping cattle. With the exception of the cross-ditch dug during mediaeval days, the defences pretty much followed the lines of those seen today; in other words, the de Laci family used the last Iron Age defences as a foundation for their own.

These people seem to have lived in rectangular lean-to huts against the inside of the inner rampart, which enclosed about five and a half acres. The entrance was at the north-east, where a large rectangular enclosure was added to the exterior, which contained at least one sizeable rectangular hut, and where further banks and ditches were added to the eastern side. A 'hollow path' led from the entrance down through the outer bank and ditch, re-built as two banks and ditches in mediaeval days. It is thought that the area enclosed by those outer defences was used for herding cattle, a similarity with some hillforts in the South-West.

The double ramparts and ditches which enclosed the summit, and formed the main part of the hillfort, had been built and re-furbished from the existing defences, bout 500 B.C. It was then that the rectangular enclosure, outer rampart and ditch and other outworkings were added. Then, within a hundred years, a fire had burned within the ramparts, as the timber supports ignited, and the whole camp was abandoned. A series of excavations undertaken between 1939-72 by W.J. Varley indicated that the cause may have been a spontaneous combustion caused by a lack of ventilation of the inner timber supports, rather than an accidental, or even deliberate, 'firing' of the defences. A strange situation indeed.

About 600 B.C., what is known as the 'bi-vallate fort' (Phase 5) was constructed; the whole of the five and a half acre summit was enclosed by two ramparts and ditches, and the present north entrance built. The outer rampart was re-built from the counterscarp bank of the existing fort, at the south end, and an outer ditch added. This period lasted until the building of the multivallate fort a century later, but was preceded, by about fifty years, by a three acre univallate fort, (Phase 4). This enclosed the south-west part of the hill, which rises to just over 900 feet. The defences for this comprised a rampart, ditch and counterscarp bank, with the northern section being in line with the bank running midway across the summit. The gap for the road approximates to the original entrance.

This univallate fort probably grew out of an open settlement, (Phase 3) of circular huts, each with a diameter of about 25 feet. These were spread throughout the summit, well beyond the boundaries of the later univallate fort, but even this was not the first settlement on the site.

At some, undated, period before, a univallate enclosure, (Phase 2) defended by a single bank without a ditch and with a guardroom at the entrance, was built on the three acre site later used by the univallate fort. There was a considerable lapse of time between the univallate enclosure and the later open settlement, as a layer of turf had grown over the ruins of the univallate enclosure. The first settlement, (Phase 1) on the site dated from c.3,000 B.C., but this had been abandoned many centuries before the first defences were built.

If you find the chronology of Almondbury's past to be confusing, you are not alone. It is a good example of a site being used and abandoned many times over a period of up to 5,000 years, and of course it is put to good use today. What is unusual is that only three pottery fragments have been found from the Roman period, so Almondbury may well have missed out on one of the most important periods in England's history.

The excavations at Almondbury, and the subsequent Carbon-14 dating of the various finds had an unexpected effect on the main excavator. W.J. Varley thought that the fort had been destroyed, probably by the Romans, and then abandoned. This had happened on many occasions following the latin invasion, but the Carbon-14 dating, even taking calibration allowances into account, showed that the various stages of building had taken place many centuries before. W.J. Varley had the good sense to fully revise his earlier dating, and theories; a highly commendable action, which just goes to show that history never stands still, and interpretations can change all the time In any case, once you have visited all the defences built over the Iron Age ones, and admired the views, you can retire to the pub to contemplate the welter of events.

Carlwark

Directions. O/S 1:50,000 map 110 ref. 258815. Leave Hathersage on the A625 towards Sheffield. Turn left at the top of the hill a half a mile east of the village. Just under a mile from this junction a Public Footpath sign stands beside a gateway on the right. Park here, and head due east across Hathersage Moor. Carlwark is a half a mile across the moor-land.

Carlwark stands gaunt and isolated high up on a small plateau on Hathersage Moor, yet it is only three miles from the south-west outskirts of Sheffield. Although it is not a difficult hillfort to reach, with footpaths arriving from all points of the compass, care should be taken that it is not too misty, as finding one's direction on the moor, in the mist, is not easy. Enclosing only two acres, Carlwark is not likely to be 'stumbled across' in such conditions.

The rectangular plateau on which the hillfort was built, is protected by natural slopes on all sides except the west. The whole was probably encircled by a single bank, and although there is little to be seen of this on two sides, it is the remaining south and west walls which make Carlwark such a worthy hillfort to visit. Unlike the ruined walls of so many hillforts, which are nowadays covered in turf, the stone revetting of the turf south wall, and the massive blocks of Millstone Grit, linked by sections of stone wall on the west, remain clear for inspection. There are precious few examples of Iron Age stone revetting still visible on English hillforts.

Although not continuous, especially on the west wall, the stones rise to over ten feet high in places. The short south wall, in particular, shows the care taken with the building, which has assisted the survival for about 2,000 years. The walls lean backwards slightly, but they were vertical originally, this being caused by the turf becoming compressed and the stones leaning rather than collapsing, as elsewhere. There is an in-turned entrance in the south-west, being about 6 yards long and 5 feet wide at the inner end, and possibly a simple one in the east.

The interior is strewn with boulders and stones, presumably from the now vanished sections of wall. Only minor excavations have been undertaken, many years ago, and nothing of certainty was revealed about whether the fort was permanently occupied. Following these, it was thought possible that Carlwark belonged to the Dark Ages. That, of course, would have precluded it from this book, and I tend to go along with the interpretation that it was in use during the first century B.C., if not before.

What became of the inhabitants, or how they lived, is not known. It is quite probable that they were a cattle herding group, and although there is a field system to the south of the fort, it was probably not contemporary with it. The inhabitants would have been few in number in what, considering the paucity of hillforts or settlements in the area, was probably a lightly populated region. Burbage Brook flows a quarter of a mile to the east, with another more accessible water source a bit further away to the south-west.

From its 1,250 feet high vantage point, in most parts of the country, you would expect to see for miles. Carlwark is on the edge of the Peak District though, and one cannot even see Sheffield, thanks to Burbage Moor, nor beyond the mass of Hallam Moor to the north. Even Hathersage is hidden from view, but the larger hills to the west sit on the horizon. To the south though, Derbyshire seems to open up before you.

It is a pity that so little is known about Carlwark, as its exposed stone walls make it well worth a visit, quite apart from the enjoyable moor-land walk. Until such a time that a full excavation is undertaken, this position will not alter, but one would not expect a hillfort of such size to have played a significant role in history, even on a local scale. Still, Carlwark has its story to tell, and no doubt one day it will reveal all.

Ingleborough

Directions. O/S 1:50,000 map 98 ref. 742745. Leave Settle, heading north on the B6479, and park in the car park at Horton in Ribblesdale. Walk to the station, and just south of this a Public Footpath crosses the track and heads north-west up to the summit of Ingleborough, four miles away.

Ingleborough is one of the best known mountains in England, its great mass towering over the Ribble valley below, and is one of the major sights from the Settle and Carlisle railway line. It is not a particularly difficult mountain to walk up, especially from Horton in Ribblesdale (waterproofs should always be taken) but it is almost inconceivable to think that people actually *lived* up there. Yet, its very 2,376 feet summit is enclosed by an Iron Age hillfort which, not surprisingly, makes it the highest in England.

A single stone wall of Millstone Grit blocks, linked-up the crags around the summit to give a triangular shaped, enclosed plateau area of 15 acres. This was thus a major settlement, probably of the Brigantes tribe, in one of the most inhospitable climates in England. It was hardly a 'highly desirable' residential area in which to live, but that was indeed its use, and not simply a fortified lookout post. This is shown by the number of hut circles, some of which are quite large, spread throughout the site, but easily found in the lee of the rampart, on all sides.

Unfortunately, the rampart itself has been greatly damaged over the centuries, by weathering and the stone being put to other uses, while more recently, the large, modern cairn, of absolutely no purpose whatsoever, has been built by robbing the rampart. No ditches were considered to be necessary, quite naturally, and the position of the original entrance(s) cannot be determined. It is a hillfort that needs to be looked for, rather than one which stands out.

One may assume that Ingleborough did in fact serve a strategic purpose for the Brigantes. There is a possibility that it was known as Rigodunum, but it was almost certainly one of the last Brigantes strongholds to stand out against the Romans, in the first century A.D. It would not have been one of the more pleasant battles the men from south of the Alps would have had to fight, but it appears that, as usual, they were victorious. The approach is long, as you will find out, but not too arduous, and once there, even in its heyday, the defences would have been weaker than most encountered elsewhere, and were probably quite easily overcome. That assumes it was used to 'hold out' against the Latin invaders.

Once its military strategic use was negated, Ingleborough was probably abandoned, quite naturally, and does not appear to have been inhabited since. It is a regularly visited mountain, with its outstanding all-round views being within an afternoon's walk, yet I have never met anyone who has been there, who realised a hillfort enclosed the summit. One just does not expect to find any sign of habitation on the remote, exposed mountain.

The walk to the summit from Horton in Ribblesdale is mostly across gently rising moor-land, between rocky outcrops. It is only in the last 1.5 miles that it becomes quite steep, although not prohibitively so, with a last short, steep walk to the summit. The rampart, although anything but complete, can be traced along its length, and many hut circles can be made out. The views are probably greater than from any other English hillfort, on a clear day, with the great mass of The Pennines visible to the north and east, across Morecambe Bay to Barrow in Furness to the west, and much of Lancashire and Yorkshire to the south. No wonder it is such a popular mountain.

In most respects, Ingleborough is quite unlike any other English hillfort: exposed on a mountain top, and a good way from any road. Once there, it is easy to overlook its defences and hut circles, as many do, blinded by the spectacular views to be had. It thus takes a bit of appreciating, and it really needs a bit of imagination to believe that it was ever permanently occupied. Yet it was, and that, perhaps, is its most interesting aspect, especially on a rough day, when you, like the Romans, will be glad to get back to the comfort of civilisation.

Stanwick

Directions. O/S 1:50,000 map 92 ref. 178123. Turn right off the A66 on the B6274, two miles west of Scotch Corner. The road cuts through the outer rampart. Turn right opposite Forcett church. Turn right after 100 yards and at the end of the houses is the English Heritage signpost to 'Stanwick Camp' on the left.

In many respects, Stanwick's fortifications do not really belong in this book. Built in three phases, only the first of these could be described as a hillfort, and this was not begun until about a decade after the Roman invasion began, a time usually considered to be after the Iron Age. Phases 2 and 3 resulted in the camp eventually covering 850 acres, yet this was not a settlement which could accurately be described as an enclosed oppidum. However, the sheer size of the final camp at Stanwick, in a part of the country with few hillforts, makes it worthy of a visit. Most impressive is the section of rampart that has been excavated and reconstructed; that is where you will end up by following the given directions.

'History never changes, does it?' That is one of the questions I have been asked countless times over the years. True, we all know that the Battle of Hastings took place in 1066 and that the Normans won. Those two facts are indisputable, but there is far more to history than mere facts. Matters such as the cause and consequences of the above battle are of more importance and relevance than the battle, and it is such things which are open to interpretation. As time passes, and more is discovered about our past, so interpretations change, and a good example of this is illustrated by Stanwick.

In the early 1950s that great archaeologist, Sir Mortimer Wheeler, to whom those interested in hillforts, among others, owe so much, *see* Maiden Castle*, undertook some excavations at Stanwick. Using information from these, and Roman literary sources, he was able to recreate the dramatic rise and fall of Stanwick and the events which caused this. A study of the plan will help in understanding what follows.

It was stated that Phase 1 of Stanwick was begun shortly after 50 A.D. as a result of a split between the pro-Roman faction among the Brigantes tribe, who dominated the north of England, led by the queen Cartimandua, and the anti-Roman faction led by the king Venutius. The Brigantes peoples, more of a confederation than a unified tribe, tended to live in small, isolated settlements or farms, rather than hillforts or other organised oppida, and Venutius had the first camp built at The Tofts area near the village of Stanwick St John. This 'hillfort' enclosed seventeen acres with a glacis rampart eight yards wide, and still seven feet high where it remains, with a 'V' shaped ditch on all sides except the north, which had a flat-bottomed ditch and counterscarp bank. This may have served as Venutius's headquarters.

Phase 2 was a much grander affair built to the north of the original camp, and included it; in fact the original camp was probably the nerve centre of the new one. Two miles of defences enclosed 150 acres, so this was clearly intended as much more than a simple command post. The new defences comprised a 13 yard wide rampart rising to over 10 feet in height, and revetted with dry-stone walls. A flat bottomed ditch, 13 yards wide and 15 feet deep, gave additional protection. The above directions lead you to the restored section of the Phase 2 defences, and although not very long, you can see what hillfort defences looked like when maintained, as opposed to the ruins you usually see today, and mightily impressive they look too. This phase coincided with an escalation of the civil war between the factions of the Brigantes, which ultimately led to Venutius controlling the tribe, in opposition to the Romans.

The final phase came after the Romans had come to the aid of Cartimandua and her supporters, and were embroiled in their own troubles over the successor to the Imperial throne. A further set of defences to the south of Phase 2 was built c.69 A.D., with a rampart 33 feet wide, 15 feet deep ditch, and 3 gateways to enclose the site. This was considered to be a rallying point for the Brigantes, and was certainly far too big to defend; as the south gate showed, it was unfinished when the final events took place. The Roman IX Legion, under Petullius Cerialis marched north from York in c.71 A.D., took the Brigantes by surprise, defeated them and slighted the great outer defences. That, at least, was what probably happened according to Sir Mortimer Wheeler.

During the 1980s, further excavations were undertaken, by C. Haselgrove and

P. Turnbull and a different interpretation has emerged, concerning both the sequence of building and the use of the camp. Stanwick is situated at the junction of the routes from the north-south, and the east-west across the Pennines, via Stainmore. As such, it was ideally situated for trading purposes, and evidence has been uncovered of metal working, perhaps the manufacture of goods or weapons on the site, while quantities of luxury pottery fragments from the South suggest a place of trade rather than war. In addition, it is now considered that the camp was planned and built in one phase, probably at the time of the Roman invasion of England, and its use fell away as treaties and trade with the Romans in the South grew. The Romans did not advance beyond York, and probably had little need to, given their own problems during the first decades following the invasion.

It is unlikely that the latter interpretation will be the definitive version of events at Stanwick, and a large hoard found at Stanwick in 1845, which consisted of a bronze sword, horse and chariot fittings and personal equipment, fits in with both interpretations. A more sinister find was a skull in a ditch, which was possibly that of a foe displayed at a gateway. The majority of the enclosed land is now farmed, so apart from the defences there is little to see, but some circular huts have been found, in the Phase 1 camp.

Stanwick encloses the village of Stanwick St John and runs close to Forcett. The defences can be seen for much of their circuit, in particular that to the north of Phase 2, under the care of English Heritage, but much of it is tree covered and inaccessible. The plan will help you with viewing.

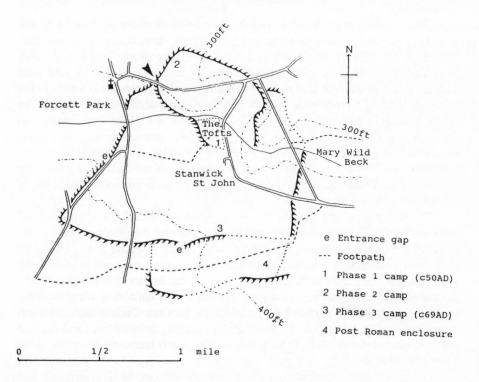

Fascinating and immense as Stanwick is, it is really the restored section of the Phase 2 rampart that is the most memorable. there you can see just how impregnable a hillfort could seem, remembering that each one differed in its defences. Perhaps just as important, are the un-restored defences, a mental comparison can be made and carried with you to all the hillforts you visit.

Hillforts along with many other pre-historic monuments, and others of lesser age, form a major part of what might be described as 'fringe' science/archaeological cults. Probably the most far-fetched of these is 'astro-archaeology', whose followers pursue the fantasy that pre-historic man, usually of the Neolithic Age, created the signs of the zodiac in the pattern of the layout of certain sites. This first came to the fore seventy years ago with the 'Glastonbury Zodiac', and others have emerged since. Preposterous as it might seem, these zodiacs have become associated with the guiding of visitors from outer space, although if such aliens can navigate across millions of miles of space, one would expect them to have equipment capable of finding a particular location on our planet, even if it were covered in forest.

A much more popular fringe activity concerns Leys, better known as Ley Lines. In recent decades the notion of our island being covered with an organised mass of linear, straight, trackways along which pre-historic man passed, has become associated with the existence of magnetic earth energies. It has been suggested that Leys were built on top of the straight routes taken by these earth energies, and that pre-historic man, more at one with the natural environment than his modern counterpart, which is quite probably true, was able to benefit from such energies. Hillforts play a major part in Ley's.

Ley theory first came to the fore through Alfred Watkins, who published his first book on the subject in 1922, *Early British Trackways.* Three years later came his best known work *The Old Straight Track,* while the 'Straight Track Club', devoted to the discovery of new Leys was founded in 1926. Watkins' idea of a linear pre-historic society was unencumbered by notions of earth energies, and was almost totally ignored by academic archaeologists. This was not entirely surprising, as anyone with an understanding of the need for *evidence* in history, either written or from archaeological digs, will know.

Watkins' theory was not backed by hard evidence, but many of the then current archaeological theories have been altered and even disproved since; for example, the 'invasion' thesis to explain the building of hillforts. All this Ley business fizzled out with World War II, but a comeback was made in the 1960s with the new, so-called fringe sciences; really elaborate theories which bend the historical evidence, and especially lack of it, to 'prove' the point. However, read Watkins' books for yourself, but do remember that these are only the first formative books on Ley theory, while never forgetting that *evidence* above all else is required in history.

The biggest single criticism of Ley theory concerns the condensing of time, particularly with regard to pre-history. The 'Golden Age' of man was supposedly pre-Bronze Age, i.e. before metals were invented to enable our forebears to become both corrupt and materialistic. Leys were supposedly in use until about 2,500 B.C., although the knowledge of their existence must have been extant if certain Roman roads, and especially the concept of 'site evolution', absolutely essential to Ley theory, were to have been built on them. Unfortunately, Ley hunters' ability to overlook hard evidence, no matter how limited, rears its head even for the Golden Age, for the excavators of the Neolithic causewayed camp at The Trundle* noted the 'squalor' of those times. Along with other evidence of widespread soil exhaustion, caused by no crop rotation, poor natural fertilisation and such-like, from the Neolithic Age, one suspects that the Golden Age of man was similar to the Golden Age of railways; when trains between cities ran every few hours, as opposed to the regular even-hour services of today.

The most common method of finding a Ley is by plotting certain 'marker' points on an Ordnance Survey 1:50,000 map. If you can find four, although five would be preferable, aligning within ten miles, the chances are that you have 'discovered' a Ley. Once you have done this, you then take to the road and seek out further confirming marker points along the way, the more the merrier. It is with these markers that hillforts enter the picture.

It would be in-correct to say that a Ley marker is 'anything old' along the route, but not too far from the truth. Bearing in mind that Leys are pre-Bronze Age, you will realise the problem regarding the dating of many Ley markers; this is where the concept of 'site evolution' comes in, which will be looked at later. Space precludes a mention of all the possible Ley markers, but I will concentrate on the main ones.

Neolithic long barrows, henges, causewayed camps, cursus avenues and other phenomena like Silbury Hill, all date from the Ley hunters Golden Age of man, and all can quite genuinely be included as Ley markers. Less certainly from this period are the stone circles, rows or avenues and the standing stones that are used as markers. Some probably do date from the Neolithic Age, but not all as the stones at Stonehenge are undoubtedly from the Bronze Age, for example.

There are thus not too many Neolithic relics left in our present landscape, not surprising given the elapse of at least 4,000 years, while the population would have been minimal in comparison with today. This is where the concept of 'site evolution' comes in. Ley hunters claim that historic sites have evolved over time, and that a site which marked a ley in the Neolithic Age has been put to use, for another purpose, at a later date(s). This we have already seen can be true in the case of certain hillforts, as some, like Maiden Castle*, The Trundle*, Hembury* and others, have previously served as a Neolithic causewayed camp. However, these would all have been abandoned for many centuries, and probably have been overgrown, so the site would not have evolved, but been chosen for its own merits in the later age.

Markers from the Bronze Age are plentiful in leys, in particular the round barrows, so common in the South. Some of these round barrows, marked on an O/S map as 'tumuli', even date from the post-Roman period. Leaving out the Iron Age from the chronological sequence, for the moment, Roman roads, forts, villas, and temples are all regarded as ley markers, although these are quite obviously from a later age. There is no real evidence of site evolution for any of these, although some Romano-Celtic shrines have been built within hillforts, like that at Maiden Castle*. With regard to Roman roads, one well-known 'fringe science' author, John Michell, claimed in his book *The View over Atlantis* that, ' . . . beneath the surface of the Fosse Way, Ermine Street and Watling Street the excavators have uncovered paving stones of earlier roads at least as well drained and levelled as those which succeeded them.' Given that we know Iron Age people paved some tracks at their hillforts, such road metaling is quite possible. However, Michell gave no factual evidence for his assertion, which is not surprising as it is totally untrue. A not uncommon encounter in the world of the so-called fringe sciences.

Moving still closer to our present time, Norman mottes ('false hills') are a favourite marker for leys, despite them having been built one thousand years after the Romans first arrived. Other mediaeval castles and even post-mediaeval moats are also considered to be ley markers. Well over 100 mottes have been excavated in the last thirty years, without one giving evidence of having incorporated an earlier mound. The same is true of moats, for no evidence has been uncovered of one being pre-mediaeval, out of well over 100 excavated in a similar period.

Churches, both pre and post-reformation, and other religious sites, such as abbeys and cathedrals are all fair game for ley hunters. Obviously, excavation of such sites is pretty rare, but some have been excavated such as York Minster and Winchester Cathedral, Jarrow Priory and a number of churches, without evidence being found of a former pagan use. Without a doubt, some churches have been built on former sacred sites, like the ruined church within the Neolithic henge at Knowlton (Dorset); the site might well have evolved, but with a gap of probably more than 3,000 years.

Markers of a more unusual kind claimed by ley hunters also feature in many leys. Ponds, and even artificial lakes, most obviously of recent construction, can be claimed to be either ancient, or have evolved, usually without there being any evidence to support such a claim. Even more optimistic claims for a marker have centred on avenues of trees, almost wholly planted within the last three centuries over land that had been landscaped and cleared of anything from the past. Even crossroads, from a road network which really only dates back 250 years, especially in areas which were subject to agricultural enclosures, are considered acceptable.

If these last mentioned markers seem especially ridiculous to include under the aegis of 'site evolution', then ley hunters will surprise you further. Notches in hills have been claimed as markers, especially by Alfred Watkins himself. This might seem perfectly acceptable, but the notches in question are usually quite small, and although visible, are not particularly distinguishable, and cannot, of course, be dated. On the other hand the Scots Pine tree, either singularly, or in a small cluster, as they can often be seen in the English countryside, can be dated. Thanks to science, and its ability to analyse pollen, it has been found, and is accepted by the tree 'fraternity', that the Scots Pine was not seen in England between the Roman period and its re-introduction in the sixteenth century. So, all those Scots Pines which act as ley markers on the sides of hills do not appear to have evolved from the seeds of their pre-historic forebears.

The real specialist marker of the ley hunter though, is the 'mark stone', which can be anything from a boulder in a hedge (usually dating from an agricultural enclosure) to a boulder beside a house. These boulders, some large, others not, are usually of a different stone to the local norm, a result of glacial movement rather than Neolithic man carting these things for countless miles, I would think. These, like Scots Pine's, 'notches' in hills and such-like, are not marked on O/S maps, and are usually found through fieldwork; they can be used to transform your 'four marker' ley on the map, into a confirmed 'five point' ley in reality.

I will return to these shortly with some examples of Ley lines, but in case you have forgotten, I skipped over the Iron Age and its hillforts. These are widely used in leys; not surprising given the sheer number of hillforts, and the large area they often cover, as even a small hillfort can accommodate several leys. Also, as the plan shows, if we make one of the markers a hillfort, then the number of leys increases considerably. Ley hunters have, however, made numerous claims about hillforts which archaeological excavations have proved to be quite without foundation.

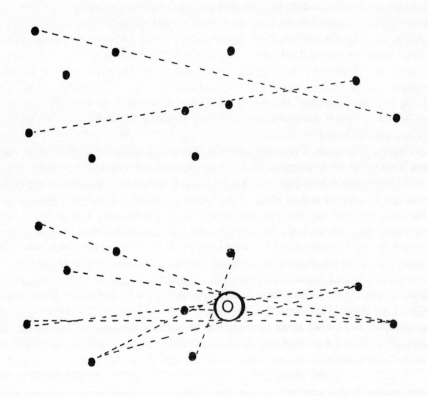

Mention has already been made of the 'fringe science' notion that Maiden Castle* would need 250,000 people, or more than 10% of England's Iron Age population, to defend its ramparts effectively. This merely demonstrates a lack of understanding about how battles were fought in the pre-Roman era. Other claims that hillfort defences are often so slight as to be useless against an attack, show a distinct lack of knowledge of such defences, and that what we see today is not a form of landscape architecture, or enhancement, but the ruins of former defences.

244

Hillforts have also been claimed to be ancient 'energy stations', where the earth's magnetic forces are gathered for use by pre-historic man. Could that possibly be true? It is all rather fanciful and, if you do not look too deeply, plausible but, despite evidence being relatively rare compared to the absolute number of hillforts, hillforts were used, and rebuilt on several occasions, for defence. As with Norman motte and bailey, and other mediaeval castles, would the inhabitants, whether defender or conqueror, allow the building of a defensive site to be determined by whatever existed before? Of course not, no more than one would build an air raid shelter today in a ruined castle simply because it was there, when an underground bunker would be far more suitable.

Although the hillforts included in the gazetteer section of this book are by no means a representative sample of all English hillforts, fifteen have provided evidence of being used in battle; many await excavation. Again referring to the hillforts in this book, over half have had some form of excavation undertaken and, with the exception of Mam Tor*, none have produced a pre-Iron Age date for the defences, although several incorporate pre-Iron Age features within the hillfort. These have not played a part in the layout of the Iron Age defences.

As for claims by ley hunters that hillforts have not displayed evidence of permanent use, well just go to Hod Hill*, Hambledon Hill*, Midsummer Hill*, Chun Castle*, Yeavering Bell*, Mam Tor* and many others and see the surface evidence of huts for yourself. Over one quarter of the gazetteer entries have surface evidence of permanent Iron Age occupation, while two thirds have provided archaeological evidence of the same. Those hillforts that have not produced evidence of permanent use have either not been excavated, or are in a distinct minority.

One might expect that leys would, as they pass through hillforts, be aligned with the true pre-Iron Age remains to be found within. This has not been the case. For example, one ley line which crossed Maiden Castle* only hits the most recent ramparts, and misses both the long barrow and the Neolithic causewayed camp. Sutton Walls (Herefordshire) was excavated in 1948 including the exact place where Alfred Watkins' ley crossed the rampart; this was found to be of entirely Iron Age origin. On the Old Sarum ley, which will be mentioned later, why does the ley pass right through the centre of Old Sarum (Wiltshire) hillfort, and just nick the edge of Clearbury Ring? Furthermore, if hillforts really were ancient 'power stations', this must have been known about in the Iron Age, two millennium after the end of man's Neolithic Golden Age. One might have expected a Roman writer to have noted this, given the supernatural nature of such a phenomena.

Various claims have been made over the years by ley hunters that archaeologists and historians 'ignore' their work, or 'rubbish' it, being afraid to look beyond their own conventional research, and many other such accusations. Indeed, when I first began to look into leys several years ago, I could find little reference to them in orthodox works; the claims of a 'conspiracy theory' against ley hunters seemed to have some grounding. It was only while trying to weigh up such evidence for the existence of leys that I realised such *evidence*, as opposed to speculative ideas and fanciful thought, rarely, if at all exists.

For a start, why are most leys so short, averaging only ten and a half miles in I. Thomson's and P. Deveraux's *The Ley Hunters' Companion?* Why are they straight?

After all, nothing else from pre-history is exactly straight, stone lines and cursus' included. How wide is a ley? A pencil line on an O/S map is eighteen yards wide in reality, which gives quite a bit of scope for re-alignment. How come these ancient sites align, surely that is more than chance? Is there anything surprising in the fact that ancient man should have pursued paths of absolute linear accuracy, using a system of markers for ten, fifty or even hundreds of miles? Not at all really. It is often easier, if walking up a mountain, to ignore any paths and to aim straight for the summit, only deviating when absolutely essential. On the other hand, if you have ever walked any tracks which have evolved from an ancient trackway, like The Ridgeway, or the South Downs Way, you will soon see why they curve and bend with the landscape. Only an idiot would try and cross the chalk downs in a straight path, which would take him over the highest points, followed by a slippery, steep descent through numerous deep, dry valleys, only to have to climb up the other side again. On the other hand, evidence claimed for such a linear ley system does not exist. To give some examples of the markers I have already mentioned in 'action', let us look at a few leys.

I have chosen to look at the following leys because of their familiarity to me. The Coldrum Ley runs for four and a half miles in North Kent. Its first marker is the Norman church of St Peter and St Paul at Trottiscliffe, although this has Saxon foundations, into which some sarsen stones are included. Local legend has it that a Neolithic site existed in the area, which is where the sarsen stones reputedly came from. This may be true, but although the stones might have come from this site, there is no evidence to suggest the site was where the church now stands. Look how many country cottages have been built by using the stones of destroyed mediaeval castles in their vicinity.

The second marker is the exposed stones of the Coldrum long barrow, of definite Neolithic antiquity. This raises a problem of visibility though, for it cannot be seen from neither Trottiscliffe church, nor marker three, a track crossing and dried up pond; neither of which show any evidence of being 'ancient'. The parish churches of Snodland and Burham are the final two markers, and both are visible from each other.

In addition, there is an ancient ford crossing the River Medway next to Snodland church, on the Pilgrims Way. The problem is, that by following the ley between these two churches, one not only crosses the Medway by the ford, but one must then re-cross the river at a right hand bend, just getting to the opposite bank, before having to re-cross it yet again. Now, I am quite a hardy person, well used to roughing it, but once I had crossed a river, I would not be too keen about re-crossing it twice more, when I could easily follow the bank and cut across land. Furthermore, rivers are always deeper on the outside of a bend, so why cross twice at such a point, when you have already crossed by a ford?

This ley, with its one pre-historic marker, also raises the question of chance, with regard to the alignment of five sites. Two computer simulations of the 400 possible ley markers in that part of Kent have been undertaken, with each mark being moved. For the Coldrum Ley not to have been a chance alignment, such five-point alignments ought to have shown up no more than in 1% of the tests. The results gave such alignments, including one seven-point alignment in 4.5 miles, in

20% of the tests. Further tests of pre-1600 A.D. markers gave five-point alignments in 16% of the tests.

The easiest way to demonstrate the possibility of chance yourself, is to take an O/S 1:50,000 map, and turn it over. Carefully put about 250 random pencil dots within the borders of the map on the other side. Then see how many four or five point alignments you can make. Incidentally, some maps have over 400 ley marker points, so 250 is a safe number.

The Coldrum Ley was only of interest to us because of the computer simulation undertaken, but the Montgomery Ley includes a hillfort; well it does not actually, but you will soon see what I mean. This runs for 5.75 miles from an insignificant cross-roads on the Dark Age Offa's Dyke, nor is it a site of any great height or distinction. The second marker is a half mile straight section of the B4385, again with no evidence of it being an ancient track. Actually, the ley runs parallel to the road over the hedge in a field, and not on its course.

The next marker is St Nicholas' church in Montgomery, having no evidence of being pre-thirteenth century, while there is a 'mark-stone' against a house in Arthur Street. How does one build a house, and especially dig the foundations, yet leave such a stone in place? Surely it was put there after building the house to protect its corner from cart wheels, or am I, as Captain Mainwairing would say to Corporal Jones in *Dad's Army* ' . . . dealing in the realms of fantasy' now?

The final three markers are Montgomery Castle (1223), Hen Domen motte, excavated in 1967 and dated from the eleventh century A.D. and it ends at a Roman camp near the River Severn, on the opposite side of a field to a glacial erratic standing stone. However, the ley misses the Ffridd Faldwyn hillfort by less than a quarter of a mile and misses the castle mound at Brompton Hall by a similar distance. Why should the ley end at Lower Cwm as well? If it continued for a couple of miles the ley could have missed the Caer Din pre-historic camp by a quarter of a mile and an earthwork at Reilth by half a mile; at least these are true 'ancient' sites.

These leys have both been discovered in the post-war ley hunting boom, and their respective lack of a genuine pre-historic marker, only one between them, is the most obvious defect. The Old Sarum Ley is different, being eighteen miles long, and the alignment of sites was noted by an eminent archaeologist, Sir Norman Lockyer, even before Alfred Watkins had evolved his ley theory. It starts off at a Bronze Age barrow, to the north of Stonehenge; then its second 'marker', none other than Stonehenge itself, is without doubt from the Neolithic Age; and it misses the Bronze Age stones for good measure. The third marker is the Iron Age hillfort cum Roman posting station cum Norman cathedral town of Old Sarum, a site that has most definitely evolved. The fourth marker is Salisbury Cathedral, and the last two markers are Clearbury Ring hillfort (Wiltshire) and Godmanescamp* hillfort, both from the Iron Age.

Among the great mass of leys discovered over the years, the Old Sarum Ley has relatively impeccable pre-historic credentials. However, remembering that leys supposedly fell from use by the end of the Neolithic Age, problems arise. A Bronze Age round barrow and three Iron Age hillforts, none of which have been excavated thoroughly but, as with all hillforts, show no outward signs of being anything other than Iron Age defensive sites, would all have post-dated any such Neolithic linear alignment. Salisbury Cathedral was, with the new city, built on virgin ground in the thirteenth century, with no mention in historical documents of there being any ancient monument present, nor indeed has such been revealed when laying foundations for modern buildings, unlike at say York or London. Furthermore, the size of these sites allows for the ley to be 'moved' and to still align, except for the round barrow. As the downs to the north of Stonehenge is littered with these tumuli, so it would not be unexpected if an alignment could be made with another, and that is the case.

However, it is pertinent to ask why should a ley simply end at an insignificant round barrow? If we pursue it northwards we would find that it misses the numerous round barrows on Enford Down, misses the large Casterley Camp hillfort by half a mile to the east, misses the large Neolithic Marden Henge by a quarter of a mile to the west, and finally misses Rybury Camp hillfort by a similar distance to the west. Going south, the ley misses all of the numerous tumuli on Normanton Down, and others on Wilsford Down; this in itself is quite a feat of non-alignment. It misses Ogbury hillfort across the River Avon by half a mile, plus yet more Bronze Age burial mounds nearby.

Once again, querying why should a ley end at an Iron Age hillfort, if one continues south one finds that the ley would miss the large hillfort of Goreley Camp (Hampshire) and several more tumuli, some by less than 100 yards, on Whitfield Hill and Shirley Common. If all these sites had evolved from Neolithic ley markers, – though how a Bronze Age burial mound 'evolves' is beyond my comprehension – surely the ley would have had more than one marker every three miles. How would a person following the Old Sarum Ley have distinguished the correct markers among the great mass of incorrect ones?

A test has been conducted at both ends of the Old Sarum Ley to find out if magnetic earth energies followed the ley alignment. A dowser and scientific magnetometer measuring equipment were used, and although the dowser's rods waved about a bit, they did not mark out anything like a straight line, which in any case did not correspond to the actual course of the ley, which was not known to either the dowser or the scientist. The scientific equipment recorded absolutely no anomalies in changes in the earth's magnetic field as it crossed and re-crossed the Old Sarum Ley, at either end. This probably established that the Old Sarum Ley, with its unusually high proportion of pre-historic, if not Neolithic, markers, does not follow a line determined by magnetic earth energy.

Most leys are of a short distance, which is not unreasonable, given that 12-20 miles would be a fair day's walk, especially when conveying wares for trade. Pre-historic long-distance paths do exist, such as The Ridgeway, which are far from straight. One well known long-distance alignment is the St Michael's Ley, which runs from St Michael's Mount, in Cornwall, to the North Sea, near Lowestoft, a distance of 380 miles. A problem with such a ley is the effect of the curvature of the earth; a straight line cannot, as such, exist.

St Michael's Mount may or may not have been a Neolithic site; it certainly seems to have been used in the Iron Age, and is a good point to start the ley. This then passes through The Hurlers stone circle (Neolithic/Bronze Age), and The Cheesewring, on Bodmin Moor. The latter has been claimed to be man-made, but there is no evidence for this. The ley then passes through a number of churches connected with St Michael at Brent Tor, Trull, Othery, Burrowbridge Mump and Glastonbury Tor, a pretty convincing alignment, until you realise that it misses all twenty churches similarly dedicated to that saint in Wiltshire.

The ley then passes through the church at Stoke St Michael, Avebury Henge, the parish church of Ogbourne St George (Wiltshire), St Michael's church at Clifton Hamden (Bedfordshire) and the abbey at Bury St Edmunds. There are thus many St Michael connections, while the leys' founder, J. Michell in *The View Over Atlantis,* suggests that both Glastonbury Tor and Burrowbridge Mump are man-made hills; no evidence was provided to substantiate such a claim, not surprising really as neither has been excavated to such an extent, so this is pure guesswork.

Unfortunately, despite the existence of only two sites which could possibly be Neolithic, i.e. Avebury henge and The Hurlers, the St Michael's line does not stand up to its claims. Othery church is not on the alignment, and that at Brent Tor is over a mile away. Finally, and most damningly, St Michael's Mount is two miles off the alignment, so this most famous of long distance leys is left with just ten markers, of varied age, in 380 miles.

In other respects, ley hunters have made, and continue to make, basic errors with the method of finding leys. We have already seen how five markers within ten miles on a 1:50,000 series O/S map is the bench-mark for a proven lay. Four markers on the map is permissible if, in subsequent field-work, other markers on the map such as a mark-stone or pond for example, are found. However, the Ordnance Survey do not mark all known pre-historic sites on this series of maps; in certain places it would not be possible. As a general rule, the O/S only mark what is visible, but they have many records of pre-historic sites only visible from the air, or even not at all these days.

So, for a hypothetical example, a ley might pass between two mediaeval church markers, despite their being no evidence of a pre-historic site, yet a non-visible pre-historic site might also be crossed, and not included as a marker. More likely, the ley misses many 'invisible' pre-historic markers, often by a not-very-great distance, on its way between two accepted markers with no evidence of pre-historic connections. Another option is that, by using a very large scale map, say one of the O/S 1:2,500 series, one can make up many more leys for a given area than by using the 1:50,000 series. In some cases five-point, or more, leys can absolutely cover a locality making any notion of a linear path or 'earth energy' carrying system ridiculous.

This appendix on Leys was included because of the importance of (Iron Age) hillforts to their existence, and because leys are connected to claims about ancient man and his ability to harbour the earth's magnetic energies for his own well-being. The mystical aspects of pre-history, backed by legends and myths, and purportedly containing druidic and other such intangible connections, can appear very convincing, particularly as supporters of such ideas can be quite fanatical in their following. Nothing wrong in that, of course, and it is good to see a bit of spirit in one's activities; I am, after all, a bit of a fanatic of hillforts. The thought that we could walk up to our nearest hillfort 'power station' for an 'earth energy' charge-up, quite appeals to me.

Regrettably, as historians, we have to deal not in speculation and ideas, but evidence, and I am afraid that, so far, archaeologists have not come with any such thing that connects hillforts with either an ancient linear path system, or a means of harbouring earth energies. Also, despite occasional claims to the contrary, until the 1960s the academic, orthodox archaeological fraternity largely ignored ley hunters and their claims. Since that time, there has been an increase in the number of archaeologists who have at least considered the claims made for leys. Unfortunately, there are other archaeologists who have openly derided the existence of leys, and their followers, in terms such as belonging to ' . . . the mumbo-jumbo of non-history . . . ', and ' . . . not worthy of consideration . . .'

My feelings about the existence of leys and an earth energy system is reflected in what has been written above. I do not think that a 'superior' attitude, as taken by certain academic archaeologists, is the correct route to take when considering such phenomena, no matter how ludicrous one might feel the subject to be. After all, until the late 1950s, it was still widely accepted that few hillforts were built before 250 B.C., and the 'invasion thesis' of ' . . . wave after wave of barbarians . . .' arriving at our shores was still well in place. It is now certain that many hillforts were built well before 500 B.C., and the 'invasion thesis' is no longer generally accepted. Archaeologists were wrong then, and will be wrong now and in the future. Such a holier-than-thou attitude is barely acceptable (and rude) if one is absolutely certain that ones theory is correct. No archaeologist, or historian, can guarantee that future works will not overturn his pet theory.

GLOSSARY

AMPHORA — Large pottery container used by the Romans to carry certain liquids for trading purposes, especially wine.

ARD — Simple, early plough without a mould-board to turn the sod. Often with metal-tipped plough-share, and either pulled by man or animals.

BANK-BARROW — Very long long-barrow.

BARROWS — Burial mounds. Usually long (Neolithic), or round (mostly Bronze Age).

BELGAE — People of mixed Celtic-German origin. Came to Britain c.100 B.C.

BERM — A flat piece of ground separating a rampart from its ditch.

BI-VALLATE — Hillfort with two ramparts.

BOX RAMPART — Box shaped rampart of hillfort, usually with a parapet.

BRONZE AGE — The 'age' preceding the Iron Age, c.2,000-800 B.C.

CARBON-14 DATING — Also Radio-carbon dating. Method of measuring the age of organic matter. Carbon-14 has a fixed proportion to carbon in a living organism, but once dead this is not maintained and falls to about half the former level in c.5,700 years; this is known as a 'half-life'. By measuring the ratio of Carbon-14: carbon in organic matter, an approximate date of death can be calculated. This cannot be determined with absolute accuracy, and is usually expressed as, e.g. 500 B.C. $\pm$100, that is between 600-400 B.C. In this book, Carbon-14 dates, where quoted, have been expressed as the middle date.

CAUSEWAYED CAMP	Early Neolithic enclosure, often with several concentric ditches crossed by causeways. They have had many uses, including ceremonial centre, meeting place and permanent settlement.
CELTIC FIELDS	Small rectangular fields often with lynchets defining the sides. Date from the Bronze Age, but in use in the Iron Age.
CELTS	Iron using peoples from central Europe. Migrated to England probably beginning in the early first millennium B.C.
CIRCA or c.	About, approximately. Used with a date.
COUNTERSCARP BANK	A bank on the outer edge of a hillfort ditch. Usually the product of clearing out the ditch.
COVERED WAY	(see 'Hollow Path').
CROSS-DYKES	Lengths of bank and ditch usually used to define territory or create internal, or ranch, boundaries.
CUP & RING MARKS	Stone carving of circular depression (usually) with surrounding rings. Mostly found in the North.
CURRENCY BAR	Usually flat iron bars of various lengths, with turned up edges at one end. In use until coins introduced.
CURSUS	Neolithic 'avenue' usually bounded by a bank and ditches. Some are several miles long.
DITCH	Get off with you!
DRUIDS	Celtic priests. Probably late Iron Age only.
ENCLOSED OPPIDUM	Large Belgic settlement, usually a 'chief's' town stronghold.
GLACIS RAMPART	Stone, earth, and spoil covered rampart.
HENGE	Circular bank and ditch enclosed earthwork from the Neolithic Age. Probably for ceremonial purposes. Some later adapted by Bronze Age peoples, like Stonehenge.

HILLFORTS	If you don't know by now, you never will.
HOLLOW PATH	(Also known as Covered Ways, or Sunken Tracks). A track usually between two earth banks, either built purposely or created by the wearing away of the trodden ground. Sometimes confused with cross-dykes.
HUT CIRCLE	The wall footings, usually turf-covered, of huts.
HUT PLATFORM	A level platform cut into the side of a hill, on which a hut was built.
IRON AGE	The period immediately prior to the Roman invasion of 43 A.D. For this book it approximates to 800 B.C.-60 A.D.
LYNCHET	Bank of soil on the downward side of a celtic field, created by continuous ploughing and stone clearing.
MULTIVALLATE	Two or more lines of ramparts at a hillfort.
NEOLITHIC AGE	New Stone Age. c.4,500-2,000 B.C.
PILLOW MOUND	Oblong shaped mounds. Date and use uncertain, but possibly rabbit warrens.
PROMONTORY FORT	Hillfort created by ramparts cutting across the level approach, with steep natural defences on all other sides.
RAMPART	The banks which, along with the ditch, defend the perimeter of the hillfort.
REVETMENT	The wood or stone facing of the rampart; now rarely seen. May or may not have been structurally supporting.
ROUNDS	Circular, multivallate hillfort, mostly found in Cornwall.
SHERD (POTSHERDS)	Broken fragments of pottery.

STORAGE PITS	Holes in the interior of a hillfort, often quite deep, used for the long-term storage of grain or salted meat. When they had 'gone off', could be used as rubbish pits.
SUNKEN TRACK	(*see* 'Hollow Path').
TIMBER LACING	Horizontal cross-timbers through the rampart connecting vertical posts at the front and rear. Essential to prevent collapse of revetment and rampart.
UNIVALLATE	Single rampart at a hillfort.
WALL RAMPART	Rampart with only one vertical face, to the outside.

+ RES
06/08